REALM OF LIGHT

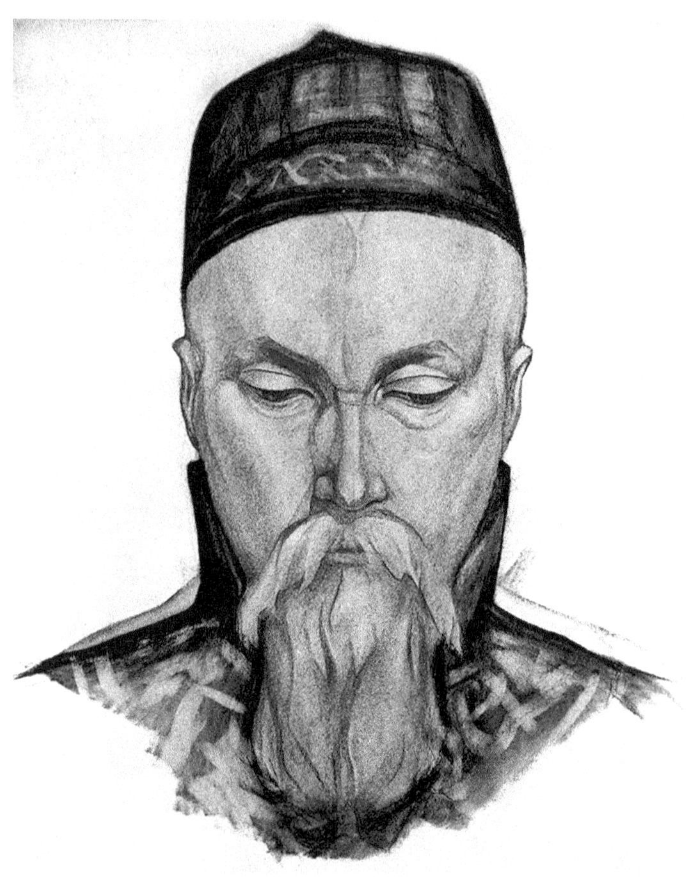

Portrait of Nicholas Roerich by Svetoslav Roerich

REALM OF LIGHT

NICHOLAS ROERICH

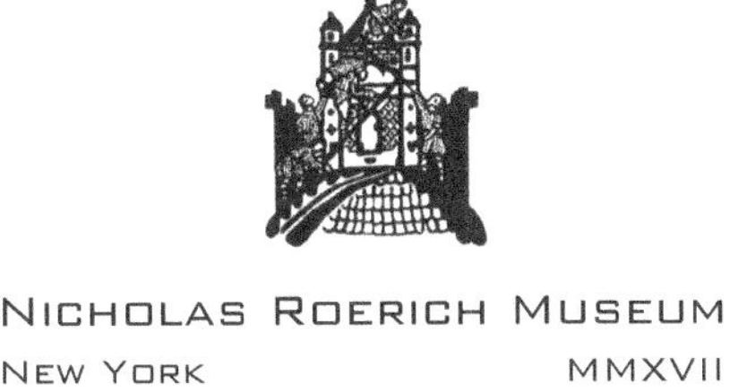

NICHOLAS ROERICH MUSEUM

NEW YORK   MMXVII

Nicholas Roerich Museum
319 West 107th Street
New York NY 10025
www.roerich.org

Cover illustration: Nicholas Roerich. *Krishna*. 1929.

FIRST EDITION PUBLISHER'S NOTE

THE "Realm of Light" is the Sixth Volume of the American Edition of Nicholas Roerich's Works. The first volume was "Adamant"; the second, "Altai-Himalaya"; the third, "Flame in Chalice"; the fourth, "Heart of Asia"; the fifth, "Shambhala."

The general device of these Books, multifarious in their contents yet united in their inner striving, is *The Call to Culture*. And by his term "Realm of Light" the author signifies the human heart.

Truly, it is a privilege to publish Roerich's evocation to Beauty, to Knowledge and Culture. The countries where Nicholas Roerich pursues his endless activities may verily pride themselves on his great creative contributions to Beauty and Culture.

It is of exceptional significance that, through the Societies dedicated to him in all continents, the name of Nicholas Roerich is so universally proclaimed and impressed upon human hearts, not only as Master of the brush but also as a thinker and a builder of life. In studying the Biography of Roerich one is confronted by a great chain of real, indisputable facts. Through his indefatigable creativeness, his daily labor and achievements, Roerich acquires in universal measure that synthesis which reconciles and solves the most difficult problems. Mark what subtle psychology and benevolent compassion is suffused through his addresses to the Societies bearing his name. He never disparages—on the contrary, his emphasis everywhere is on the most positive, creative foundations.

These volumes, covering the complete editions of Roerich's works in English, may be justly called missals of the rites of Culture. In one of his addresses, the author asks: "In what country do you desire to live?"

His answer is: "Certainly in the country of Culture." And for Roerich himself, such a country is not an abstraction but an immutable possibility and a beautiful necessity for humanity.

It is but natural that this vital call to Culture has attracted multitudes of followers to Roerich. His Banner of Peace is truly an Oriflamme of invincible Culture around which the all-constructive and positive elements may gather without differences. If Roerich has his enemies, let us recall how in his evocations, he names the insatiate enemy of all light-imparting aspiration—the homunculus of ignorance. He regards ignorance as the most heinous crime; but he welcomes with an all-containing benevolent cordiality everything which indicates the striving towards Knowledge.

The author says: "Let us abandon the past for the future. Let us impel our entire consciousness into the future and let us suffuse it with radiance, for this is within the access of humanity."

Roerich presents his book for the Fund of the Bio-chemical Laboratory of the Himalayan Research Institute, founded by Roerich in 1928. To the same Common Welfare of humanity is dedicated also his all-embracing thought for the remedial and salutary foundations of man's evolution.

CONTENTS

CONTENTS

REALM OF LIGHT

REALM OF LIGHT

"ANGEL—the Blessed Silence!" Who has not been exalted by this flaming mystery in the image of a fiery Angel? Who has not been imbued by the all-penetrating message of this ever-awaited, yet never-expected guest? His is the silence of the heart which has attained. He is the keeper of the eternal beauty of spirit. The beauty of the eternally silent and merciful spirit. He guards and blesses.

The old Christian book, "Mirror" says: "The Angel is the impalpable, the fiery and the flame-bearing" ... "That which is not in need of word for his expression, nor ear for his hearing. Without word, or hearing, the Angels communicate to one another their wise understanding" ... "In a dream-like body the Angel clothes Itself for manifestation to the people."

In silence that vision was manifested: Translucent became all objects. And the Image of the Great Guest appeared effulgent. And his lips remained silent and he crossed his hands, and from each hair streamed light. And unfathomably, piercingly, glowed his eyes.

Zealously the Flaming One brought the message of the renewed and blessed world. Mysteriously he ordained the sign of Bliss. Daringly he recalled the Never-expressible. Untiringly in the hours of day and night he awakens the heart of humanity. He ordains the victory of spirit. And all will cognize and accept it with the language of their hearts.

Who then embodied the Image of the Angel—the Blessed Silence? This Image came from the Northern Sea. But this mystery is known not only in the midnight sea. In it is evident the veiled image of the Messenger of the East. Within it is also the mystery of the Cross. The very Hand and Thought which created the Image of Sophia, the Almighty's Wisdom, made manifest the Angel of Silence. Flaming are the wings of the ever-striving Sophia—the Wisdom; of the same flame are the wings of the Angel, the Blessed Silence. Fiery are the steeds of the chariot of Elias. So is the fiery baptism preordained by the Apostles. In all is the very same fire; Agni Omniscient and all-ascending, all-penetrating, and before which human word is superfluous.

Sparks of the dynamo imbue space. In tension they flower into spirals of ascension and glow like a tree with its branches and fiery leaves. The Logos of thought intensifies the *prana* and man stands humble, trembling before the radiance of the command of lightning. The fire of Kundalini kindles. The wheels of Ezekiel revolve. The Chakras of India rotate. Austere is the eye of Kapila. The Egyptian High Priest proclaimed "Sekhem Ur am Sekhemmu." Where is the limit of Radiance? Where is the measure of Might? Light itself reaches the invisible and sound immerses...

No glimmer stirs; not even the fragrance of *prana*. This is the highest tension. Inaccessible to the eye, and inaudible to the ear. Only the heart knows that silence is calling and that the Chalice is brimming. First lightning and thunder and whirlwind and tremor; and only afterward, in silence, the Voice ineffable. Agni Yoga says: "The first call is as thunder, but the last is accomplished in silence." At first, a flaming Messenger; and after, the purest Sophia, the Wisdom. ...

It is said: "Bliss is a timid bird"; impetuous are the wings of Sophia. Woe to him who did not perceive; woe to him who did not comprehend; woe to him who rejected. Why shall the flaming wing, which became. manifest through Bliss, appear again to the timid or cruel eye?

But how many fires are already apparent even to the inexperienced eye? Humanity dreams about the Abodes of Light. It dreams in silence. In the darkness, it daringly confesses to itself. Even by night humanity believes; but by day it does not profess. Although it is aware of the law: "I have faith and profess." Oh, they themselves know that faith without deeds is but a phantom. Only abstraction! But bliss is attraction and affirmation. Otherwise for what are all misty sighs? Otherwise for what is Science itself, if the spirit does not dare its application? Nicodemus in the night is but the symbol of faith without deeds; a spark without flame or warmth.

Ghastly is decay. Unbearable is the frigidity of ignorance. It is inadmissible because of its harm, its contagion of accumulations, its destruction of the very foundation. Many a time the frightened Bird of Bliss fluttered with its white wings against closed windows. But we fear everything that assaults our ignorance and we depend upon door-bolts. Even when the eye perceives, we call it an "accident." Even when the ear hears, we say "coincidence." For us even the X-ray and the qualities of radium are ordinary, and electricity is only a lantern for our comfort. If one is told that thought alters the weight of a body, even this does not amaze the mechanistic ones of civilization. Irregularity of the blood circulation and harmful blood pressure are increasing amazingly. The latest form of influenza burns the lungs like a plague. The throat seems aflame. Asthma ravages. Meningitis is on the increase and incomprehensible heart symptoms are multiplying. But to us these signs are only fashionable diseases, not deserving of any special attention. We already hear of the hyper-saturation of Space by radio waves; of poisoning through gasoline; of signs of over-electrification ... it is discomforting to think of the future. Hence the fate of a golf ball is regarded as equal in importance with the destiny of that small ball—our planet. Unlike the wise Queen Hatshepsut, we fear to address those "Who will live in the years to come, who will develop their hearts and will look into the future"—even if the terrifying concept "the future" is pronounced through ideas so fossilized that the way to it is at once transformed into a subterranean dungeon.

However, the first condition for the attainment of knowledge is freedom from methods of study. One should not insist upon standardized methods. The true knowledge is attained by inner accumulations, by daring; for the approaches to the One Knowledge are manifold. The description of such calls and milestones of life would make a most needed and uplifting book. One must not insist, not deprive, not subdue by conventionalities, but should constantly recall the light, the fires of space, the high energies, the predestined victories. All facts not within the elementary school books should be collected. Such facts should be threaded with full honesty, without conceit and disdain, or hypocrisy, behind which lurks fear—truly speaking, ignorance. One may never know whence the useful seed will come: the physicist, bio-chemist, botanist, physician, priest or historian or philosopher or a Tibetan lama, or Brahmin-pandit, or Rabbi-kabbalist, or Confucian or an old medicine woman, or, finally, the fellow traveler whose name we failed to ask without reason—who will make the most important contribution? In each life there is so much that is remarkably inspiring, unusual. Only to remember it! In these reminders sparkle so many of the best stars only temporarily obscured. Thus, once more without renouncing our daily labor, we approach not the things forbidden but the possibilities which illumine life. Only it is not our task to insist, lest we coerce. For nothing is achieved by forcing. But, I repeat, it is necessary to recall the possible joys. The names of these spiritual joys are inexpressible in the language of the material world.

Saint Isaak Siryn ordains: "The hope of ease, in all times, forced the people to forget the higher." He also says: "Who is unaware that even birds approach traps in the hope of rest?" Happy are those who, realizing Infinity, love daily labor. After the Holy Scriptures let us also remember the last book of Prof. A. S. Eddington, "Stars and Atoms." Speaking of the condition of other constellations beyond earthly conditions, the Professor points out that it would be more accurate to say, the reason of a given manifestation lies in that it is earthly, and does not pertain to the stars. Even recently, people tried to ascribe earthly conditions to all far-off worlds. Freedom from prejudice is needed. The creative flame is needed. The bonfire summons the travelers in the desert. Likewise, the reminding call resounds and, through all encasements, reaches the heart which is ready. The milestones are manifold. The calls are unexpected. Untiring vigilance and thoughtful attention are the keys to the sealed gates. Where universality and sincerity of study, and veneration of the blessed Hierarchy are ordained there is no place for negation.

Nonetheless into the life of science must enter the unprejudiced. With difficulties, under scorn, in various countries, those fearless souls already strive to the predestined synthesis. Soon perhaps congresses of these creative workers will be possible. Already centers are being erected where without fear of the condemnation of ignorance or jealousy, one may interchange these viewpoints in full confidence. Let us then gather with all care these multi-colored flowers of the great garden of culture, remembering that "I shall not reveal the mystery to the enemies, nor shall I give the kiss of Judas." Without the coldness of condemnation, without repelling ignorance, shall we welcome each seed of Truth.

We interpret the flaming ecstasy of lofty spirits as "Hysteria Magna with high temperature." Vishudha, the center of the throat, is for many only "a hysterical globe." The fires of Saint Teresa, Clara, Radegunda; the ardent warmth of the Fathers of merciful love; of Tummo of the high Tibetan lamas; or the custom existing even today in India of walking upon fire (the Agni-Diku—the throne of fire was likewise in India, where rise the thousand summits of Maha-Meru). For many these all mean either an abnormal rise of temperature or the loss of sensitiveness. Even the difference in weight of a potato before its dissolution and the loss in weight at the summarizing of its particles does not impel us to ponder upon certain energies which have been overlooked. However, each sincere chemist will admit that at each reaction some unaccountable condition is present—perhaps the peculiar qualities of the experimenter himself. For instance the presence of a certain personality in the laboratory of Sir Jagadis Bose prevented the death of plants. As Sir Jagadis is a great scholar, he at once noted this fact. But few are those who pay attention to the influence of human nature upon plants. Few are far enough advanced to accept a fact as it stands, unprompted by prejudice, superstition, selfishness and self-conceit. Verily, rare are such great self-sacrificing scientists as Millikan, Michelson, Einstein, Raman, Marconi, who untiringly carry the torch of enlightenment and betterment of life.

The light-bearing quality *(Tejas)* of the manas is as real as the radiant emanation created by the tension of a thought of high quality. The masters of Christian iconography, as well as the Buddhist artists, expressed these radiant emanations with great skill. Studying these images you will find an evident exposition of the crystallization of light. It is time to study and apply this reality of the value of thought—the value of light. It is time to realize that when we pronounce the great conception of Bliss, we are not falling into abstraction, but affirming a high reality. The time has come for the establishment of the evaluation of the rays and energies now being discovered. Ahead of us, for decades, lie carefully-planned experiments into the influences and consequences of radium, X-rays, and all that power which invisibly permeates and magnifies the atmosphere of the planet. Without question, one must found laboratories for untiring, decade-long experiments. There psychic energy will also be studied as will physiology of the spirit and thought, and the quality of light-bearing agents, life-givers and life-preservers. It is a vast creative field, and during these researches, fearlessness before Infinity will be manifested.

Fire and Light. The entire progress of humanity is

concentrated upon this all-penetrating and omnipresent element. If properly evoked it will be realized and lawfully applied; otherwise it will burn the consequences of ignorance. In this search for the synthesis of knowledge once more the excrescences of the East and West, North and South will be erased. Everywhere we shall find the very same "subtle pain of the cognizing heart," "the very same attainment by the innermost heart exertion," the "same exaltation of spirit." And together with the Apostle we shall say, "it is better to say five words from the depths of the heart, than a torrent of words with the tongue." Let us not leave the real values in abstraction, but let us unhesitatingly apply them without prejudice. The transferring of reality into abstraction is one of the most deplorable crimes against culture. There are many who still do not distinguish between civilization and culture, and thus they are committing the values of culture into misty un-attainability. How much of that which is predestined has already been rejected by fear and hypocrisy? But sooner or later one must be cured of fear; it is necessary to liberate the enormous amount of energy usually dissipated in fear, irritation, lying and treason. Let us hasten to affix our radiant emanations on a film—thus we shall obtain the true passport of spirit. Agni Yoga says: "The darkness shrieks, deafening in its regularity. Darkness cannot withstand the daring of light."

Saint Teresa, Saint Francis of Assisi, Saint Jean de la Croix, were levitated in ecstasy to the ceiling of their cells. Some may say that this is absolutely impossible. And suppose even today there should be witnesses of levitation and changing of weight? The Flaming One took part in the Service with Saint Sergius, according to tradition. From the flaming Chalice, Saint Sergius took his Communion. In the great Fire, he realized the invisible Truth: The uplifted consciousness was illumined by tongues of flame. During the prayers of Saint Francis of Assisi the monastery was so aglow that the travelers rose, thinking: "Is it not the dawn?" The radiance glowed above the monastery when Saint Clara prayed. Once the light became so luminous that the peasants came running, thinking: "Is there not a fire?"

Many traditions exist. But here is a simple story told about the Pecherski Monastery in Pskov:

"Our monastery is an unusual one. Walking out from the monastery, and regarding it from a distance, impenetrable darkness surrounds one. But above the monastery light gloweth. Many a time I myself have seen it.

"Some one inquires, 'Perhaps this is from the monastery fire?'

"So also do others who do not know:

" 'What fires are in the monastery?'

" 'Two kerosene lanterns and two oil lamps burn before the icons. This is all the lighting.'

" 'In our city, electricity is used, but nevertheless in the darkness, one cannot discern on which side it lies.'

" 'No, this is a special light above the monastery.' "

Likewise, in the Himalayas, the people came running to what they believed to be a fire, and in the same way, instead of destructive flames they found the radiance of the spirit. Likewise the mountain stood crowned by the blue petals of the fiery Lotus. Thus in the Bible the unconsuming fire was kindled. Many fiery signs have appeared, such as the special manifestations of electricity. And what is electricity? This also has not been explained.

During the last earthquake in Italy many people saw the entire sky ablaze in tongues of flame. Over England a fiery cross was seen. Was it superstition? Or did somebody see that which in other cases passed unnoticed?

Try to test the attentiveness of people and you will be shocked at the rarity of those who know how to apply their vigilance and power of movement. Even the power of thought, the mighty magnet, is shamefully neglected. Smile, smile, but just the same you do not try to think precisely.

Boxing, golf, cricket and baseball truly do not require the power of thought. Racing also is not precisely thinking.

One may invent still other occupations which will justify the neglect of thought, but yet one will sometimes have to turn back to the creativeness of thought. Therefore even small experiments in attentiveness are not useless. Verily, in schools one ought to establish special courses for developing concentration and thought. Rare is the person who is able to dictate two letters at once, or write with both hands, or to master two conversations simultaneously. Often a clear image of an object cannot be retained and even a simple interior cannot be described. For some people even all foreigners look alike. But even a slight attentiveness could be of great assistance in life. In the study of the hygiene of thought we notice some things which are called phenomena by the average person, whereas, they are simple manifestations of the law. Thus honest study will once more replace the despair of unbelief by a glorious possibility.

In any case we cannot avoid the era of Fire. Hence it is better to value and to master this treasure. It is advisable to question any statement when it assaults our reason, but doubt springing from ignorance will be destructive. However, the entire world is now strikingly divided into builders and destroyers. With whom shall we side? We have heard repeatedly of many luminous radiations; nevertheless we deride anything concerning human and animal auras. Even if a photographic film catches them we prefer to hint about a defect in the film, rather than to admit the well-known ancient law.

When remembering the strange experiments of Keely, we rather prefer to class him as a charlatan, than to consider the specific quality of his nature. The apparatus invented by him worked in his presence but refused to act in the hands of others. Why then does a machine become more "fatigued" in some hands than in others? Every experienced engineer notices this. Why does the fatigue of a horse depend upon the rider? Why does the quality of a hand shorten the life of flowers? We talk about psychic energy. We are aware that, as the ancient *Militia Crucifera*

Evangelica gathered about the symbol of the Cross, we must gather around the sacred conception of Culture.

Complicated but beautiful is our Era when, in new combinations, shine new multi-colored stars. The experienced Fathers advise us of "the wondrous exertion in the innermost heart." "We have ceaselessly to revolve the name of the Lord in our hearts, as lightning whirls in space before rain. This is well known to him who is experienced in spiritual fights. This inner battle has to be carried out like actual war."

"But when by the Sun of Truth, sensual desires will be dispersed, then usually are born in the heart luminous and celestial aspirations."

In another part of the ancient Teachings, it is said: "The pure heart of him who has affirmed himself in full consciousness, is transformed into a mental sky with its own sun, moon and stars. Such a pure heart becomes a receptacle of the inconceivable God through the mysterious vision and exaltation of mind."

Further the Fathers of Mercy teach: "Be seated or, better still, stand in a half-lighted corner in silence, in a prayerful posture. Do not relax, transfer the mind into the heart. Guard thy attention and do not permit either good or bad thought into thy mind; keep calm patience. Keep reasonable moderation." ...

"In order to assist in this task, the Holy Fathers pointed out certain means qualifying them as practitioners of art and even the art of the arts. This natural art, that of entering into the heart by means of breathing helps greatly the exaltation of thoughts." Continuing the advice for this special *pranayama*, the Holy Father counsels: "Breathing through the lungs conducts the air to the heart. Thus, be seated and, concentrating the mind, lead it in this direction; force it by breathing inward, to penetrate into the very heart together with the air inhaled: and keep it there, not permitting it to leave, much as it would want to. Keeping it there, do not leave it idle, but give it sacred words. Try to become accustomed to this inner concentration and watch lest thy mind leave there too soon, for at first it will be under depression, then it will be joyous and happy to dwell there and it will itself want to remain there. Shalt thou succeed in penetrating into the heart by the means I have pointed out to thee, abide by this exertion forever. It shall teach thee that which thou never hast conceived."

"Thus it is necessary to find an experienced preceptor (Guru). Saint Gregory Sinaite says: 'An active and heartily intelligent prayer is achieved thus: Be seated on a low chair, half a foot high; transfer the mind from the head to the heart and keep it there and from there invoke with hearty intelligence: Lord Jesus Christ, have mercy!'

"Know that all such special postures of the body are prescribed and are needed until pure and concentrated prayer is enrooted in the heart. And when, through the Bliss of the Lord thou shalt attain this, then, laying aside much special exertion, thou wilt be united without words with the Lord, in pure and concentrated heart-felt prayer, no longer necessitating special preparations. Besides, do not forget that when at times thou art inspired for a pure voluntary prayer, do not by any means destroy it by the usual prayer precepts. Cast aside these precepts and as far as thy inner forces reach, try to adhere to the Lord and He will enlighten thy heart in the spiritual attainment.

"Even in deep sleep the fragrance of prayer will ascend from the heart without effort. Though the inner voice be silent during sleep, yet within, the sacred service shall ceaselessly act. For only this sacred dagger ceaselessly rotated in the heart, liberated from any other image, can force the enemies to retreat and destroy them and consume them as does fire applied to straw."

One may quote endlessly from the Holy Fathers of the Church and the rules of the covenants of the hermits; and one feels that these rules are created for life and applied in reality. Again speaks an experienced voice: "When the spiritual gifts are realized, then, under a constant bliss, one becomes radiant and becomes unwavering in the contemplation of the spiritual treasures. Such an one is freed from all earthly things and forever is liberated from death into the eternal life. Inexpressible in words is the radiance of the Divine Beauty. Neither can word express it, nor ear contain it. Even if thou shalt compare it with the glory of dawn, the luminosity of the moon, the light of the sun—all these do not equal its divine glory. Poor are all these before the true Light, deepest night or densest darkness before the purest light."

Thus can he alone speak who has experienced what is the "spiritual man of the heart"—"a light which even in the darkness shineth and is inextinguishable by darkness."

When Makary, the Egyptian, wrote the following, he depicted, not abstract symbols, but vital realization: "Those who are the sons of Light and the sons of Service in the Holy Spirit, they shall learn nothing from men for they are inspired by Divine Wisdom. For Bliss itself inscribes in their hearts the laws of spirit. They need not be induced by writings inscribed with ink; but upon the tablets of the heart the divine Bliss inscribes the laws of spirit and the heavenly mysteries. It is the heart that rules all the organs of the body. And if Bliss reached the valleys of the heart, then it rules all the organs of the body and dominates all thoughts."

An ancient Egyptian papyrus says: "The beginning of the physician's wisdom is the knowledge of the heart's action."

He who knows the spiritual heart, knows also "the subtle pain of the physical heart," about which the Holy Fathers speak so inspiringly. He who knows this "subtle pain" has cognized also the fire of love—not the love of sighs but the real love of action and attainment. That love which, since antiquity has been called the Love of God-man, which purifies and uplifts the human sensations. Agni Yoga says: "What sage of knowledge would not be a Lord of Love?"

"The subtle pain," the heat of the flame of the heart, is known to the experienced one in the highest tests of life. It is known to those to whom enlightened labor has become the daily prayer; and prayer transformed into the ceaseless rhythm of heart, into the rhythm of light. Some will ask what is rhythm and why is its realization so important? It means that he who inquires does not know what is the "subtle pain" of the heart and is unaware of the music of the spheres, and has not hearkened to the hymn of nature. Without his own striving, he shall not cognize the sparks of attainment, which will bring his heart closer to the Cosmos and Love. The center of spirit is linked with the center of the organism. ... "This unity, known for ages, is not deciphered scientifically, nor philosophically, but is nonetheless quite evident."

The Chalice of experience! In this way we again approach the creation by thought—the mysterious but immutable, "the Word become matter." This way the Logos is embodied into the physical. This mystery is manifested in each man, in each incarnated spirit. "God breathed eternity into the heart of each man"—the Realm of Light is immortal, eternal through all incarnations. And it shall cognize the Light; for it is the very source of Light itself. The "subtle pain" is the manifestation of subtle energy and the luminosity is one of the prime qualities of the action of such energies. When this light is intensified, it becomes visible even to our eye. This moment remains forever the long awaited and unexpected. It is ordained to keep the torches aflame, but the moment of the great Messenger is inexpressible. Likewise inexpressible is the "subtle pain" of the heart and the covenant that "Joy is a special Wisdom." Alongside with this one can remember the covenants of the Bhagavad Gita, and Agni Yoga and the Kabbala and the prophecies of the Bible and the Fire of Zoroaster.

The "Sun-likeness" of Plato belongs to the same untold but luminous conceptions. When the experienced ones meet, they are not in need of a vocabulary, for, even in silence, they will understand the language of the heart.

Hence, gain experience and proclaim it—because you are not aware of your best hour, nor do you know when the flame will flash over the Chalice of accumulations. Only the high quality of thought will guide you and insatiable impetuosity will be the wings of Light of Sophia — Wisdom. It is ordained to radiate, but not to be consumed.

The resounding of the Center of the heart, heard by Socrates, harmonizes with the rhythm of Good. The high matter of Spinoza is ozonized by the same waves of light. The luminous center of the heart can radiate with the all-illumining flame—the fabulous stone of the legends of the Grail.

Agni Yoga says: "At the basis of the Universe, search for the heart." ... "The creativeness of heart is strained by the Chakra of the Chalice." ... "The greatest Might is in the Magnet of the Heart." ... "The word not containing the affirmation of the heart is empty." ... "The pearl of the heart is the subtle tensity." "An Arhat as a flame carries in his heart all fires of life."

Origen affirms: "With the eyes of the heart we can see Be-ness."

"All is pure to the pure," fearlessly ordains the Apostle Paul. He knew the purity and activity of the heart, when it knows only the good and as a magnet attracts around itself only the good. The similarity between heart and magnet is often mentioned, although scientifically it is not yd acknowledged. However "the treasures of Wisdom and knowledge" are attained only by the wisdom of the heart, by the chalice of love and self-sacrificing action. "There, where is your treasure, there is your heart," says the Apostle. The luminosity of the heart is similar to fluorescence of the sea, which in motion produces numberless visible luminous formations. Likewise the action of creative love kindles the flames of heart. "There shall be Light," says the Thought of the Great.

The "inner man" wishes only good and at the moment of hearty radiation he knows without doubt where is the good. And from the hearty radiation springs forth only good. And this emanating light smites all excrescences of ignorance; because sin and ignorance are the brothers of darkness. To live in spirit means to radiate, to do good and ceaselessly to attain. To live only in the body means to obscure, to condemn, to be ignorant and to prolong one's path. But it must not be overlooked that in retarding our own progress we obstruct the progress of those nearest us —hence every display of egotism, selfishness, self-pity, false pride, ignorance—is the stronghold of darkness. In the name of those near us, we must not disturb the rhythm of the waves of Light and Good.

Useful are observations upon flowers. The garden of light is likewise in need of constant care. The streams of pure thoughts are its best nurture. The more intense is light, the weaker the darkness. Even the radiant heart of the Angel could choose the freedom of gloom instead of the freedom of service and glory. Therefore without delay is needed the nurture of the garden of Light, otherwise the spotted tongues of tiger-lilies will devour the Lilies of Annunciation and the treacherous Belladonna will over-power the Fresias of the shiny summits. One must radiate. One must generate and strengthen the light of the heart. One must remember that co-radiance and co-resounding of light are mutually strengthened. Immeasurable is the might of the thoughts united by Benevolence. For every one, is the Light prepared, but we may extinguish it with an empty vessel. It is said, "At the fall of a rose petal, the far-off worlds tremble" and "the feather from the wing of a bird creates thunder upon the far-off worlds." What a vast, beautiful responsibility! Let us not turn the thunder born through light-mindedness towards the Earth.

From this inspiring responsibility issues a radiant attempt honestly to study without any disillusionment all which surrounds us. Even an accomplished virtuoso is in need of daily exercises. It is repeated: "If thou art tired, begin again. If thou art exhausted, begin again and again." And like a Shield invoke Love.

"The warmth of Love" is as real as the "subtle pain" of the heart. The radiance of the thought is not only tangible to the eye, but is even accessible to the film. It is necessary to study at once, without superstition, fearlessly and altruistically. Evidence relates to the physical body, but not to the spirit. Truth is in the very reality, but not in the pathology of evidence.

The heart, this great transmuter of energies, knows where is the convulsion of horror and the tremor of ecstasy. The spirit distinguishes the spots of terror and the radiation of exaltation. Wherefore to be scorched and carbonized if it is preordained to radiate immortally? "God is the fire which warms the hearts," says Saint Seraphim.

"He knows the depths of the heart," chants the Psalmist King. When we speak about the Beautiful, about the depths of the heart, then first of all we have in mind the beautiful creative thoughts. As the most delicate flowers they must be cultivated. They must be unceasingly watered by the joyful streams of Bliss. One must learn daily how to think clearly and benevolently. One must nurture the aspirations—these loftiest seedlings of thought. Let us dare. Let us not be afraid to aspire upon heights. From the summits we can see afar. From the summits come the Tables of Commandments, From the summits come the heroes and achievement. Radiant is aspiration. The flaming aspiration is the threshold of Bliss.

Agni and Thought.

Fiery are the wings of "Sophia—the Almighty's Wisdom."

Himalayas, 1930.

CULTURE

D EAR Friends:
We shall say briefly wherein the substance of our tasks and strivings lies. Everything which is defined can be expressed briefly: We are helping Culture. And if some one in a moment of audacity should take upon himself the burden of saying "We are constructing Culture," then he will be not far from the truth. Does not every one who helps appear to be a co-worker?

We are asking our friends, each day to think, to pronounce and to apply the understandings of Beauty and Culture. And this is not new, because there is nothing new anywhere. But we are gathering around these precious understandings a new effort; we are striving to help towards the tension of creative energy. We are striving to learn and to reincarnate the so-called abstraction into reality. It is very easy to make an abstraction from each action, and in this abstraction to lose the possibility of action. We see constantly that the most real teaching of life is being transmuted by clever rhetoric into an unapproachable abstraction and for the appeasing of the weak will it is being transported into an intangible cloudiness. To make this artificially created abstraction a reality and substance of life, is the next task of Culture. It is impossible for one to imagine that the true perception of substance, the true teaching of life is only something forbidding, obstructing or deadening.

Truth will be there, where will be manifested without obstacles a constructive broadening containment and love towards the untiring achievement. Our enemies say that we are forming of ourselves a special race. If we understand by this a nation of culture, then maybe this hostile definition, as too often happens, comes very close to the truth. We shall not be afraid of this truth, if as the highest condemnation, the Black Century—which has already spent itself—will tell us: "Here are gathered dreamers, and they imagine they can help humanity." Namely, in this help to humanity we are being reproached. But each of our companions-at-arms, who are scattered all over the world, will smile at that and say: "Does not every natural labor appear to be a help to humanity?" Because it would be abominable to think that every one who labors, labors only for himself. No, he works for some one unknown to him. And this unknown one will accept the nameless labor as an expression of Benevolence which makes his passage along the earthly path easier for him.

Not dreams, but embodiments of thoughts; the dream flies away into the shoreless ocean of the air, but the embodiment of thoughts creates substance and cements space with the coming creations. Of the creation by thought into multiple forms, all religion, all teaching has spoken. Many thousands of years before our era the Egyptians knew the creativeness of thought. And it has been said everywhere: "Thought and Love." And under the sign of the Heart and the Serpent and the Chalice in all its multiformity of benevolent symbols is being given also the wise, preordained inscription, "Thought and Love." Because from a thought, an emanation absolutely real, we contrive to make abstractions. We forget that it is not the hand, but the thought which creates and kills. And of Love we have made either a sour sigh or an abomination of fornication.

It has been told us that certain branches of the Christian Church recently sanctioned abortion. This unhappy ordinance must be understood as the highest negation of spirituality. Just think, if the Church will recommend murder, instead of the wise distribution of strength and abstinence. If the division of the world into Constructors and Destroyers is constantly talked about, then this measure would be a terrible sign of destruction. But Culture in its essence does not know destruction as such. It is impetuously, constantly creating, it is constantly covering with a newer, higher dome the imperfections of yesterday. But here it comprises that stone which would be of use to the wise builder, which meets every possibility.

Verily, in all parts of the world, at present is rising the tension of constructive energy. The lines of new workers cry out: "We are tired of destruction, we are overburdened by senseless mechanization. We want to create, we want to do that useful work which unites us with the resplendent future." In ancient teachings, there has always been pointed out the bridge which unites the old and the new worlds. And nowhere have destruction and violence been mentioned.

If one is to ponder over the spirituality of the future, although this spirituality seem an abstract one, it shall again assert its visibility, its tangibility and its immutability. And again Benevolence will become objective, just as Thought is objective and can be weighed. If one ennobles his life, if instead of vile calumny, one tries to turn again to the resplendent creation, is this laughable? Because only ignoramuses will laugh—for them, knowledge itself has already become an abstraction and Beauty also has become an unnecessary luxury, and Benevolence itself has become a childish fairy-tale. But the most serious scientists long ago came to the conclusion that a fairytale is a narrative. And a narrative is an historical fact which one can perceive only through the smoke of ages.

The same scientists have pointed out to us that Culture and the achievements of empires have been constructed by Beauty. Take away the monuments of Beauty and the whole aspect of history will be depleted. The virility of Beauty, the age-long inviolability of Culture tell us of the true transmutation of abstraction into manifested life. And we are not dreamers at all, but workers for life, and our apostolate above all is content in that we are striving to say to the people, "Remember Beauty. Do not exile its image from life, but also actively call others to this feast of joy! And if you see allies, do not bid them depart, but find the full measure of benevolent containment in order to call us to the very same peaceful, measureless field of labor and construction. In Beauty and in Spirit shall our strength be multiplied. Look into the heights, and spread thy wings as the conqueror of the predestined Light." ... In the day of spiritual disturbances and tremor, we shall repeatedly affirm the very same construction and the same benevolent Light. And there are no conditions which could turn one aside who has entered the path of construction. And we shall not be afraid in the name of the Beautiful; and we shall remember that the ridicule of ignorance is only a torch of achievement. If we will eschew egotism, if we will strive not only ourselves towards the path of the Beautiful, but also by all possible means open it to our nearest ones, then we shall have already fulfilled the next task of the enlightening of Culture—the ascension of the Spirit.

1930.

THE BEAUTIFUL

Address to the Dalton School

IN Bombay I was once asked what was the difference between East and West, and I answered, "The best roses of East and West have the same fragrance." So, while we are speaking about opposition and differences, essentially we have the great "One," because really all law is One, and under this Law, everything is One. We have only to serve this One and if we are unable to do so, we may say *"Mea culpa,"* for we are guilty of having failed to follow the law.

Very often we are trying to discover how to build the next life—how to build the evolution to come. Well, that is our duty. And you will all very soon wish to build up your own lives, and certainly you will wish to build up a happy life. What is the best medium to reach this happiness? Fortunately, after visiting more than twenty-five countries, I can tell you from my own experience—only through the Beautiful. We are divided in so many experiences, and yet everywhere is this same feeling of the Beautiful. You note that I am underlining the *Beautiful,* not Beauty, because I am speaking not only about art, or about some expression of art, music, drama, song, but I am speaking about the *sense* of the Beautiful, and it is our duty to introduce in our lives this general sense of this great conception.

Perhaps some one could ask me, "Well, it is very good to have such a dream—to make life somehow beautiful. We often think that this Beautiful is only for those who are rich; and he who must work—how can he dream about the Beautiful? And certainly, we all have need of this dream about the Beautiful."

In various countries, I have seen many collectors, real workers in art, and some of them have been very poor.

They have been of the working class, and still this sense of the Beautiful was so strong in them that, even with their modest means, they found the possibility to approach the Beautiful.

I remember one very prominent collector, a colonel in the army—and you know that the income of a colonel is not large—but he was a born collector. He understood that not only the painting exists, but that before it, a sketch is made and very often in these sketches the conception is expressed far better than it is in the painting. So this ardent collector began to gather various sketches. He came to our studios, saying he could not pay much, but would like this first thought, this first expression of the painting. He was very persistent—in ten years he gathered a most remarkable collection of these various expressions, and perhaps this collection was sometimes far more precious than a huge collection of finished paintings.

The chief thing is to have this inner sense of the Beautiful. Because not every one has a medium in art, but practically every one has thought, and very often our creation in the realm of thought is far greater than reflections in some medium of art. I am underlining this because very often people come to me, saying over and over the same story: "I have no prospects in life, how can I dream about something beautiful—I have no time to study." But in a few moments you can see that this man is really gifted—that he has wonderful conceptions and thoughts, and really can project his thoughts and his conceptions into space.

We have to remember that every thought is recorded in the space. So the chief thing is to create in thought—to be real cooperators in this beautiful creation of the whole universe. Because in this way of creation we will reflect the best creative powers and we will then be true cooperators and co-workers toward the Supreme.

After visiting various peoples of Asia, with varied customs and varied lives, I can affirm that this idea is very vital. Because while we think very often to introduce art in life—there you find everywhere that art is part of life.

When some one asked us, "Is it possible for you to be away from a theater for five years?" the answer was that we have the theater in life itself; we have music in life itself; we have song in life itself.

Several times in Central Asia, in the desert of Mongolia, we heard a Mongolian singing a beautiful song. When we asked him to repeat it, he answered, "That is impossible, because we are singing only for the desert." We are dreaming of having art in life, in the most vital way.

In the Roerich Museum you have seen my expression of the Sacred Dances of Mongolia. You ask how to introduce the theater? There they have as a stage-setting their beautiful sacred banners, exquisitely painted; a huge orchestra, with gigantic trumpets; powerful choruses. For days and days they are performing the sacred dances, sacred rituals. For days and days every one takes part in the ceremony. So all of life is transmuted into beauty.

How can we introduce this spirit here? Difficulties and possibilities are alike—there and here. To do this in a vital way, we have to realize the power of thought. We speak often about will-power, but very seldom do we employ this power. We speak about telepathy and we think that it is something very difficult and supernatural, phenomenal; but there are no phenomena, and there is no occultism.

To children, even the telephone is a most occult thing. But when you know how energy is employed, you know that there is nothing extraordinary involved.

We should introduce these possibilities into our lives.

In Asia, they speak about Agni Yoga, the Teaching of Fire. Is it something supernatural? No. They are explaining how to use this element of Fire—the flame of Space — this all-embracing element. And you will be told that very soon the Era of Flame is approaching our land. You will hear it in a quite scientific way, and then you will remember that Professor Millikan discovered the cosmic ray, and is about to discover the keenest application of that ray.

In Asia, for ages and ages, they have spoken about this

same beautiful energy. And this discovery will soon be given to humanity.

In the time of Buddha, they knew about the iron birds which would serve humanity. They knew from the most ancient times about iron serpents, also for the sake of humanity. So you see how, for ages, real knowledge was being given out, but in another language, or with other symbols, for if we analyze our prejudices in full honesty, we can have a multitude of very useful facts. But the problem is how to approach facts honestly. "We have to take science as science without any prejudice or superstition." At the same time, not infrequently, the scientists themselves fail to regard facts in the pure light of honesty. We should take these facts through ourselves —through our own understanding, and sometimes we will find ourselves more superstitious than some of the people in the desert. But all this does not matter. When we have such scientists as Einstein, as Millikan, we feel that our coming evolution is in good hands.

You have probably read the articles by Prof. Millikan. Is it not a great joy to see how this eminent scientist speaks in so broad a way? In him there is no superstition. And he is experiencing this same state of the Beautiful, because every scientist, in the moment of discovery, is the same as the artist, because he is in the same spirit of the Beautiful. Sometime you can ask a discoverer how his discovery was made—what happened in the moment of discovery. And if the man is honest, he will tell you that something happened at that moment. It was not an accident. At that moment, he touched the Supreme—the highest Cross of Eternity.

I have seen your beautiful room dedicated to chemistry and to science. You know how electricity is created by the crossing of two energies. That is a beautiful moment when two immeasurable energies create something physical and measurable.

You see how important it is to create your essential energy. You will hear about scientific energy, occult energy, Agni energy. These are all symbols for the same thing—creative energy.

Some big bankers, big business men, are also artists, and it is very easy to speak to and to receive understanding from a big man, because his consciousness is already expanded and if you are speaking to him about something difficult, still his experience is so big that he can understand everything, and from this understanding emanates his tolerance. Please remember this quality—tolerance. You will need it. So many things have been broken through ignorance.

Intolerance is ignorance. And having dispersed essential ignorance with science, we may feel that science and art are one. Because everything is one. And creative energy is one. In this way you can forever keep your enthusiasm. Sometimes we think we are tired. But we are not tired. We are only using the same nervous center too long. If we are tired, it does not mean that we need relaxation—that we need to sleep. We should only change our work —change the center, and in this change of different nervous centers you will become rested.

Remember, the chief poison is the poison of irritation and anger, and this is a most powerful poison. For with every irritation, we physically create in our nervous system some emanation.

Our best scientists, physicians, know already that something physical is created through irritation. In Asia, they will tell you about this crystal of anger. How can we be happy if we know that through our anger, we are creating poisons? The remedy is only not to be irritated—not to be angry. When you remember forever that anger is something hideous, then it is not so difficult not to be irritated. If you know some one comes to irritate you, you must encounter him with a smile. And when you know that, you are already strong.

I should not like to feel that some of you today think that I am speaking of something abstract, or occult, or something mystical. What is "mystical?" Something from mist. But we have nothing to do with mists or clouds—only with facts and light. And with facts we can enlighten our life.

We are speaking about the Beautiful because when you will realize this scientific energy, the greatest power which is in each of you—then you shall release this energy, and energy will grow.

Very often people ask how to release this energy. This energy is our property. One time a young group asked how to release this energy. I asked them—"Each of you, please tell me something unusual about your life." They all became silent. There was nothing unusual to tell! "Our lives are routine." ... "I am working in a bank." ... "I am working in a factory." ... But is it not strange that Boehme, one of the great philosophers, was a shoemaker? And One was a carpenter! Certainly this routine of life is our *pranayama.* This word, new to you, means the using of the energy, the processes of learning how to use the energy. You can achieve through this—and I can tell you that your routine work is the *pranayama.* Only we must maintain the quality of work. When we keep the quality of our work, we begin to be successful. He is the highest artisan who can attain the quality of art in work. We can even wash the floors spiritually. For then some one will at once remark it saying: "This man is doing this work in such a beautiful way, that he is not in his place. Something higher should be given him." And when we refine the quality of our work, another thing happens—we have the joy of work. The greatest misfortune is that people often work for rest, for a holiday; but when we know the joy of work, then we need no conventional holidays. We can celebrate our holiday in labor, with the clearest conception, and with the best thought. And we shall not be tired, because we shall be so enthusiastic, we shall keep our enthusiasm. We shall not sleep too much, because we shall not need to sleep much. When we are sleepy, when we are not thinking, then everything bad happens. But if you are producing this work for the quality of the work, in this creative enthusiasm, you are strong and you are impersonal, and perhaps this feeling of the impersonal is the greatest aspect of the Beautiful.

You have some beautiful examples of art in your school —where is the name of the author? There is no name; no author. If the name had been written, perhaps it could be ascertained only for a few hundred years. But you have these objects for thousands of years.

So this impersonality is the greatest central aspect of the Beautiful. Then we can understand that "I" is isolated, and that "We" is strong. Through "We" comes the real beginning of organization, and the real cooperation.

Everywhere in Asia you have this beautiful conception of Guru-ship, the Teacher—it is not a feeling of slavery — on the contrary, it is a great feeling of cooperation. In this way, a chain of cooperators can be created. You know your Master and some one considers you as a Master, and in this way there is one chain to the Supreme.

And when you know this one Road, so many things are easy to you. I hope that sometimes you will remember what I have told you—how practical is the quality of work. We have to remember how much of waste there is in anger, so we can avoid it.

We know that at one time America and Asia have been one country. Some cataclysm occurred, and they were divided. In this connection, the Mongols tell a beautiful tale of how the earth was split, and how some fiery iron birds are soon to bring them news from their lost relatives. The scientists have made this story come true and the people of the desert knew the same thing, only in their own language.

It would be the greatest mistake to think that the people in the East had forgotten their memories. They have many things in their own symbols. How beautifully they can speak about art and art objects! I wish many art critics might have so beautiful a faculty of expressing their feeling before art objects.

I remember in Kuchar in Central Asia, somebody told a beautiful tale about art:

How one artist wanted some money for his painting, and when he came to the money lender the man was absent, and only a boy was there. This boy gave the artist a very large sum for the painting. When the money lender came back, he said, "For these fruits and vegetables you gave such a great sum!" and he discharged the boy.

Time passed, and the artist returned, and asked for the painting. When he saw it he was horrified, saying, "That is not my painting. Where are the butterflies? Go find the boy, that he may help us find my painting. This painting you show me has only cabbages."

The boy came and said, "Now it is winter and the butterflies come only in the summertime. Put the painting near the fire, and we shall see the butterflies return." And so it was; the paint was put on the canvas so delicately that during the cold weather the colors receded, but in the warmth they returned.

Thus beautifully do these people speak about the perfection of art.

Remember the sense of the Beautiful. I again advise you to keep your enthusiasm, and to keep this creative thought—to remember that thought is the chief thing—that power of thought is the real possibility and it is the most practical thing to have pure thoughts. So please have pure thoughts.

New York, March 27, 1930.

SPIRITUAL TREASURES

IF, in gathering the beauties of spirit, we begin to remember the events of the last years, We are astonished by one basic circumstance, which prompts special consideration. For the last few decades we have seen many remarkable personalities passing on to the far-off path. It has been valuable to perceive also what sincere regrets have been called forth by their loss in the hearts of the most varied peoples in the different continents. As though something precious, needed, that constructs the ascending foundations of life's structure, is passing away. In the eyes of the most apparently impartial people glimmered tears—those pure gems of impersonal vibration. We remember how we marked the passing of Leo Tolstoi, of Pasteur, of Wagner, of Mendeleeff and many others equally significant in the betterment and purification of human consciousness.

We remember also, another fact no less valuable: namely, the welcoming of experiments, discoveries and cultural achievements which took place. It is not a soulless chronicle which pointed out and hailed the new conquests of mankind. The enthusiastic praises as well as the inevitable condemnations which followed these events ignited an explosion of sparks which in their turn created and aroused attention.

How does it stand at present? The chronicles point out discoveries, and devote even greater space undoubtedly to the stock exchange and sport. The appearance of great people is met by suspicious doubt, and their departure is accompanied by a formal rising and an artificial silence, and no one knows the quality of the thoughts during that moment of prescribed silence.

What does this mean? Perhaps it is a sign of unusual spiritual riches? Perhaps giants of thought, giants of creativeness have become so usual, that their departure can no longer occupy or attract public attention?

Is this really the case? Or does it rather signify the very opposite? Does this not mean contempt of spiritual values? Does not this fascination with material, physical and passing concepts during which the light is veiled as if by a dusty cloud, indicate that the values of culture are being pushed into the mist? For us it is not necessary to convince ourselves of the true causes of the visible manifestations which take place. We gather together in the name of culture and each of us of course, feels keenly the need of true unity around this understanding which leads the forces of evolution. But if we, in any measure, feel the truth of what has been said, then is it not our duty to manifest it? Each person according to his own sphere must direct the attention of those who surround him, to any negligence of spiritual value.

It has been repeatedly inscribed on the scrolls of command that a spiritual garden is daily in need of the same watering as a garden of flowers. If we still consider the flowers as precious adornments of our life, then how much more must we remember and prescribe to the creative values of the spirit the leading place in the life which surrounds us? Let us then with untiring, eternal vigilance, benevolently mark the manifestations of the workers of culture; and let us strive in every possible way to ease this difficult path of heroic achievement.

Equally so, let us mark and find a place in our lives for the passing heroes, remembering that their names no longer are personal, with all the attributes of the limited ego, but have become the property of pan-human culture, and must be safeguarded and firmly cared for in most benevolent conditions.

Thus we shall continue their self-sacrificing labor and

we shall cultivate their creative sowing which as we see, is so often covered with the dust of non-understanding and overgrown with the weeds of ignorance.

Very few are the spiritual discoveries of creative revelation. Hence we cannot excuse our negligence toward the leading lights because of the advance of the standard of life. Even though electric lights, which were a rarity not so long since, now burn upon every street, there still remains a treasure of new, and still-untried energies to be brought to us. Their manifestation in all branches is bound with the same self-denying sacrifices and labors, which should occupy public attention, because in this attention we seemingly collaborate with the creator, and in our benevolent thought-sending, intensify the possibilities of his discovery.

And so among the activities of our cultural associations, let us assign a place worthy to mark creations and discoveries in all branches of art and science. Let us dedicate sincere thought to the progressive labors of the bearers of light—of those who come anew as well as those who pass on. Let it not be a doubtful shrug of the shoulders. Let it be not a cold obituary. But, as an honor-guard, let us protect these sprouts of light. Liberated from prejudices and superstitions, serving victorious beauty, uplifting knowledge, we shall apply in all measures and for all branches the zealous thought of affirmation of bliss, by thus helping the further branches of research and betterment of life.

How precious that our associations are in various countries! Thus it is easier to watch universally for the manifestations of creative power and researches, the easier for mutual interchange, to enrich each other with useful and encouraging information which otherwise might merge in the shoreless currents of closely printed chronicles. No one knows why it is absolutely necessary for the creators of true progress to be exiled and to depart from the earthly plane condemned.

The covenant repeatedly says not to be embers but to glow. Even the evil blazing, may be easily controlled by the conscious efforts of united cultural associations which are sincerely dedicated towards the creative cognizance.

Of course our basic problem of action is to interchange all artistic expression between all our branches as well as all scientific discoveries, thus mutually acquainting ourselves with the spiritual values of all nations. And therefore, among plans of scientific and artistic discovery and the intercourse with which we are mutually enriched, let us not forget the noble work of gathering and establishing the cultural standards which so often may be ignored in the ebb and flow of life's tides.

And so, friends, let us introduce into our immediate program this interchange of constructive achievements already realized. And let us remember that the ignoring of cultural values is a shameful crime of ignorance. Therefore, let us untiringly and fearlessly strengthen each other and illumine the path which brings us closer to life.

Himalayas, January 1, 1930.

TRANSFIGURATION OF LIFE

L AST summer a robot was placed at the busiest cross-streets of London to direct traffic. At first this mechanical man performed his duties conscientiously and some people remarked jokingly in this connection that robots could be used for many tasks heretofore done by man. But after a cloudy day the sun appeared and its hot rays beat upon the robot, and apparently caused a local short circuit, for the robot, who was so splendidly replacing man, suddenly seemed to have gone mad, began frantically to wave his hands and for an entire hour threw into turmoil the most important traffic point of the metropolis. Policemen and mechanics were forced to apply extreme measures to put an end to this madness. Headlines in the newspapers commented on this extraordinary incident.

Another case was also recorded by the newspapers. During a boxing bout a robot was employed to keep the count and as a result confusion reigned in this favorite sport of today and even—horrors—money was lost. Again a very characteristic occurrence.

We must, however, see in this something which goes far beyond the limits of a street incident. The boundary of mechanization. The boundary of madness. How indispensable it is then to ponder over the necessity of establishing an equilibrium between spiritual energies and mechanical appliances. It is precisely now that the world civilization is deciding this most important problem. Not so very long ago people thought that photography could kill art and we still believe that the gramophone and the "talkies" can kill music and the theater. Did not wise men prophesy that in our day mankind would become blind from electricity and deaf from the telephone? A short time ago, motors were considered an impractical invention and the failure of the wireless telegraph and aviation was predicted. And now, when so many remarkable conquests have been bestowed upon humanity, how quickly people have succeeded in making an abominable standardization even out of the application of energy and of the elements, thus killing the possible enhancements of these conquests. Let us try to turn the regulator of an ordinary radio to see what there is on the air and infinity shall respond with a pandemonium, with Bedlam broken loose. In the same way all the maledictions of hate and envy are hanging in space and are destroying the healing *prana.*

We have reached the point when a human word can go around a planet in two minutes. But what does it impart at such speed? The news either of the stock exchange, or of sport or of clownery. Therefore, how necessary it is to use all means at our disposal to purify the quality of human thought so as not to depreciate and disfigure the splendid conquests of man's genius. At times one already hears mention made in the schools of the need of developing the creative impulse and of organizing thoughts. If a deadly standardization is not made of this beneficial enterprise, then perhaps somewhere there might be felt a shock which will make the school generation ponder over the questions of elevated thought, of heroism, of self-denial and self-sacrifice. And then only will people understand the simple truth that in giving we receive and in sacrificing we are enriched. And this will not be understood in a narrow, material sense, but its spiritual meaning will be revealed in all its true wealth. This physiology of the spirit, of which one has to speak so often nowadays, will be a practical life principle which will once more bring the abstract into reality.

In our communities let us not be afraid of such syntheses of the idea of life, without pseudo-occultism and mysticism. Yes, we greet each great conquest of the spirit and of knowledge and we understand that mechanics may become true mechanics when the understanding of art is united to it.

Therefore, through our friends, let us explain the all-penetrating understanding of the beauty of art, which shall save us from death-imparting standardization and from the pernicious debris of life. Over and over again we repeat that these are not commonplace utterances. We repeat that the idea of nobility and the dignity of thought is not hypocrisy, but a sign of true creative impulse brought forth by the Divine spark of the spirit in man. Mutually fortifying ourselves, let us say these same words to the school generations. And let us show them, at the same time, that we are not trying to humiliate them by giving them toys, but that we are earnestly calling them to cooperation. Does not every child feel proud when he is entrusted with the work of an adult? Only then does he act with circumspection and care, trying not to disgrace himself in the eyes of the grown-ups. We would like to call attention to the fact that children prefer the books of adults far more than the artificially "stylized," so-called children's books, in which some adults try to pull on children's rompers. These reflections apply also to the mob, which, in fact, is far better than it is reputed to be. Only ignoramuses think that vulgarity is demanded by the mob. Thousands of examples could be cited to show that heroism inspires the crowd in a greater and more efficacious way than clownery or an insipid joke. Let heroism and nobility of thought be not an abstract notion for us, but let them become honored guests at our daily intercourses. And again let it not be an empty sound when we say that we shall devote all our strength to the positive principle of creative work. In studying the history of art, we see exactly what signs followed the constructive and the destructive moments. Unprejudiced and cautious, let us choose these sparks of positive creative impulse and let us try to bring them into our every-day life.

Himalayas, February, 1930.

TO WOMANHOOD

Dedicated to Woman's Unity of Roerich Museum

THE Mother of the World. How much of that which is tremendously stirring and moving is blended in this sacred image of all ages and all peoples.

In cosmic waves this great conception moves toward the consciousness of man. In the spiral of accretion it appears sometimes as though receding, yet it is not a regression, it is only a phase of movement, inaccessible to our vision.

Teachings speak of the epoch of the Mother of the World which has now begun. The Mother of the World, Near-to-all-hearts, Revered-by-all-minds, again takes Her place at the great helm. And he, who understands this Visage of Evolution, shall be happy and protected.

In an impressive and stirring way Christianity has consecrated the following legend to the Mother of God:

The Apostle Peter, sacristan of Paradise, was disturbed. And he said to the Lord God: "All day long I watch the gates of Paradise; I do not let anyone in, yet in the morning there are newcomers in Paradise."

And the Lord said: "Let us make the rounds at night, Peter."

So they went in the night and they saw the Holy Virgin lowering along the wall Her snow-white scarf, up which souls were climbing.

Peter took this to heart and wanted to interfere, but the Lord whispered: "Sh ... let be..."

The Orient has consecrated the following hymn to the Mother of the World.

"Above Them is She Who veiled Her Face, She Who wove the Web of the far-off Worlds, She the Envoy of the

Unutterable, the Ruler of the Intangible, the Bestower of the Unrepeatable.

"By Thy Command is the Ocean silenced and the Whirlwinds trace the Invisible Signs.

"And She Who Veiled Her Face shall stand Alone in Vigil, amid the Splendor of Her Signs.

"And none shall mount the Summit. None shall witness the Effulgence of the Dodecahedron, the Sign of Her Power."

The cult of the Mother of the World has been discovered in the ancient city of Kish, and the oldest literature of China has greeted the Mother of the World in inspired hymns. She is the Quick-to-Aid, She-of-the-Hundred-Hands and Of-the-Thousand Eyes, She Who protects by Her Veil all those who come for help. She, the Mother of the World, whether in the image of Kwan-Yin or in the bright colored mantle of the Madonna.

The marvelous Russian artist Maria Germanova, the Russian Duse, sent me last summer the following stirring and appealing letter which I am citing as a remarkable monument of the fiery heart of a woman.

This letter was the more appealing to the aspirations of our hearts, since the thought of a Woman's Unity had crystallized itself with Mme. Roerich and myself into the forms of new organizations which, in the broadest measure, could summon the world to new constructions. In March, 1930, Mme. Roerich wrote to America of the need to organize a Woman's Unity. And long before, the idea was formulated for the Altai Sisters—Sisters of the Golden Mountain. Frequently I hailed the women's organizations. I also had written of the Great Mother of the World and the mysterious veil of Woman, and in this article, I asked, "Why, since antiquity, has the wreath been the true adornment of the woman's brow? The wreath—that crown of achievement!" ... Hence, in the name of this crown of Achievement, the letter of Mme. Germanova responded so greatly to our previous decisions. I quote it:

"We lift our hearts to the Mountains...

"There is an old proverb: 'When the children are small, they are a burden for a Mother's knees; When they grow up, for her heart.' And, verily, children grow up, they outgrow us, they fly away from the nest; there is no more need to bathe, feed, clothe them; yet a Mother's heart is just as full of cares, worries and prayers for her beloved ones.

"A Mother's heart, a woman's heart, is a great treasure. It kindles us, it lights up the family. Who taught you to pray? Who will understand and forgive? The Mother. The Woman. Who will inspire to a great task?—The Beloved One, The Friend—The Woman.

"Oftener and oftener, firmer and firmer, it is now being realized that the Era of the Woman has come, and many glowing lamps of the women's hearts are kindled in solitude, in secrecy, and often in the bondage of darkness; but they are kindled by one fire—Love, by the beauty of Motherhood, of Womanhood.

"If only we could unite in the time of this Fire, if only we could know that we are not alone!—how lightly and joyously the flame of our hearts would rise.

"We, the Women, old, young, mothers, wives, friends, the happy and the lonely ones, if we were to gird ourselves by the might of Love, what a divine power would be erected, what resplendent harmony would take up arms against darkness and evil, to help all humanity, which at present is in unprecedented danger.

"We shall save the earth. We shall transform life. In the Unity of our hearts we do not have to gather in clubs and societies; read reports, give lectures; and abandon for these our dear ones and our homes. No. Verily in the Home we shall carry our Light.

"How much we can do! We shall cast ugliness, vulgarity, out of our everyday life, and we shall invite Beauty to come as a Guest into our homes.

"We shall sweep away the dust and the spider-webs, not only from the corners of our houses, but also from our relationships, words, thoughts—in order that our spirits may breathe easily; we shall think not only of the meal but also that there should be no poison for the spirit. Let us cast out the poison of quarrels, gossip, slander, and give the honored place at our table to the laughter of joy.

"When departing on a journey, or to work, let us not only take care of trunks and expenses, but also send forth pure, benevolent thoughts and prayers.

"Yes, one cannot enumerate at one time all the possibilities of achievement which as a Promised Land lie before the Woman.

"We shall lay down our souls for our beloved Ones.

"Jeanne d'Arc saved her country.

"We, if united, shall save the earth. There is no resurrection without a Golgotha, and so this call has a reason, because it comes out of the pain of one tortured woman's heart, the heart of Madame Helena Roerich, who is in a foreign, far-off country, to which she came so self-sacrificingly to bring her service to Enlightenment. She is ill, alone, longing for her dear ones; separated from her husband and friends, who, because of inexplicable, unjust, incomprehensible reasons, are unable to secure visas and the possibility of consoling, calming, healing this sacred pain and sorrow of a Mother. Let us rise to the defense of this suffering heart. Let it be our oriflamme. It is purged by the fire of eternal suffering, and shall be as a Beacon Star which will lead us to Victory."

* * *

The letter was partly addressed to Helena Ivanovna Roerich who has written and spoken so glowingly of the Mother of the World. I am citing her inspiring reply:
"Dear Maria Nikolaevna (Germanova),

"I have received your inspiring letter and rejoice in spirit. Verily, the idea of creating an unity of the women of the world is at present more than timely.

"During the hard days of cosmic cataclysms of human

disunion and disintegration, of the forgetfulness of all of the highest principles of existence which give true life and lead to the evolution of the world, a voice must rise which calls to the resurrection of the spirit and to the carrying of the fire of achievement into all actions of life. And of course, this voice should be the voice of Woman, who has drunk the chalice of suffering and humiliation and has become forged in the highest patience.

"Let Woman, Mother of the World, say, 'Let There Be Light.'

"Then what will this light be, and in what will the fiery achievement consist? In the lifting of the banner of Spirit upon which will be inscribed 'Life, Knowledge and Beauty.'

"Yes, only the heart of the Woman, the Mother, can gather under this banner the children of the whole world without difference of sex, race, nationality and religion.

"Woman, Mother and Wife, witness of the development of man's genius, can appreciate all the great significance of the culture of thought and knowledge.

"Woman, the inspirer of beauty, knows all the power, all the synthetic might of Beauty.

"And so at once let us assume the carrying of the Great Banner of the New Era—the Era of the Mother of the World. Let every woman expand the boundaries of her own hearth so as to encompass the hearths of the entire world. These multiple fires will strengthen and embellish her hearth.

"Let us remember that each limitation leads to destruction and each expansion gives constructive energy. Therefore with all forces let us strive toward the expansion of our consciousness and the refinement of our thoughts and feelings so that through this fire we will be enabled to kindle our hearth.

"Put into the foundation of this Woman's unity the striving towards the true knowledge which does not know human demarcations. 'But how can one reach the true knowledge?' you will be asked.

"Answer that this knowledge lies in your spirit, in your heart—be able to awaken it.

"Striving toward beauty will be as the key to knowledge. This knowledge lies in each striving towards the General Good. This knowledge is scattered in all great teachings which have been given to the world. This knowledge is poured out in manifestations of the Cosmos, in each phenomenon, and only people who have lost the gift of observing Cosmic manifestations have lost the key to many of the mysteries of existence which could give them the understanding of the causes of all calamities which take place at present.

"Therefore, gathering women-warriors of Spirit, direct them toward the carrying of this knowledge.

"Humanity should realize the great Cosmic law, the law of Majesty, the law of greatness and equilibrium—of two as the basis of existence. All principles deprived of these two beginnings, call forth a lack of balance and destruction. But let the woman who has realized this law, and who is striving toward the equilibrium of the Beginnings, preserve all beauty of the Woman's Image, let her not lose the tenderness of the heart, the finesse of feeling, the sacrifice and courage of patience.

"You, my Dear, who have accepted with a sensitive heart the Teaching of the Lord, can become the calling and the leading one, kindling the souls of those who are ready, with the fiery Word of the Greatest Heart. Be able to give to each woman according to her consciousness and broaden the consciousness by light, careful touches without impeding the natural and individual growth of each one. Let each one develop herself in the direction closer to her, and bring out what is possible according to the level of her consciousness. Beauty is contained in manifoldness. Give all to one general foundation—the foundation of striving toward the General Good. Because the broadest cooperation is inscribed upon the Banner of the Lord. His Cupola contains all and everything! Let us manifest the broadest tolerance.

"Sisters of the Golden Mountain, before us is a difficult and wonderful time. I send you the Call of the Heart. Be armed with the fire of striving, patience and courage, through all obstacles carrying the Banner of the Mother of the World—the Banner of Self-Sacrifice and Beauty—so that in the hour of victory, you may erect it upon the Peaks of the World.

"My dear, I feel your heart, I feel our future united work, and I send you strength and joy of spirit for the creation of the great Unity. The Lord of the Heart is with us.

"In spirit and heart with you,

"H. R."

* * *

In great joy I answered Germanova with the following words:

"Dear Maria Nikolaevna,

"Verily I rejoiced at your note about the foundation of the Woman's Unity of Roerich Museum. This thought is truly ever dear to me; and the dedication of your thought to Madame Roerich deeply touched me.

"Who, if not woman, must now rise and unite in the name of Culture and the Beautiful? Because it was precisely a Woman who was destined to be first to proclaim the Resurrection.

"To enumerate all that was accomplished and inspired by woman would mean to describe the history of the world. If we speak about the bringing of the Beautiful into the whole fullness of life; if we know that the predestined evolution rests upon the cornerstones of Beauty and Knowledge; then who shall be the most faithful ally and transmitter of these foundations into the depth of human consciousness?

"A beautiful legend speaks about the coming Era of the Mother of the World. Under manifold garments human wisdom molds the very same image of Beauty, Self-sacrifice and Patience. And again must the woman ascend a new mountain, telling her dear ones about the eternal paths.

" 'Sisters of the Golden Mountain' will speak in the West. 'Sisters of Altai' will speak in Asia. Mothers, sisters, beloved ones—all this is impressed above tongues and earthly boundaries. Once more in this unity will be shown to us the one meaning of Beauty, the one achievement, the one all-binding and strength-giving Benevolence.

"Better than others, the woman knows the element of fire, that element with which is bound the nearest future. From ancient times, the woman was called to the most sacred tests. And so now she is called to the most broad knowledge, because with her heart she will understand how variedly and cautiously one should kindle the fires of understanding and response.

"Reaching the extreme line of disunion and demarcation, humanity again thinks about collecting and constructing. The paths of destruction already reach the abyss. The way of Evil already seems to show boundaries. And to measure the boundary of Evil against the boundlessness of good can only be achieved by comparing the relative limitedness of Evil with the infinity of Good. When all attempts of Evil have already been distorted in the horror of their impotence, then still boundless and unlimited will be the Legion of the Warriors of Light.

"Verily, it is not only the gatherings of women, regretting something or condemning something, which have already become conventional; but the union of women in the valiant, living exchange of all creative possibilities of unity, calling for the realization of the Good through united work, that will give the desired results.

"There have already been many different unions and societies; and yet we feel clearly that the unity of women which will weave the sparkling threads from the hearth through all Hierarchies into the Infinite, is especially needed now.

"Life itself, in all its complexity, imperatively calls for builders. In the various comers of the earth women are dreaming: 'Great countries are beyond the seas.' It is just this image of the woman, striving toward the distant shore in the realization of the predestined treasures of the Spirit that I felt in this picture; and as the apotheosis of this spiritual striving, in the painting: 'She Who Leads,' I wished to give the resplendent striving of the woman who leads the seeker of achievements to the glorious peaks.

"And the first distinction of this unity of women from any other unions, should be that its participants will come together with the purpose of bringing each one within her own boundaries, within her own knowledge and possibilities. This chalice of the soul-offering will illumine the gathering and transform the hard everyday life into the festival of labor and attainments.

"It is a joy for me to feel that women are striving toward these great strongholds of Spirit. And to strive in the right direction means already to approach Victory.

"And therefore, I wish you, Sisters of Altai, Sisters of the Golden Mountain, to conquer all fiery obstacles, to reject all fear and doubts—and unwaveringly, untiringly, heroically, patiently, to build the resplendent Zvenigorod erecting the Indestructible Kremlin of Beauty. And the sighing shall become the inspiration of Benevolence and in the Victory of the Spirit shall shine daring and exultation and Beauty.

"In spirit with you,

Nicholas Roerich."

Thus, the Woman's Unity has already been formed, erected not through business calculations, but because of fervent, heart-felt yearning—because of the impulse of the heart which gives life to things on earth and above it.

Presidents of the Branches of this Society have already

been selected both in North and South America, as well as in Europe, and the new creative seeds again shall sprout on the Field of the Great Achievement.

How good it is that beauty and knowledge blend so indissolubly with the highest and greatest ideals and gain more strength on the steps leading to the great transfiguration of life.

Now is a hard time.

No one should think that we have enough schools. No one should be satisfied with the fact that something has already been done. Creative work is insufficiently appreciated. Only to a small degree is it understood that ideas are not made with money. The world is living through a materialistic crisis of tremendous significance. Everybody feels that it is impossible to remedy currency by currency. Of course it is necessary to counteract it with other values. The treasure of the spirit, of the mind, of the conception of creative work and of illumination will be the only adequate panacea at the collapse of the superficial, mechanical civilization. The conventionality of uncognized life can be transformed only by that bright, affirming conception which is expressed in the word culture.

Action cannot be deferred.

Remember women, remember mothers, wives and sisters, remember that you are united by the beauty of spirit. Beyond the confines of everyday life a great feast is awaiting you. In the night the preparations have already begun; the lamps are being lit which are to illumine the Great Ascent of the Mother of the World. A marvelous spiritualization by Her resplendent Veil.

Women, it is you who are to weave and unfurl the banner of peace. You shall stand guard over the amelioration of life, you shall light at every hearth a beautiful fire, creative and inspiring. You shall tell your children the first word about beauty. You shall teach them the blessed Hierarchy of knowledge. You shall explain to the little ones the creative power of Thought. You can preserve them from disintegration and at the very beginning of their lives inculcate in them the meaning of heroism and self-sacrifice. You shall be the first to speak to the children of the advantages of spiritual values. You shall say the sacred word Culture.

A great and beautiful work is entrusted to you, Women. Greetings to you!

1930.

ROOTS OF CULTURE

On the Tenth Anniversary of the Master Institute

TEN years have already passed since we laid the foundation of the Master Institute of United Arts. How unnoticeably these ten years have gone by! Because during a multitude of circumstances and events, time moves with especial rapidity. As if it were yesterday one recalls how with M. M. Lichtmann we were hurrying to rent space in the Hotel des Artistes in New York. By accident we found ourselves delayed on the way, and due to this accident, as we entered the subway, we were accosted by a Greek artist with the unexpected extraordinary exclamation:

"I have been looking for you for three months already! Do you need a large studio?"

"Of course we do. Where is it?"

"In the building of the Greek Church on 54th Street."

"All right, tomorrow we will go to look at it."

"No, impossible! I cannot keep it any longer; if you wish to see it, let us go at once!"

And so instead of the Hotel des Artistes, we are seated with Father Lazaris of the Greek Cathedral, who insists that I must be of the Clergy. And here we decide to rent the space. And under the Cross of the Greek Cathedral is laid the foundation of the long-since conceived Institute of United Arts. It is a large studio, but only one room.

Some one says to us: "Could you possibly dream of having an Institute of United Arts in one studio?"

I answer, "For the conception of creation, one does not need a room larger than the cell of Fra Angelico. Each tree must grow. If the work is vital, it will develop, if it is destined to die, in any case it will have to die in one room."

And so the first piano studies resound through the studio, and the first dreams about painting, vocal and sculpture classes are realized. Soon the studio has to be divided into three parts, and life itself supports the idea of unity.

Those connected with us are such experienced, creative guides as Giles, Such, Mordkin, the Lichtmanns, Grant, Germanova, Bisttram, Andoga, Wagenaar and Appia. Already we have seventy co-workers, working in different departments and hundreds of students fill the classes and halls. Already the new generation of teachers is growing, and Ellen Kettunen, Frieda Lazaris, Linda Cappabianca and others of our pupils form the second line of attack. Twelve years ago, based on long academic experience, I decisively affirmed the following statement:

"Art will unify all Humanity. Art is one—indivisible. Art has its many branches, yet all are one. Art is the manifestation of the coming synthesis. Art is for all. Everyone will enjoy true art. The Gates of the 'Sacred Source' must be wide open for everybody, and the light of art will influence numerous hearts with a new love. At first this feeling will be unconscious, but after all it will purify human consciousness, and how many young hearts are searching for something real and beautiful! So, give it to them. Bring art to the people where it belongs. We should have not only Museums, Theaters, Universities, Public Libraries, Railway Stations and Hospitals, but even Prisons decorated and beautified. Then we shall have no more prisons."

I remember that at that time, certain friends smiled to each other, whispering, "Beautiful dreams, but how will life react to them?" But our chief principle is: "Admittance and benevolence." We and our co-workers do not like the dead, "No"; and with each possibility make the effort to say, "Yes." It is not without reason that all people express their affirmations by an open sound, and for negation have chosen the dumb, semi-bestial, "No."

What other considerations have been confirmed by the experience of the last ten years? Life has confirmed that all unity is useful; confirmed that it is practical (we do not fear this word) to have various branches of art under one roof, having one common library, a common office, a common artistic activity, common guidance and the closest intercourse between the separate branches. It is practical to afford the students the opportunity of trying their forces in various branches until they finally make their choice. It is practical that there be interchange of musicians, artists and designers. It is practical to show full trust in the teacher, letting him manifest his methods in life. The results will indicate whether he is right, because as in one's entire life, we must judge by results. It is practical to give opportunity to students as soon as possible to try their forces in life, teaching them courage and safeguarding them from vulgarity. It is practical as was carried out by Howard Giles and Emil Bisttram, to have music during the work in art classes and to give lectures which by their artistic and philosophic content, may raise and unite the spirit of the entire artistic working guild.

It is practical to give examples from the history of art; thus we will once more learn to what extent art was the creative, peaceful basis in the entire life of the State. Chiefly, one must reject less, remembering that the majority of denials have ignorance as their basis; thus the teachers turn into guides, transmitting to the students not only technique, but also life's experience, sharing with them the valuable acquisitions which will prove a strong shield for the new generation.

How often humanity, entangled in its problems, attempted to deny the significance of the teacher. In epochs of decadence, it was seemingly possible to shake the basic conception of the spiritual hierarchy. But not for long did this darkness last. With the epochs of renaissance again the great leadership of teaching was inevitably crystallized and people again began to feel the ladder of ascent and the blessed hand of the Leader. Many times small minds hesitate, fearing that they may be oppressed by the personality of the Teacher. Especially those who have little to lose often worry lest they lose something. In this regard, we now enter a very significant epoch. In certain strata of humanity, the spirit of denial has just succeeded in evoking a protest against the Teacher. But as always happens, denial can arise only temporarily, and the creative origins of humanity again lead the wanderers of life into the path of affirmation, of fearless search—to the path of creation and beauty. People again remember about the Teachers. Of course these teachers must not pertain to a grandfather's study with all its petrified remains. The Teacher is He who reveals, enlightens and encourages. He who will say, "Blessed are the obstacles. Through them we grow." He who recalls the beautiful Golgothas of knowledge and art, because therein lies the creative achievement. He who is able to remind, to teach the means of achievement—he will not be rejected by the strong spirits. He himself, will realize the value of the Hierarchy of knowledge; and in his constant movement will create the ascending researches.

So many schools and useful disseminators of knowledge can be organized in our societies. To all of them the same advice can be given; each tree can be planted only as a small sapling. Only gradually it will become tried and find steady roots. Therefore, if there is heartfelt desire to help the dissemination of knowledge and beauty, let it be fulfilled without delay. Let it not be handicapped by small possibilities. Practicality is not in the measure, but in the inner substance of the seed.

Himalayas, 1931.

COLLECTING

FROM ancient times collecting has been a sign of stability and introspection. It is very instructive to survey the various means and ways of collecting and of studying art from our days down to the heart of antiquity. Again, as in all the spirals of accretion, we see almost completed circles, yet at times, an almost elusive heightening of consciousness forms another step which is reflected in many pages of the history of art. We see how specialization and synthesis alternate. Collecting molded by the inner consciousness of the collector and united by one general idea is replaced by a classification almost pharmaceutical, sometimes destroying completely, by its pedantry, the fire of new discoveries. Not so long ago the combining of Gothic primitives with ultramodern aspirations would have been considered a proof of dilettantism. It would have been regarded altogether taboo to have simply a collection of beautiful medals and coins. Pedantry was wont to confine its scope of vision to a certain epoch, limiting it to objects of a certain type and character. Thus icons and primitives glowing with color, were turned into iconography in which the descriptive part obliterated the true and artistic meaning.

Thus, not very long ago the history of art was taught as a collection of anecdotes of painters' lives, while the exposition of sculpture and the technique of painting were reduced to a summary of proportions and to the mechanics of construction, diverting and distracting attention from the essence of creative work. Peculiar text-books began to appear in which one would come across such chapters for instance, as: "How to paint a donkey," in connection with which gray paint—which does not exist—was recommended. I remember that my attention was arrested on a boat by the typical argument between a mother and her little girl in which the mother earnestly asserted that the mountain in the distance was black, while the child affirmed candidly that it was blue. It seems to me that the mother's eyes must have been dimmed by some text-book she was studying about the way to paint donkeys.

What a joy it is for children, when, from their tenderest age, in their homes they see objects of true art and serious books. Of course, it is necessary that these artistic objects do not cease to "live" and do not find themselves in the pitiful situation of remaining upside down, sometimes for an entire decade—which means that the soul of the collector has long departed for the cemetery and that his heirs have for some reason become morally blind.

During the very recent years we have had occasion to rejoice many times over the synthetic system of collecting which has again come into existence. Not afraid of being called eccentrics or dilettantes, the sensitive collectors have begun to group their treasuries of various objects according to an inner meaning. Thus, the most modern pictures could be combined with those masters who, in their time, burned with the unquenchable fire of bringing new ways to creative work.

In the newest collections one sees such giant pathfinders as El Greco, Giorgione, Peter Breughel and all the noble galaxy of those who were not afraid to be considered the seekers and innovators of their epochs...

And how convincing among modern paintings are the forms of Roman art and the collaborators of Giotto and Cimabue, and the icons of Novgorod and ancient Chinese artists.

As all the conventionalities of division and demarcation vanish, the combined creative and spiritual findings shine before you like beacon lights, outside the conventional boundaries of the nations. If circumstances do not permit the bringing of originals into the homes, then sketches and even well-reproduced copies would permit one to entertain happy dreams about the future.

I have had occasion to write the stirring story of those collectors who began their activities when still at school. Probably many painters have had experiences like mine of having little boys, coming to one of my exhibitions, who would bashfully hand me a dollar, asking to be given a sketch in return.

Another still more moving case was when public school pupils raised a collection in order to purchase a painting. That meant that within them ardor was stirring and taking shape, and that they wanted to transmute meaningless words into facts, into conscious action. Without such an imperative impulse to action, how many light-winged, thought-butterflies singe themselves in their flutterings!

In various countries we can help by experience and advice, in the question of how to begin collecting. To open the door to those who knock timidly is one of our immediate obligations. And not only to open the door, but also to explain that they should knock with a firm hand without entertaining the prejudice that the use of art is a privilege only of the rich. No, first of all it is the privilege of bright and courageous spirits, who long to beautify their existence and who have decided—instead of taking the deadly hazards of gambling—to strengthen themselves by the manifestations of the spirit of man which, like an infinite dynamo, breathes life into everything made by it. Great joys are to be found at this feast of creative impulses. And many dark places in life can be so easily brightened by the brilliant rays of admiration. It is our sacred duty to help in this.

We are speaking about collecting. Some one smiles wryly: "Is it timely? Is it timely to speak of artistic values when even the richest countries are horror-stricken by the general crisis?" Let us answer him firmly and with the realization of the import of our words, "Yes, it is timely!"

According to the latest reports, in spite of the tremendous business depression in America the prices for art objects have not suffered any depreciation and this does not surprise us in the least; on the contrary, we consider this to be a characteristic sign of the existence of the crisis.

We have seen that during the most acute upheavals in Russia, Austria and Germany, the prices of art objects did not fluctuate noticeably. In some cases it happened that the objects of art were instrumental in bringing an entire State out of financial difficulties. We preserve this irrefutable fact as a proof of the true value of the spirit of man. When all our conditional values are shaken, the consciousness of man instinctively turns to that which, amidst the ephemeral, proves to be relatively the most valuable.

And the spiritual, creative values which have been neglected during the triumph of the stomach, again become a shelter of refuge. Although it is always timely to speak of the growth of spiritual creative power and to lay stress upon collecting and preserving, this becomes especially needed when evolution passes through difficult moments and does not know how to solve the actual accumulated problems. To solve them, however, is possible only in spirit and in beauty.

In my address on the significance of art, in 1921, I gave formulae which have become the motto of the International Art Center of Roerich Museum. I said: "Humanity is facing the coming events of cosmic greatness. Humanity already realizes that all occurrences are not accidental. The time for the construction of a future culture is at hand. The revaluation of values is being witnessed before our very eyes. Amidst ruins of valueless banknotes, mankind has found the real value of the world's significance. The values of great art are victoriously traversing all storms of earthly commotions. Even the 'earthly' people already understand the vital importance of active beauty."

And I closed the address with the following: "Not on the snowy heights, but amidst the turmoil of the city we pronounce these words. And realizing the path of true reality, we greet with a happy smile the future."

These words were based on thirty years' experience. Ten more years have elapsed since. Have the formulae then expressed changed during the period? No, the experience of many countries confirmed and even strengthened them. And we must base our conclusions on experience, and on nothing else. Theory for us is only the consequence of practice. And that same practice brings forth the happy smile with which we greet the future. May the smile of knowledge and courage become the banner of our meetings. We unite to make application of knowledge and may each crumb of knowledge add spirit to our smile.

1930.

WISDOM OF JOY

AND we shall have enemies. Even in great number. The great Emperor Akbar used to say that enemies were the shadow of a man and then, counting his enemies he would add: "My shadow is very long." Like the ancient Romans let us say: "Tell me who are your enemies, and I shall tell you who you are."

But whence will our enemies chiefly come, when we are engaged in peaceful cultural work which, it would seem, neither belittles nor violates any one? Could this hostility arise from lack of understanding or envy? Of course not. We must search for it in another, deeply-rooted human quality which also emanates from ignorance. We must speak unceasingly about making objects of art a part of our everyday life. We shall have also to speak about books, the friends of our lives, which are neglected in so many homes. And we shall have to appeal to the rulers and presidents of many countries, asking them not to place the Department of Education and Fine Arts as the last in their list of State Departments. In this connection, we shall encounter many comments affirming that these two most vital factors of evolution do not in the least merit first place. Often this will be said not because of some particular hatred of education or of the beautification of life, but simply because of obsolete preconceptions and petrified traditions. This circumstance therefore, will procure us a great number of enemies. Yet in going over the list of their names, we shall feel proud that precisely these people have proved to be the enemies of culture rather than the reverse. Moreover, as I have already said in the article, "Praise to the Enemies,"[1] no one is as helpful in our lives as enemies of precisely this quality. Our keenness of vision, our indefatigability, our capacity for work, we owe in a great measure to them. These enemies, as you know, do not stop at small formulae; on the contrary it is precisely they who are liberal with exaggeration. They possess a magnificent dictionary of hatred before which the language of friends often pales and seems faint. Too often in life do we lose our vocabulary for good, for gratitude and for praise. We are often ashamed even to think that some one might suspect us of gratitude; we are often afraid of being suspected of revering the Hierarchy of Good. Yet enemies, urging us to indefatigable activity, also forge for us the armor of heroic achievement.

I remember that once a great painter, when told that some one had slandered him, pondered for a while, then shook his head and said: "That's strange, I have never done anything good to him." This remark gave proof of great wisdom of life. And the same wisdom of life could also suggest to us, that in spite of everything, we should untiringly promote in life the simple truth concerning the preservation and the unfoldment of culture.

Many years' experience have demonstrated to us that art and knowledge have bloomed forth in places where they were recognized by those at the helm of government as the greatest stimuli of life. There where the rulers of States, the dignitaries of the Church and all teachers of life united in striving towards the beautiful, a renaissance took place, a regeneration on which volumes of appreciation are now being written. If we know exactly what outside factors have promoted art and knowledge, would it not be the easiest way, in the name of culture, to apply these same methods again? For the embryos of all these possibilities do exist, and are only crushed by the deadened traditions of unsuccessful epochs. But we know that activities in this direction prove always to be true, noble activities.

---

[1] N. Roerich. *Shambhala.* New York, 1930, pp. 150-155.

And therefore, in full sincerity, we can strengthen each other in this great achievement. Think what happiness it is to realize that we, scattered in various countries, can feel the invisible, friendly hand always ready to extend spiritual aid and support. When, in the name of the beautiful, in the name of culture, we turn to the rulers of States and Churches, we bring them help also, for many of them would like to be a Lorenzo the Magnificent in the highest sense of this word, did not petty superstitions and prejudices interfere with their excellent impulses.

Someone might ask—is it timely, right now, at the moment of general material crisis, to speak about art and science? Yes, precisely now is the time.

The blooming of art and science brings on the solution of life's crises. It changes the deteriorating production into one of higher quality. It forces men to ponder life's problems which can be solved only by means of a bridge of beauty. It gives wings to those men, who otherwise, under the yoke of convention would become a herd of *Panurges.* In a word, the blooming of art and knowledge spiritualizes man's individuality. How very old is this truth and how much needed just now, when destructive forces are so active! It is precisely now that one cannot, even for an instant, forget the advantages of a true cultural epoch, in order to advance bravely into the future, leaning on these guideposts of the past.

To criticize and criticize greatly is always possible, but critical disintegration has already brought many misfortunes upon mankind. At this time it is an imperative need to build, to assemble, to meet and to draw from each other mutual courage in the realization that everywhere, beyond mountains and oceans, our friends are ready to rejoice with us.

1930.

THE CAREFUL KEEPER

To the International Conference of Museums' Experts in Rome

Mr. E. Foundoukidis,
Secretary of the International Office
of the Museums of the International
Institute of Intellectual Cooperation.

DEAR Sir:
I was very happy to receive your kind invitation to the Conference of Experts which will take place at Rome under the auspices of the International Institute of Intellectual Cooperation during next October.

To my great regret, important work will not permit me to participate in person in the Conference, but I should like to express a few of the ideas that the program of the Conference suggests to me. I should be grateful if you would bring these remarks to the attention of the members of the convention at Rome.

The questions mentioned in the Daily Schedule of the Conference are not only important but absolutely urgent.

In the course of the last few years, the safeguarding of artistic treasures has begun to be organized according to new methods which must be examined with attention and also with prudence. The introduction of the X-ray—that new and powerful factor in the study of works of art—causes us to admire the new possibilities placed at our disposal by science for the search of truth, but also obliges us to wonder whether this method will not produce certain effects on the colors as much as on the other elements of works of art. No one can doubt that the powerful X-rays produce consequences that may be either beneficial or destructive. But the highest authorities are unable to certify that this energy applied to works of art will remain "neutral and without effect." The time which has passed since the introduction of X-rays is too short to permit a definite conclusion as to their effects. Thus, although no one had any intention of inventing varnish or pigments that would be harmful, yet, various effects of these "perfections" are revealed after several centuries, as bringing harm to magnificent productions of human genius.

Certainly it does not follow that we should take a definite stand for the old methods without searching new means of approaching the truth. Everything must progress. Among the enterprises that are most useful in this respect we count, for example, the laboratory which is now being organized at the Louvre and where, thanks to the energy and gracious initiative of M. Henri Verne, new scientific methods can be determined and verified. I believe that I should here salute this extremely useful enterprise by expressing the hope that similar laboratories, organized in accordance with the most recent scientific principles, be installed in all countries, in order to study the effects of local climates and pigmentations, as well as the technical methods of use, adapted to the particular conditions of each place. It is important in this respect for the laboratories in question to coordinate their work and exchange the results of their experiments. It is also necessary that researches of long duration be undertaken. Undoubtedly, one human life would not suffice for the study of certain results of these experiments; but, for the good of the future, it would be necessary, beginning now, to commence coordinated research work that others would continue until a very far-distant time.

We must reconcile modern discoveries with the experience of past ages brought down to us by the works preserved, and also take into consideration the preparatory works of the old masters: for example, the methods by which the oil used for painting was purified during a period of several years; the preparation of varnish and "olifa" by the primitives and iconographers; finally the choice of woods for the panels, not to speak of colors. All this obliges us to fix our attention on the qualities of ancient methods, allied to modern improvements.

If the Conference adopted the principle of coordinating the artistic research laboratories affiliated with museums, I could propose that our Museum at New York join in this useful and necessary cooperation. The idea of Intellectual Cooperation in itself indicates that this International Institution could proceed to the revision and to the exchange of research work and of its results. Thus, with the end of serving future generations, still another fertile collaboration would be realized.

Aside from the perfecting of technical methods, it is certainly necessary in addition to take into consideration another essential question; that of the exchange of works of art, and especially the exchange of exhibitions of older creations.

This question causes contradictory thoughts to arise.

On the one hand, everyone understands that a better international agreement can be developed on the basis of art and science. Nothing in this world could take the place of these forces of peaceful enthusiasm and cordial fervor. But, on the other hand, one must not lose sight of the considerable risks and dangers that the transportation of works of art entails. Without counting the danger of the transportation itself, which is great, in spite of the most careful precautions, we know that works of art, like living organisms, are divided into migratory and stationary. Strange though it may seem, works that are migratory by the will of Destiny, withstand the perils of travel much more easily than those that have passed centuries in one fixed place without risking the hazards of life. How often have I seen manifested, with sudden malignancy, following a transfer, an "illness" which, under other conditions, would not have occurred. Everyone knows the surprises occasioned by the transporting of a work across the ocean. Even with thick boards, in spite of the most careful wrapping, the linings become bloated and crack. The original coating heaves up, and often imposes the operation, always undesirable, of transferring the painting to a canvas. All linings (maroufles) become bloated frequently. Similar injuries also ruin sculptured woods and ivories. These are the risks that no insurance can cover. Also, without diminishing in the least degree the great task of art, whose role consists in being the intermediate agent between the peoples of the world, it is necessary to think of the intensification and of the rationalization of traveling, rather than of increasing the transporting of works of art into different climates, which breaks in some way the secular vibrations that surround the work of art.

All those who have charge of artistic treasures know that painful feeling which comes over them in seeing the injuries suffered by works confided to their care. We know how many just regrets arise following each transfer of works of art. Undoubtedly, particular care and judicious choosing, not only in accordance with their quality, but also in accordance with their physical nature can, to a certain degree, keep the productions of genius from the perils of these long voyages.

The coordination of the researches organized by museum laboratories, which was discussed above, would be useful in all respects, and it would particularly please me to know the opinion of the Conference on this point, which our Institutions would be happy to study towards their imminent realization.

I beg of you to confer my cordial greeting to the Members of the Conference at Rome, and to accept my kindest regards, as well as my thanks in advance for whatever communication you care to make to me on the subject of the work of the Conference.

We are continuously receiving from all countries numerous letters and articles in which is expressed the greatest sympathy towards our flag for the protection of the arts and sciences.

Paris, August 25, 1930.

HEALTH

A CERTAIN worldly-wise uncle bequeathed the following advice to his nephew: "Love yourself more than your neighbor. Never do today what you can do tomorrow. And never do yourself what you can make others do. Do not pay your debts until taken by the throat. Remember that man has been created to lie on something soft, to suck something sweet, and to listen to something agreeable. But above all you must remember that you cannot exist without your stomach."

Made wise by a peculiar worldly experience, the uncle could not think above his stomach and the latter suggested to him these misanthropic formulae which he expressed in a jest. But there are a great many such uncles and an infinite number of worshipers of the belly of Moloch. And misanthropy springs forth from this all-devouring belly. All its worshipers take great care of their health. Notice that the conversation nearest their hearts always concerns the taking of unknown medicines. And these patent medicines, usually containing some variety of narcotic and poison also prove to be an offering of some kind to the belly of Moloch.

However, it is not specified anywhere that mankind should despise health. On the contrary, the preservation of health in some form or other, is affirmed very emphatically in all teachings. He, who said that in a healthy body there is a healthy mind, was right. But the question is— what is a healthy body and what is a healthy mind?

Again in many teachings the possibility is mentioned of the approach of new diseases, destructive to many. Influenza, cancer, meningitis, sleeping sickness, asthma, all forms of throat, heart, lung and nerve diseases, nervous spasms, often taken for appendicitis, are actually assuming proportions sometimes far more dangerous than the old epidemics, against which other prophylactic methods have already been discovered.

All these new diseases draw our attention not to uncle's stomach, but somewhere above—the heart, the throat, the brain. When we take heed of these higher centers, the healthy body and the healthy mind both appear in a different light.

Sports and exercise in the open air, which of course, are good for health in a certain measure, could not entirely furnish nutrition for the nervous system of mankind. It is true that humanity is fatigued, but it is not fatigued because of the amount of work it has been doing, for work intelligently regulated can never tire. True rest is found not in inaction, but in a wise distribution and change of the quality of work.

The sanitation of the body, especially at the present time, when so many newly-discovered energies and rays have been introduced into daily use, demands a different, more careful attitude than the crude regulation of one's digestion or primitive and often one-sided sport.

Human beings reach out for culture. They suffer from the intolerable perversion of life. If we cannot get away from this distorted life, we can at least bring into it manifestations of inner sanitation. It is imperative that we remember the ancient truth that sound and color (which in fact are one and the same) have a tremendous influence on us. I remember in London, how Dr. Young investigated the influence of the color of paintings upon various diseases and also applied color rays, and of course the observations thus obtained were very instructive. It is interesting also to recall the pamphlet written by Leontine Hirsch Meyers, the blind pupil of the Master Institute of United Arts in New York, who, in spite of her total blindness, was able to recognize the tonality of paintings.

Moreover, let us remember all the extraordinary experiments of Sir Jagadis Bose and all the various observations of the effect of color and sound upon animals and plants. Also let us remember that Institutes for treatment by color are already being established in America, Germany and India.

Even today an ordinary truck gardener understands the value of color rays for his truck garden. Is it possible that the human organism, the most sensitive of all, could fail to react in the strongest degree to that which is felt even by a cabbage?

Setting details aside, let us stop within the dimensions of culture. Whence shall come the exquisite sound and the refined color if not from a generally cultured understanding? Therefore, if you are told that in speaking about culture you are thinking only of the spiritual, let us reply:

"No, we are also thinking of the body, so as to make it actually healthy, according to the demands of true culture. Populating the planet with monsters, prodigies, giants and dwarfs has long since ended. Mankind understands that right now not only is the expansion of consciousness most urgently needed, but especially its refinement."

Without the refinement of consciousness we shall never solve those intricate problems of life which have assailed mankind and are provoking various destructive excesses. Thinking constructively we shall inevitably arrive at the introduction of cultural principles into life. These principles will not remain within the bounds only of special phenomena but will especially reach the masses, bringing light into daily work and spiritualizing the meaning of each task.

Agni Yoga gives insistent advice to physicians to pay attention to the peculiar new illnesses which, if not foreseen, can overwhelm mankind with unheard-of calamities.

A radio station in Paris complains that the saturation of the atmosphere is a direct obstacle to transmission. In Belgium, the fog imbued with poisonous exhalations caused many deaths. Extend this single occurrence into infinity, and you will have a new calamity which can threaten the population of entire cities. The heart cannot endure poisonous fog. Man's heart weakens; even by keeping up the functions of the stomach it is impossible to impart life to the heart. Not only life-preservers and life-givers are needed, but one must also cognize the powerful psychic energy which is so closely connected with the quality of our mind. In order to apply this high energy so beneficent when rightly understood, one must also understand the fundamental ways of obtaining it. And here again, without any preconceptions we have come to the same necessity— that of introducing the principles of high culture into all the manifestations of life.

In London, Sir James Jeans, broadcasting over the radio, announces to the entire world that we are living within a continual explosion of the universe. Dr. Martin Gil, head of the Argentine Meteorological Station, remarks with reference to the recent poisonous fog, that such phenomena are the result of profound cosmic causes. He recalls similar manifestations in Europe, Northern Africa and Bolivia, connecting them with stellar dust and points out that in addition to their poisonous effects, they also promote outbreaks of various epidemics. Senor Gil explains that the passage of a mass of stellar dust through the atmosphere of the earth, forms an unmistakable stratum of intensive electromagnetic activity which causes organic and respiratory disturbances in people whose nervous system is very sensitive.

Dimitry Merejhkovsky says: "Scientific inventions, the marvels of mechanics, can become the marvels of the devil ... a learned troglodyte with the marvels of the devil—is the wildest of all savages. ... I wish I could be mistaken, but it seems to me more and more that ... the universal ship is sinking..."

He also cites the words from Avesta: "During the last days the earth will be like a sheep in fear falling down before a wolf."

Rabindranath Tagore, always so sensitive, exclaims in

his latest article on America: "I know that I am as one crying in the wilderness when I raise a voice of forewarning. At the time when the West is occupied with the organization of a machine-made world, it continues to feed by its injustices the underground forces of earthquakes."

In a recent speech Dr. Albert Einstein advises an intensified study of the hidden forces of nature. It is there that the searching glances of Millikan and Michelson are also directed. Thus, on different continents and urged by different causes, the best minds turn to the factors of the reciprocal action of the cosmic forces on the destinies of the earthly peoples. The question of true health stands out in a new light far beyond the limits of one-sided sport or of "misunderstood" rest.

The best minds guide man's thinking in multifarious ways, toward the expansion of consciousness, in which alone is confined true prophylaxis and the foresight of the possibility of bright, constructive work. The time of deadly scholasticism is at an end. The dark prejudices are dying out. Bright minds call for constructive synthesis in which the old precept—*Mens sana in corpore sano*—assumes a special meaning, and it is actually possible to understand that a clean creative spirit does inhabit a clean, healthy organism, and in the conclusive synthesis, assuming the indivisibility of spirit and matter, the circle can be completed in the reverse position—a clean, creative spirit can make the body healthy. Thus the question of health expands from the medical aspect into the sphere of true national education and inspiration.

1930.

MASTER VIRGO INTER VIRGINES

To the Chicago Art Institute

WITH the utmost interest I have read the article by Mr. Daniel Catton Rich in the March issue of the *Bulletin* of the Chicago Art Institute. In his article Mr. Rich says: "Where so many paintings of this period have suffered drastically from wear or over-cleaning, this 'Ecce Homo' (by the Master of Virgo inter Virgines) has come down to us fresh in color and surface."

This just remark has special meaning to me. When in 1923 in Rome we were choosing this remarkable painting for the collection of the Roerich Institutions, I was attracted not only by the rare characteristic quality of this painting, but also by its beautifully preserved condition. At first I attributed this unusually fine condition to the fact that this painting had been in the possession of the San Lucas monastery for a long time, where no retouching or transportation harmed it. During the last International Conference of Museums' Experts in Rome under the auspices of the International Museum's Office of the League of Nations, I expressed my opinion, unanimously approved by the Conference, about the irreparable harm which comes to paintings from frequent transportations.

But in the case of "Ecce Homo" another very important factor was told to me which ascribes the excellent condition of the paintings to the fact that for a long time "Ecce Homo" was covered by another subject painted on it in a later period. The difference in their age permitted the upper layer to be taken off later on without any harm to the painting itself. I often met similar conditions during my collecting and more than once I smiled to see how such acts of vandalism as using the surface of old paintings for new ones preserved many originals, for the old *vernis* constituted an impenetrable shield against intruding new layers of colors. I remember a similar case in my collection with the painting by Bernard Orley, which was covered by a horrible portrait of an old man, also with the painting of Abraham Bloemart "Adoration of Shepherds" where the entire sky was covered by heavy clouds evidently painted later, under which appeared to be an untouched colorful choir of cherubim. A similarly vandalistic over-painting also preserved a very fine work by Roeland Savery, "Noah's Arc," which was hidden by a castle, huge trees and ugly rounds of bacchanalian dancers. Another painting still remains in an equally hidden condition, but it was over-painted by Correggio himself with a subject "Ecce Homo." Through the colors of Correggio you can quite clearly distinguish the outlines of the portrait of a man in an armchair. It could be the portrait of a Pope, or Cardinal, but the "Ecce Homo" of Correggio's brush is so remarkable, that the hidden painting, perhaps still more beautiful, remains inaccessible.

These occurrences remind us once more of the meaning of a passing fashion, which has caused even the most outstanding masterpieces to pass through a period of exile, often being veiled by ugly strata. However, this unjust banishment served only to enhance their glorification bringing to us the creations unspoiled. Certainly to our regret the hand of the vandal did not always have mercy on that which he conceitedly over-painted. We can see how sometimes to paint over it, the original was scratched off, and it is only the branded seal of the Saint Lucas Guild on the back of the panel which now reminds us of the destroyed masterpiece. But one can rejoice that in the case of "Ecce Homo," which through the generosity of Mr. Ryerson is now a part of the Chicago Art Institute, the temporary veil of the painting has preserved for us intact the beauty of this masterpiece.

Himalayas, 1931.

LEGENDS

PROFESSOR ZELINSKI, in his very interesting work about the ancient myths, comes to the conclusion that the heroes of these myths are not only legendary figures, but actually existed. Many other authors also have come to the very same conclusion, thus overthrowing the materialistic tendency of the past century, which sometimes actually tried to prove that even historical figures were also only myths. Thus Senard, the French scholar, tried to prove that Buddha never existed and was nothing else than a solar myth. Likewise attempts have been made to deny the existence even of Christ, despite the fact that we have evidence very close to His own epoch; besides, there have also been discovered the Roman inscriptions with the edict against the first Christians in Syria, so very close to the period of the Great Manifestation. In this fight between those who acknowledge and those who deny, is revealed a trait of universal psychology. It is instructive to see herein how those who deny are gradually defeated and those who defend heroism, truth and reality find support in the very facts themselves.

Besides, those who have heretofore appeared as dreamers of heroes and myths suddenly appear as the realists, whereas the denying skeptics gradually come to occupy the position of dreamers who place their trust in slander or in a spurious source. Thus, slowly but surely, the wheel of evolution revolves, carrying with it the revelation of the forgotten truth.

Let us look back and see how quickly and easily humanity forgets events and personalities which are even recent. Only recently, such personalities as Paracelsus and Thomas Vaughan were listed as impostors even by the encyclopedias. But those who were impartial, undertook to read the works of these men, and discovered instead of the pronounced charlatans, profound scholars who benefited humanity by their discoveries. I remember in my childhood how I was fascinated with the book, "The Martyrs of Science," by Gaston Tissandier. Those who perished at the stake in tortures and on the scaffold, are regarded now as great scientists. But false skepticism continues work, and in place of these martyrs, hastens to create new ones, in order thus, in a sure way, to honor them by monuments and celebrations.

In recent years a social manifestation has become apparent, which gives hope that sometime—perhaps that time is even at hand—the harmful denials will be bridled and set in their deserved place.

People have become eager to read biographies. Truly even here the skeptics try not to give in. Shrugging their shoulders, they will say, "How can we be sure about the true motives behind the actions of these portrayed personalities?" or "How can we be certain what accidents created the circumstances which marked the lives of the portrayed personalities?" or "And how can we be certain of the impartiality of the biographer?"

Let us say that these remarks are true to a certain extent. Let us even allot a certain part to the personal mood of the biographer. Even so, the collection of historical documents reveals exactly the same milestones of true reality. Likewise, until recently, chronicles were considered to be inadequate documents not worthy of serious consideration. But a detailed study of chronicles, documents and discoveries, has shown that chronicles deserve much more esteem than usually was supposed. Certainly, one also hopes that humanity will not permit entire centuries to go by before taking note of outstanding manifestations.

Through reading biographies, humanity will learn also to inscribe them. Naturally, it is a fallacy to think that heroes are the attribute only of antiquity. The synthesis of our era will likewise crystallize its heroes and we may hope that the stake, prisons and executions will no longer be the portion of these great souls.

Having ascertained that the gods of antiquity were heroic personalities imprinted upon the memories of the peoples, we shall affirm ourselves in the knowledge that in our days individuality and personality are likewise laying their hand upon the rudder of humanity. Ascertaining the existence of such personalities, we shall learn, as did the ancients, to accompany them by an affirmative exposition of their lives. We must not forget that in future, these life-descriptions shall reach the schools as the torches of history. Hence, let our youth not only enjoy reading biographies, but also let them learn to write them or rather to discern which of the manifestations of their contemporaries is to become history.

Through reading legends, youth also learns to dream. And this is a great capacity: to know how to dream, filling one's heart with the best fires. With these fires of the heart, youth will learn also to discriminate wherein lies truth. No mechanical calculations can disclose the truth— it is the language of the heart alone which knows wherein abides this great truth, which despite all, leads humanity upward.

Are not legends the collection of the best flowers? Of that which is small or insignificant, humanity does not create legends. Even in seemingly negative legends, is often contained in great part a reverence to power. In any case, each legend contains something of the unusual. And does not this "unusual" lead us beyond the twilight of mechanical standard? Evolution is not built through this machine-like standard. But the legend which liberates us beyond the limits of the oppressive daily routine refreshes our trend of thought and permits us to merge into new depths of knowledge, with an eternally inextinguishable youthful ardor.

Ask a great mathematician, a great physicist, a great

biologist, a great astronomer, whether he knows how to dream. I do not even mention artists, musicians, poets, for their entire being is composed of the capacity to dream. And a great scientist, when truly great and when unembarrassed by the presence of a witness, will reveal to you in beautiful terms, his ability to soar in dreams and that many of his discoveries have at their base not only calculations but, precisely, dreams.

We then remember that legends are not abstractions, but usually reality itself. We also remember that dreams are not signs of illiteracy, but are the qualities of refined souls. Let us then encourage in our youth this aspiration towards the inspiring and creative legend, and remaining young together with youth, let us pay tribute to dreams as to the guiding, uplifting medium of regeneration and perfection.

Striving, Hierarchy, Infinity, Beauty—only under these milestones we progress indisputably. All which constitutes the activity of our Societies must be immediately applied in life. Paying tribute to dreams, we must not become dreamers.

Let ours be the dream of a creator. In this dream there is no intoxication, nor vacillation, but the immutable knowledge gathered in the depths of our spirit. And, first of all, we shall remember that the word "Culture" signifies Cult-Ur or the *Cult of Light.*

Himalayas, 1931.

BURNING OF DARKNESS

*Read at the Meeting of Young Idealists,
New York*

THUS we will not grow weary of repeating that at the base of Existence lies creative thought. We will consciously realize the significance of rhythm as the underlying dynamo of our work. We will remember the covenant of Light—that, of all things, the first in importance for us are spirit and creation; second, comes health; and third, wealth. If, however, you hear the sweet-voiced whisperer, creeping through darkness say, "First wealth, then health and last, creation," then say, "We know thee, disguised homunculus! Thou hast again crept in. Thou hast taken advantage of the door unlocked while the caretaker was absent for his morsel. Thou art reckoning once more on human weakness and inconstancy, and again thou hopest to revive the seedling of treason. No matter what thy disguise, we will recognize thee. With thy materialistic revaluation of values thou hast revealed thyself and thy decaying influence. The next evolution is not built according to thy foundations, homunculus! Verily, thy ornate disguise will not help thee. We know without question that the values of spirit and creation lie at the base of Existence and can be the only salvation of humanity!"

Vigilantly penetrating into the laws which govern humanity, we see redeeming sparks everywhere. Observe that the homunculi, as prototypes of the treacherous *Mime,* who dreamt of annihilating the heroic *Siegfried,* always reveal, in one manner or another, their hidden intentions. You remember how *Mime* sweetly stills the vigilance of *Siegfried,* whispering to him how he brought him up. He even speaks to *Siegfried* about heroic achievement, obviously with the motive of appropriating the rewards of this gigantic task, whereas *Siegfried* will be killed through his treason. But in some miraculous way, *Mime* begins to tell, not what he would like to tell, but what he actually thinks. Verily, watching closely, you will discern the true formulae of homunculus, which, sooner or later, he pronounces in your presence.

Sharpen your attention; in small things learn to intensify your concentration and be always alert, so that at the required moment, you will not be obscured by your own foggy, petty thoughts. It is said that a criminal is always attracted to the scene of his crime and thus exposes himself. Likewise will homunculus betray himself, for in the final analysis, everything which is destructive, will be exposed. Homunculus dreads the future, just as many people become atheists merely to reject all thoughts about the future.

The idea of a "Guiding Spirit," the idea of "High Leadership" passes through all ages, for in this concept is contained a counter-balance to the dark homunculus. Beginning with an address to the exposed homunculus we remember some of the covenants of Light which unwaveringly and eternally guide struggling mankind.

This is what the Eastern Wisdom ordains:

"In the construction of affirmed beginnings, one must remember that construction always proceeds upward. While constructing in the name of the Lord, there is but one path—that which leads to the Creative Source; the path of mighty Hierarchy, the path of the mighty Leadership of Great Service; hence the contact with the creative principle impels the spirit to the affirmed law of Hierarchy. Each construction requires upward striving. Therefore only the law of obedience to the Hierarchy can give the lawful tension. Therefore what is given for the foundation must be guarded, for without the stones of foundation the structure cannot stand.

"How then to affirm oneself in the Teaching? How to come close to the Highest Law of Hierarchy? Only through the refining of thought and expansion of consciousness. How can the Command from Above be attained if the affirmation of conformity is not present? One must be able to accept the vastness of the Teaching. Conformity alone can permit the vessel to be filled. Hence, the manifestation of tolerance is worthy of a broad consciousness. On the way to Us one can attain only through Hierarchy. Thus only through the power of Hierarchy can We send that which is given, therefore all armors must remain pure. How can new possibilities and new people be attracted if one does not proceed in the Name of Hierarchy?

"With Us certainly one can achieve through the saturation of the heart. He who attains this, is privileged, for the source of the heart will not wear away. The Image of the Lord centered in the heart will not be blurred, and at any hour is ready to help. This method of using the heart is most ancient, but requires considerable expansion of consciousness. One must not speak about the heart in the very first talk, because it is possible to overburden it without result. Likewise it is useless to speak of love, if the heart does not as yet contain the Image of the Lord. But the hour strikes when it is necessary to point out the power of the heart. I advise recourse to the heart, not only because there the Image of the Lord is near, but also on account of cosmic reasons; it is easier to cross abysses if the bond with the Lord is strong. Thus it is not easy to go without the Lord. Not only with the lips repeat the Name of the Lord, but revolve It in your heart, and He shall not depart, but shall be as an image carved into a stone by the mountain streams. We say *Cor Reale* when the King of the Heart enters the predestined abode. One must protect oneself with the Image of the Lord.

"The omnipresent fire imbues each vital manifestation. The omnipresent fire strains every action. The omnipresent fire impels each striving, each beginning, therefore how not to imbue oneself with the omnipresent fire! The cosmic might which is subsistent in each impulse of man, and in creative power, is directed towards conscious creativeness. With what great care should we gather these corresponding energies for the creation of a better future! Only a conscious striving toward the possession of the power of co-measurement can manifest creativeness worthy of future progress. Hence every one on the way to Us must strive to attain creativeness, consciously directing his discrimination.

"When the consciousness prompts your recognition of the necessity of having an Image of the Lord constantly before you, retire into a quiet place and direct your eye upon the chosen Image. But remember that you have to decide irrevocably, for the constant Image will be a constant reproach in case of treason. After a fixed contemplation of the Image, close your eyes and transfer It into the third eye. Exercising thus, you will receive a vivid Image and you will feel an intensive tremor, especially in the heart. Soon the Image of the Lord will abide with you inseparably. You can test yourself against the sun and you will see likewise the Lord before you, sometimes colorless, but again vividly, and even in motion. Your prayer will lose its words and only the tremor of the heart will fill your understanding. Thus, one can achieve in life something very useful, but the consciousness must correspond.

"How important it is to preserve the fire of impulse; without this incitement one cannot imbue the very basis with the best potentialities. The forces applied in the beginning, multiply through the fire of impulse. Therefore, it is very necessary to strive to multiply the given Forces of the Primary Source. In all constructions it is necessary to observe harmony and co-measurement; hence to imbue Our beginnings it is necessary to co-measure the given with the applied measures. Fire and impulse sustain life in every beginning. Without these, the beginnings lose their vitality. Thus let us strive to the affirmed Fire, given by the Lord. Thus one can attain the fiery saturation. Yes, yes, yes!

"Embarking on a ship a traveler was robbed of a purse

containing his gold; every one became indignant, but the loser smiled and said, 'Who knows?'

"A storm arose, and the ship was wrecked. Only our traveler was thrown ashore. When the islanders regarded his rescue as a miracle, he again smiled saying, 'I simply paid more dearly than the others for my passage.'

"We never know when the good seeds will sprout nor how long it takes for the harvest of poisonous thoughts to ripen. They also require time to ripen. Therefore, beware of poisonous thoughts; not one of them will be lost without leaving traces.

"But where is that country, where is that hour, where an ear of poison will ripen? Even though small but stinging, there will be no pieces of bread which would not tear one's throat.

"Is it possible not to reap from one's sowing? Let the seed be a good one, otherwise poison will generate only poison. Much can be avoided, but the treasury of thought is finest. Thought, being the highest form of energy, is indissoluble, and can be deposited in sediments. The manifestation of an experiment upon plants proves the power of thought. Likewise a scientist whose thought is tense, can take from a shelf the needed book.

"Therefore one must develop the wondrous impulse of fire, which gives life to everything. Thus the imbued fire can attract all corresponding energies. In the culture of thought one must, first of all, nurture the fiery impulse. As the creative impulse attracts reverberations, likewise thought attracts correspondences. Thus guard the impulse of fire.

"The main mistake of people is in considering themselves outside that which exists. From this misconception arises the lack of cooperation. It is impossible to explain to the one who stands without that he is responsible for what happens within him! The manifested father of selfishness has sown doubt and deceit in order to sever the link with the treasury of Light.

"One can enroot oneself in world thought, and thus

grow for oneself wings in heaven and in the foundation upon earth..."

Study without prejudice the history of humanity, and you will see that however he may be disguised, homunculus despises Light, and most of all hates the Hierarchy of Bliss and Knowledge. With this light-bearing Hierarchy, homunculus begins, in his own confusion, to reiterate his own concealed formulae. But all which has already been pronounced is no longer dangerous. The thin cobweb of the net of darkness will be instantaneously destroyed by the fire of space.

In the service of great Culture one should not limit oneself to a uniform program. Every standard leads to tyranny. The fundamental flame of Culture shall be one, but its sparks in life shall be extremely manifold as well as preciously individual. Like a careful gardener, the true culture-bearer will not ruthlessly crush those flowers which enter life outside his garden, if they belong to the same precious kind which he safeguards. The manifestations of culture are just as manifold as are the manifestations of the endless varieties of life itself. They ennoble Be-ness. They are the true branches of the one sacred Tree, whose roots sustain the Universe.

Should you be asked of what kind of country and of what future constitution you dream, you can answer in full dignity: "We visualize the country of Great Culture." The country of Great Culture shall be your noble motto. You shall know that in *that* country, where Knowledge and Beauty will be reverenced, there will be peace. Let all ministers of war not be offended if they have to concede their priority to the ministers of public education. In spite of all homunculi who spy from their holes, you shall fulfill your duties of great Culture and you shall be fortified by the realization that only homunculi will remain as your enemies. Nothing can be nobler than to have the homunculi as your enemy. Nothing can be purer and more elevating than the striving for the future country of Great Culture.

Himalayas, 1931.

BANNER OF PEACE

New York Times, March 11, 1930

HUMANITY is striving in divers ways for peace, and every one, in his own heart, realizes that this constructive work is a true prophecy of a new era. In view of this it might seem incongruous to hear discussions on the comparative desirability of various bullets or on whether one type of ship is closer to the conception of world unity than the cannons of two battleships. Let us, however, consider these discussions as preliminary steps toward the same great peace that will tame the belligerent instincts of humanity by the resplendent and joyous creations of the spirit.

The fact remains, however, that the shells of even one of these cannons can destroy the greatest treasures of art and sciences as successfully as a whole fleet. We deplore the loss of the library of Louvain and the irreplaceable loveliness of the Cathedral of Rheims; we remember the beautiful treasures of private collections which perished during the world's misunderstandings. We do not, however, wish to inscribe above them words of enmity; let us simply say, "Destroyed by human errors, and re-created by human hope." Nevertheless, errors in this or any other form may be repeated, and other precious milestones of human achievement can be destroyed.

Against such errors of ignorance we should take immediate measures; even though these may be only preliminary measures of safeguarding, some very successful steps can be made. No one can deny that the flag of the Red Cross proved to be of immeasurable value and reminded the world of humanitarianism and compassion.

For this reason, a plan for an international peace

pact which would protect all treasures of art and science through an international flag has been outlined by the Roerich Museum for presentation through America to all foreign governments. The purpose of the project, which has been submitted to the State Department and the Committee on Foreign Relations, is to prevent the repetition of the atrocities of the last war on cathedrals, museums, libraries and other lasting memorials of creation of the past.

It is the plan of the project to create a flag which will be respected as international and neutral territory, this to be raised above museums, cathedrals, libraries, universities and any other cultural centers. The plan, projected by the Roerich Museum, was drawn up according to the codes of international law by Dr. George Chklaver, doctor of international laws and of political and economical sciences, Paris University; lecturer in the Institute of International High Studies, in consultation with Professor Albert Geouffre de la Pradelle, member of the Hague Peace Court, vice president of the Institute of International Law of Paris, and member of the faculty of law, the Sorbonne. Both are honorary advisers of the Roerich Museum.

As set forth in Article I of the pact, "educational, artistic and scientific institutions, artistic and scientific missions, the personnel, the property and collections of such institutions and missions shall be deemed neutral and, as such, shall be protected and respected by belligerents.

"Protection and respect shall be due to the aforesaid institutions and missions in all places subject to the sovereignty of the high contracting parties, without any discrimination as to the State allegiance of any particular institution or mission."

When the idea of an international cultural flag was first propounded, we were not surprised to find that it met with unanimous interest and enthusiasm. Experienced statesmen wondered why it had not been thought of before. When we asked our honorary advisers, Dr. George

Chklaver and Professor Albert Geouffre de la Pradelle, to frame this idea into an international formula, we received not only a splendidly formulated project of international agreement, but also many answers full of pan-human sympathy.

This international flag for the protection of beauty and science would not in any way demean any interests or lead to misunderstandings. On the contrary, it elevates the universal understanding of evolutionary discoveries, as though new human values had been created and we were moving on to a path of progress and peace. And this understanding of a creative striving toward peace becomes more real. Above all else, this guardian of peace reminds one of the necessity for impressing cultural treasures in the world annals. This is not difficult and in many countries it is already accomplished, although there are gaps and each enrichment in the universal consciousness must be greeted. As the Red Cross flag needs no explanation to even the most uncultured mind, so does this new flag, guardian of cultural treasures, speak for itself. It is simple enough to explain, even to a barbarian, the importance of safeguarding art and science.

We often repeat that the cornerstone of the future civilization rests upon beauty and knowledge. Now we must act upon this thought, and act quickly. The League of Nations, which has progressed toward international harmony, will not be opposed to this flag, for it expresses their aims of a world unity.

That the idea was originally conceived in the United States is not an accident. By its geographical position the United States is least personally affected by such measures of protection. Hence, this proposition comes from a country whose own art treasures are in no particular danger, illustrating the better that this flag is a symbol of peace, not of one country, but of civilization as a whole.

The flag designed for this project has three spheres within a circle on a white ground, symbol of eternity and unity. Although I do not know when this banner may wave above all the world's cultural institutions, the seed is already sown. Already it has attracted many great minds and travels from heart to heart, spreading once again peace and good-will among men.

Really it is imperative to take immediate measures to preserve the noble heritage of our past for a glorious posterity. This can only come if all countries pledge themselves to protect the creations of culture, which, after all, belong to no one nation but to the world. In this way we may create the next vital step for a universal culture and peace.

PEACE PACT CONFERENCE IN BRUGES

Letter to M. Camille Tulpinck

DEAR Colleague:
Mme. de Vaux Phalipau has informed me of the contents of your letter of March 25th, and I want to thank you sincerely for your invitation to me to take part in your Conference. Unfortunately, I will not be able to assist this summer, as my work takes me to Lahul, in the chain of the Himalayas. Your noble idea to call an International Assembly in Bruges to support the Peace Pact proposed by me, has touched me profoundly. It is most precious to hail each new initiative in the realm of Culture for the defense of the treasures of human genius. Certainly, heroic Belgium, as well as glorious France has profoundly historic interests in this question. Belgian heroes have been witness to the destruction of superb churches, historic mansions, libraries and other artistic monuments which can never be replaced. And it is not only in time of war that such human errors may occur. With each insurrection or internal hostility the monuments of Culture are equally menaced by dangers as grave as those in time of war.

At this time especially, humanity should concentrate all its efforts for the protection of the treasures of creative power. If the Banner of the Red Cross has not always served as a guarantee of complete security, nevertheless it has introduced into human consciousness a most powerful stimulant. Similarly true with the Banner which we propose for the protection of the treasures of culture; for although it may not always succeed in safeguarding these precious monuments, at least it will always and everywhere, call to mind our indispensable duty of caring for the fruits of creative genius. It will give the human spirit another stimulant—the inspiration of culture, the inspiration of esteem for all that concerns the evolution of humanity. We, who have shared in the work of museums and collections; we, who have watched over the works of creative power, have experienced the innumerable Calvaries of Art and Science. No one will dare say that the project of safeguarding the treasures of human genius is superfluous, exaggerated or useless. Beyond deepening the sentiment of protection and respect for the monuments of Culture, our project offers the possibility of revising and cataloguing once more the treasures of creative power, and of placing them under the protection of all humanity; because, I repeat, not only during war, but daily, is it necessary to protect the most beautiful and precious works of creative genius.

It is valuable to note that our project has been instantly acclaimed with exceptional response in all parts of the world. I know you will be happy to learn that besides the great representatives of Culture and the governments of the world, there are among the social organizations inspired by our idea, powerful societies numbering millions of members. Thus, at a meeting on March 24th in New York, dedicated to the Peace Pact, Mrs. Sporborg, President of the New York State Federation of Women's Clubs, spoke of the Peace Pact in the name of the Federation, which includes over four hundred thousand members. Moreover we have received proofs of interest and sympathy from organizations which have over three million members. Thus, the plan for the protection of Culture is supported by public opinion. A number of the institutions supporting our plan are ready immediately to raise the all-unifying Banner of Peace, guided by public opinion. For these institutions as well as for us, the essential thing is the fact itself—the seed itself—which will grow by its own irresistible vitality. Is it possible that some one will dare oppose this emblem of the amicable union and protection of Culture? Such a one would thus reveal himself the opponent of human evolution. Such a denial would forever remain a shameful negation. But the true workers in all the domains of Culture are never negative, and by their constructive positivism, they create indefatigably, since without creation life does not exist. I know that in talking thus, I express your own sentiments, as well as those of all our friends in various countries.

I wish to hail your noble idea with all my heart and that of His Excellency M. le Ministre Jules Destree and of His Excellency Dr. Mineitciro Adacti. I also want to express to you and all those attending the Conference that we have a multitude of friends throughout the world who hope to see the all-unifying Banner of Culture float over their institutions. For there where we rise in defense of righteousness, beauty and culture we are invincible enthusiasts.

It was not by chance that the Conference will meet in Bruges. Unique is the appeal of the beauty of antiquity typified in your city, that living treasury of human genius. May the chimes, which inspired me and which I so greatly admired when visiting your beautiful city, accompany all your solicitous decisions with their victorious carillon. I am often reminded of the music of the opera "Princesse Maleine," dedicated to me and based on the beneficent harmony of the bells of old Bruges.

In the name of World Peace, in the name of Culture and luminous creation, in the name of the heroic aspirations which ennoble humanity, I send, dear Colleague, my heartfelt greetings to you and to all the members of the Conference and to the heroic people of Belgium.

Himalayas, April 24th, 1931.

BANNER OF PEACE

For Visva-Bharati, Santiniketan, 1931

AT THE end of Kali-Yuga, wearying and seemingly unconquerable difficulties obscure humanity. A multitude of problems apparently insoluble, burden life and divide nations, states, communities, families... People try desperately to face them with materialistic inventiveness, but even the most formidable colossi of mechanical civilization are shaken. Every day brings news of commotions, confusions, misunderstandings and misrepresentations. Life is filled with a multitude of petty lies. Everything uplifting and calling becomes, in the eyes of ignoramuses something shameful and depreciating. Thus do the Vishnu Puranas describe the end of Kali-Yuga. But the same Puranas announce also the blessed Satya-Yuga.

What great conception, what bliss lies primarily at the base of this purification and transformation of life? Certainly it is that bliss, in which are united the all-embracing, the all-beautiful, the all-inspiring and all-uplifting. Verily, it will be that great conception which humanity envisages under the name Culture. To this great conception let us undeferrably direct all our best thoughts and creativeness. In this realization, let us reveal the ancient wisdom in the cause of a glorious future. For the glory of this treasure let us realize our great mutual responsibility and let us not impede each other from solemnly upholding this tabernacle of Light. Let us consider our routine work not as hideous shackles, but as the *pranayama* which awakens and coordinates our highest energies. Let us lose neither the day nor the night in sowing the blessed seeds of refinement and implanting Culture among the broad masses.

To this great Service was our Peace Pact with the Banner of Peace consecrated for the protection of all cultural treasures of humanity. Our great Rabindranath Tagore, who is one of the most enlightened protectors of Culture, thus writes to us about the Peace Pact: "I have keenly followed your most remarkable achievements in the realm of Arts and also your great humanitarian work for the welfare of the nations, of which your Peace Pact idea with a special Banner for protection of cultural treasures is a singularly effective symbol. I am very glad indeed that this Pact has been accepted at the Museums' Committee of the League of Nations and I feel sure that it will have far-reaching effects on the cultural harmony of nations."

I am not astonished that we receive so many enthusiastic responses to our Peace Banner. Our past is filled with deplorably sad and irreparable destructions. We see that not only in times of war but also during other periods of error the creations of human genius are destroyed. At the same time the elect of humanity understand that no evolution is possible without the cumulations of Culture. We understand how indescribably difficult are the ways of Culture. Hence the more carefully must we guard the paths which lead to it. It is our duty to create for the young generation traditions of Culture. There, where is Culture, is Peace. There where is the right solution for the difficult social problems, is achievement. Culture is the cumulation of highest Bliss, of highest Beauty, of highest Knowledge. In nowise can humanity pride itself on having done enough for the flowering of Culture. For after ignorance we reach civilization; then gradually we acquire education; then comes intelligence; then follows refinement and the synthesis opens the gates to high Culture. We must confess that our precious and unique treasures of Art and Science are not even properly catalogued. And if our Banner of Peace be the impetus which will urge such an achievement in behalf of the universal treasures, this alone would be the fulfillment of a colossal task. How much of the useful and beautiful could be easily attained! Let us imagine a universal Day of Culture, when simultaneously in all schools of the world will be extolled the true treasures of Nations and Humanity. Amidst the varied works of enthusiasm must be pointed out the great sympathy of the women of America. At a recent celebration dedicated to the Banner of Peace, the representative of four hundred thousand women, Mrs. W. D. Sporborg, pledged their support for the Peace Banner. Vast is the list of organizations, societies, museums, libraries, schools, statesmen, who have expressed the great hope that this project will enter into life. Several organizations have already raised the Banner of Peace. The International Museums' Office of the League of Nations under the Presidency of M. Jules Destree, Belgian Minister, have unanimously accepted this project. And now thanks to the initiative of M. Camille Tulpinck, under the protectorate of Dr. Adatci, President of the Permanent Court of International Justice, a special Conference is being organized in Bruges, for which a broad program is being planned. In connection with this Conference, of great interest is the proposed League of Cities united under the same Banner of Peace. M. Tulpinck and other enlightened minds have enlisted in this idea. A letter from Paris indicates that our friend the poet, Marc Chesneau, will represent the old city of Rouen. I have just received an important article by Dr. George Chklaver, "Le Pacte Roerich et la Societe des Nations," an excerpt of the *Revue de Droit International,* which highly recommends the Pact from its legal aspect. Verily, the protection of treasures of Culture belongs among those all-unifying foundations which permit us to gather in friendship without petty feelings of envy and malice.

We are tired of destructions and negations. Positive creativeness is the fundamental quality of the human spirit. In our life everything that uplifts and ennobles our spirit must hold the dominant place. The milestones of the glorious path must from childhood impel our spirit to the beautiful future. Be assured it is not a truism to speak about the undeferrable and urgent strivings of Culture.

If some ignorant person find this idea superfluous and needless, we shall say to him: "Poor ignoramus, you are outside of evolution. But remember, we are a legion! And in no way shall we abandon our plan for a Peace Banner. And the obstacles of your making we will transform into possibilities."

Let us realize how many highly useful projects can be easily introduced into life. I return to my long cherished idea of a World Day of Culture, when simultaneously throughout the world under one Banner a day may be dedicated to the recognition and appreciation of the treasures of Culture in one's own country and the entire world. Cenotaphs recall the past. But everything connected with Culture, with innumerable glorious martyrdoms and magnificent attainments, impels our minds towards the future. Only think with what simple means, if acting in primary unity humanity could establish traditions which would guide the young generations.

Verily I would like to hail our Conference in Bruges as the beginning of a true League of Culture and I would wish that all members and friends of this Conference should joyously welcome this all-enfolding, all-uniting, all-glorifying idea. In such a movement we could set an example to all those who in ignorance divide, disperse and destroy.

Doubtless the inner import of the Conference in Bruges will be highly significant and will open new gates for all the superb future constructions in the realm of Culture. The Conference in Bruges will not resemble a fleeting moth which has singed its wings at the first candle. It will form a radiant legion whose fiery wings will grow in consonance with the achievement of great Beauty and glorious Necessity.

In the Museo Civico of Padua there is a panel of Guariento, "Angels of Peace." In a solemn circle the angels hold their council. Each angel carries a sphere as an all-embracing sign and the palm of peace which in the angelic hand, is austere as an irresistible sword. This panel rises before me as I think of our Conference. These angels are benevolent but indomitable. Thus benevolent and invincible, I visualize our legion of Peace and Culture.

Let us gather those who, surmounting all personal difficulties, casting out petty selfishness, propel their spirits to the task of preserving Culture, which above all, will insure a radiant future.

Let us exert all means to make paramount the beautiful necessity of Culture. No superlatives are too great in speaking of the most essential conception in the world.

We must not fear enthusiasm. Only the ignorant and the spiritually impotent would scoff at this noble and unsullied feeling. Such scoffing is but the sign of inspiration for the true Legion of Honor. It would be outrageous, if in touching on the great manifestations, such attributes as "small" and "little," were used. Thus we should beware of committing that most hideous of all acts—disparaging. This would signify decay. Nothing can impede us from dedicating ourselves to the service of Culture, so long as we believe in it and give to it our most flaming thoughts. Do not disparage! The great Agni singes the drooping wings. Only in harmony with evolution can we ascend! And nothing can extinguish the selfless and flaming wings of enthusiasm!

GREETINGS TO
THE BRUGES CONFERENCE

HEARTIEST salutations to all assembled in the name of the Banner of Peace, in the name of reverence to all cultural treasures!

I have already expressed my admiration for the noble project of M. Camille Tulpinck to convene a Conference in Bruges to spread and enforce in life our Peace Pact. M. Tulpinck will undoubtedly acquaint the honored assembly with some of the considerations, which I have outlined in my communications to him.

Now, I should like to address all present and in this salutation, to bear witness to the enthusiasm already transmitted to us from countries throughout the world for this cause. To me, this Conference appears as the foundation of that long-anticipated *League of Culture.* This League will sustain the universal consciousness in its realization that true evolution is constructed only upon the foundations of Knowledge and Beauty.

Only the values of culture will solve the most complex problems of life. Only in the name of the treasures of culture, may humanity prevail. At the very root of this concept, so sacred to us, is enfolded the entire veneration of Light, the true service to Bliss. For it is precisely the concept of culture that must be regarded, not as sterile abstraction but as the virility of creativeness; it lives, nourished by the indefatigable achievements of life, of enlightened labor and of creation. Not for our own sakes because we are already mindful of it, but for the sake of those growing generations to come, let us repeat again and again that during the proudest epochs of human history, a renaissance and efflorescence were achieved where the tradition of reverence for culture grew. And we know that this tradition cannot be strengthened instantaneously. It must be tended daily by the benediction of light. For even the worthiest garden withers in darkness and in drought.

Hence the Banner of Peace is indispensable for us, not only in the hour of war but perhaps, even more, as a necessity each day, when unmarked by the roar of cannons, irrevocable errors are committed against culture.

Of universal significance are the cultural spiritual values of mankind; and an equally peace-imparting unification is effected by the cordial handclasp in the name of the glorious treasures of all generations.

In our wide program, the multifold ways of how to care for Culture are to be discussed. Multifold also will be the useful suggestions, we shall undoubtedly hear, all so needed in this universal movement. And the question which concerns us is only how best and in what order to apply them. We shall also hear of a Universal Day of Culture, when simultaneously in all schools and educational institutions, a day shall be consecrated to the full appreciation of all national and universal treasures of culture. We shall discuss which monuments of culture and which cultural collections shall be protected by the Banner of Peace. We shall discuss a universal inventory of all treasures of human genius. We shall discuss the entire complex of protective measures for Beauty and Knowledge, which must verily become the responsibility of all rational humanity, introducing firm foundations into life. There will certainly also be discussed the organizing of special Committees in all countries, the representatives of which have already expressed, or are prepared to express their endorsement of this cultural work. The organization of such a Committee has already begun in America. In our first Annals, which we have had the pleasure to offer to this Assembly, are outlined the measures which have thus far been fulfilled by us for this Pact. We are of course certain that not only will the Annals indicate the development of the Peace Pact, but that another edition will be issued, dedicated to all questions pertaining to the universal inventory of cultural treasures.

Beginning with this Fall, on the basis of the sympathies and approval of the Pact by organizations numbering millions of members, we are inaugurating a Fund for the Banner of Peace. A special meeting dedicated to the Banner of Peace in our Museum in New York, proved once again what powerful sympathies fortify our idea. One must also mark that some institutions have already flown the Banner of Peace above their treasures, thus confirming the urgency of this decision. It is necessary to emphasize that all these actions must proceed along one channel. The concept of Culture must arouse in us also the consonant concept of unity. We are tired of destruction and of common misunderstanding. Only Culture, only the all-unifying conception of Beauty and Knowledge, can restore the pan-human language to us. This is not a dream! It is founded upon my experience during forty-two years of activity in the domain of Culture—Art and Science. And in unison we may pronounce an irrevocable oath, that we shall never abandon the defense of culture and the League of Culture, neither we, nor our associates. Nor can we be deluded, for our experiences in the domains of art and knowledge have filled us with an unquenchable enthusiasm. Not only one nation, nor one class is with us, but multitudes, for, above all, the human heart is open to the Beauty of creativeness.

From the snowy peaks of the Himalayas, in the name of all-embracing and all-conquering Beauty of creativeness, in its vastest conception, I greet you! I greet the friends-devotees of Culture. And this Union in the Beautiful will multiply our strength, it will imbue our thoughts with harmony and with its impelling power as a Beautiful Necessity will attract to us multitudes of co-workers for culture.

The conception of Culture belongs among the invincible synthesizing concepts. Only ignorance can be hostile to Culture; and wherever it reveals itself, we must regret it. However, we must remember how slowly even the most evident ideas enter the consciousness. Let us remember that even the Banner of the Red Cross, which has since rendered incalculable service to humanity, at first was received with derision, mistrust and ridicule. Similar were the cases also with numerous examples of the most useful discoveries and innovations. But these deplorable facts serve to imbue us with conviction of the necessity and vitality of the Banner of Peace and League of Culture.

After all, what we propose in nowise belittles anyone or anything, it does not involve complicated measures, but is feasible through very simple means. Certainly, great works cannot be carried through instantaneously—long and indefatigable labor is needed. And for this we are prepared. But fire is ignited instantaneously, thus let this sacred fire, the fire of the Chalice of Ascent, unite us all without delay to join and unfurl in friendship the Banner of Peace, the Banner of Culture.

1931.

INAUGURATION
OF THE FRENCH ROERICH SOCIETY
IN PARIS

FRANCE and Paris are so intimately linked to the best memories of my life that I have learned with a very particular pleasure that a French Association of Friends of Roerich Museum has just been founded in Paris.

It is there that I completed my artistic education; there that exhibitions of my paintings were organized. The decorations which I conceived for the theater were realized on the stage of the great Parisian theaters. I recall that the eminent Jacques Blanche pronounced his admiration for the "Danses Polovtsiennes."

Is it not to France, to Paris, that each one comes to refine his judgment and to pay tribute to Beauty?

The ties, which shall link the American Museum to its French friends, have in my opinion, an especial significance.

Already, the American hearts are enthusiastic about the magnificent art created by French genius. In the United States, the Museums and collections reserve a chosen place for these brilliant and infinitely diverse works, the splendid flower of the French soil. These works are not only viewed but are enfolded in an intelligent and respectful devotion.

France and America are impelled together by the sure instinct of the People's feeling.

I have always believed that Art and Science are the firmest foundations for real Peace between Nations; supported by these bases, France and America comprehending each other better from day to day, will evolve towards a complete understanding.

Did not Confucius say: "If each day I bring a mound of

earth, I will be able to raise up a mountain." It is by multiplying the relations of personal friendship, by esteeming the creations of art, by pursuing with perseverance the realizations of science that we will be able to raise this mountain which humanity will ascend with firm tread.

It is not for our personal gain that, uniting our efforts, we gather the chosen materials which may serve to construct a future happiness.

We labor for those who are unknown to us, the men of the future who shall know how to value all that has been achieved in securing the Peace for the world.

I do not consider your Association as a mere gathering of individuals, accidentally united. It is a new link created between France and America; a new desire for mutual comprehension is being dispatched through space.

For, each time we act without personal motive, the creative power transports itself to the level of the general welfare. Hence, there is no need to desire success, because success is already here. Success never fails an action undertaken for the benefit of all.

This is why the goal of your Association is not solely artistic. The work which you are founding acquires an international importance since, by its peace-effecting cultural labor it can contribute to the consummation of an era of veritable peace.

In thanking my Friends of France for the sensitive thought which has inspired them, I express to them my best feelings and I rejoice in the anticipation of advising our American Friends of the broad plans of the distinguished French personalities who are consecrating themselves to the common tasks of civilization.

Himalayas, May 1929.

SALUTATION TO FRANCE

Paris Press, 1930

IT was a joy for me to renew an ancient tradition by visiting the sanctuary of Notre Dame on the day of my arrival in Paris. Under these noble arches and in the splendor of the rose-windows, once again I felt vibrate the heroic soul of the French nation and the "French Spirit," under whose emblem has been gathered the French Association of Friends of Roerich Museum in New York. During the course of the ceremony, M. le Consul General, Maxime Mongendre, and Professor Meillet, of the College of France, delivered addresses which were interspersed with those sparks of brilliance that inspire a secular culture.

When M. Meillet spoke of the lives of other planets, he revealed all the breadth of an intelligence which liberates itself from narrow prejudices and freely evolves towards a creative conception. I remember that one member of the audience who was seated too far away from Professor Meillet to be able to hear him well told me later: "His address must have been most beautiful!" "Why?" I asked him. "His face was so inspired!" replied my friend. In truth, the sensitive image of the French savant has become still more ennobled by the long years of scientific study, by a transcendent reflection acquired only through daily contact with the treasures of Beauty and Knowledge.

Recently, when M. Henri Verne did the honors at the Delacroix Exposition at the Louvre, I had the direct sense of a triumphant synthesis.

The Centenary of Romanticism! Who knows? Is it not rather its millennium which should be celebrated at this moment? I think of the flowering of Roman style, of the heritage of the Druids, enriched through the course of centuries by new beauties. I think of the Sacred Mother of the Druids enrobed with the brilliant mantle of the *Mater Maxima.*

The Centenary of Romanticism! Romanticism was not born with Eugene Delacroix; he already is revealed as the product of a consciousness evolved through centuries, but its point of departure is the heroic Roman style. Romanticism is perhaps only a synonym for heroism, and this is not a kind of spasmodic activity, but above all, the ennobling of an infinite succession of actions, of thoughts and of enhancements which are spiritualized in the gradual effacement of all traces of egotism in human nature.

As multiple as are the manifestations of the genius of Delacroix, it is his spirit of synthesis which we most admire. It is this sacred synthesis which has liberated the artist from the narrow frame of an individual consciousness and revealed to him the unifying Cosmos. It is this which permits him to reproduce with veneration the sunset and to portray with equal mastery the images of men, their sufferings, their actions and their aspirations. Perhaps, the artist himself, did not intend to express himself thus diversely. He was simply hastening to throw upon the canvas the ecstasies of his soul. But his creative genius was supported by centuries of tradition. The artist did not fear to resemble others, nor to preserve a first sketch. He allowed himself to be guided uniquely by the surrounding reality, by this triumphant reality which should have equally illumined the road for the younger generation. Among multiple manifestations of the art of Delacroix one can find material to justify the most diverse and sometimes contradictory conceptions.

How useful are such expositions! One can sincerely congratulate the director of the Louvre, in the person of M. Henri Verne, thanks to whom the Museum is not a mortuary chamber of treasures of art, but a living institution which does not hesitate to modify the aspect of its very walls. Thanks to the reuniting of so many masterpieces scattered in distant collections, many new parallels may be established. How greatly our understanding of Delacroix' powers as an artist has been enriched! Besides his great works, one sees in the glass cases his note-books, little known, in which he inscribed his thoughts, in a style totally different from his habitual style. Sparkling new facets have been added to the precious gems of Romantic Art. In truth, it is not the centenary, but the millennium of Romanticism which one should celebrate in these manifestations. And this Romanticism itself is only a particular aspect of the French spirit, which cannot be summarized in the volumes of a library nor in a series of pictures. But this polyhedron reflects an effulgent light from the radiance of Romanticism, that is to say, of heroism.

Perhaps this is the road towards the very essence of the French Spirit, to which neither the logic of reason nor the exactitude of calculation, nor analysis of the sequence of facts would be able to guide us. But, if we possess the key of heroic Romanticism, this magic key will permit us to penetrate up to the very sanctuary.

Should this essential quality of man—heroism—be considered as conducive to perpetual tremors, or on the contrary, as a powerful aid in the constructive effort of the French nation?

In the present state of infinite complications, of deviations, of contradictions and of ambiguous formulae, one is obliged to make a choice between all that which is positive and everything negative and destructive. So many new factors appear in our lives, so many old conceptions are effaced, that psychology, like the artist seeking a silhouette, is constrained to proceed by categories and to follow some fundamental lines. We are advancing through an entangled jungle where the vines and other parasitical plants enlace too tightly the massive trunks; and the ephemeral orchids absorb an inordinate part of the sap of the roots. Once having traversed this forest, we come to a crossroad. There, as in the old tales, a laconic inscription indicates the road of Salvation. This road is the road of culture—not the culture of a material civilization, but of true culture—which from time to time opens to Humanity.

Despite the delays, new discoveries are achieved, a new wind sweeps away the ancient dust; and we are forced to advance on this road which is marked with the milestones of destiny.

It is not necessary to complicate the affairs of life, nor to distort them, nor to coldly imitate them, but to accumulate the elements of culture and to attempt thus to attain the next step.

And in this way we will arrive at the conception of the French Spirit. Thus above all doubts and calculations appear the outlines of a heroism which advances towards the future. During the years when the entire efforts of the nation were aimed towards victory, France gave proof of her heroism, her self-denial and her incomparable endurance. Once again, one was able to value the quality of her soul, bright and firm, as a sword. We, who have been witnesses to these memorable years, are able to affirm that they were not the effect of a passing paroxysm. A new magnificent page has been inscribed in the annals of the country.

When we feel the Spirit of France vibrate, we seem to perceive the powerful winds which sustain her and lift her toward new summits. At certain moments of life, to be content merely with pronouncing criticisms becomes at once useless and dangerous. Only positive action is fruitful. It reminds me of the Siberian peasants, who said: "We do not know what is going on in the capital, but we are certain that we must construct. We no longer are content to live in huts, we want two-story houses." This was not egoism, but the manifestation of a constructive and practical spirit, which was expressing itself by the organization of co-workers and a true collaboration. We are equally impressed by this same spirit in France. One glance suffices to realize that everywhere in France construction goes on. Is there not a French proverb saying that: "When building is going on, everything progresses"?

This popular opinion summarizes admirably the character of a constructive epoch.

The noble project of M. Briand, for the unification of Europe pertains to the same constructive spirit which animates the French nation. Not long ago, such a thought would have been considered an abstraction, but at the present time, this action is so advanced that we are able to greet this new phase of international organization as a positive reality.

Thus, I take pleasure in recalling the benign features of the French savant addressing an American audience, the creation of a Delacroix, the achieving spirit of the French people. This trinity expresses to me the culture which we find, above all, on ancient roads. It is through the purification of the ancient formulae that we are coming back to the triumphant emblem of culture. It is not accidental that at this moment, in the most different countries, men in diverse walks of life evoke these elements of culture and unite in its name. They want to forget that which divides them; they want to rebuild on the foundation of this victorious principle. In fact, their conceptions of culture do not differ so greatly. After all, human consciousness grasps these elements as perfectly as it perceives the principle of honesty, for example. Even if some one admitted himself unable to define honesty, one can be sure that deep in his heart he would know how to discern an act of abnegation. It is not a question of idealism or an abstraction, but a question of the daily nourishment of the spirit. Some may be inclined to call it occasionally civilization, or progress or achievement, instead of culture. But, civilization and progress are only circumstances brought about through culture, and as to achievement, it is synonymous with true culture, since the latter is really living, perpetually evolving, containing the ideas of "yesterday" and "tomorrow," while the element "today" is scarcely noticeable. This constant evolution accepts all initiatives and rejects all deceiving negations.

New roads open through space, infinite roads. We will

not fear this infinity of the future where our spirits, saturated with experience of the past, will vibrate only to the influence of heroism.

Yes, verily, one feels happy to be able to find in heroism the very essence of the French spirit, because there, where the principle of heroism prevails, the human heart resounds to the call of the Infinite.

Likewise must we express our gratitude to all those who provide us with the opportunity of invoking once again the sacred principle of heroism.

CONSTRUCTIVE WORK

To the Committee of the French Roerich Society

THIS day is especially memorable for me; just thirty years ago, I left Paris, after having finished my art studies there under the direction of Fernand Cormon. I carried away with me, not only Master Cormon's teachings relative to art, but in addition his friendship and his advice—the fruit of his experience of life —which later I had many occasions to remember.

Among the eminent French artists that I met at this epoch, I was often struck by the quality that true culture alone can give. When Fernand Cormon or the illustrious Puvis de Chavannes expressed their views on Art, they always gave proof of an admirable tolerance. Thus, for example, I remember that in visiting an exposition with Puvis de Chavannes, I was surprised to note how he could find kindly and positive words for the most diverse artistic creations. From time to time, the Master passed by a work in silence —this was the only sign of his disapproval.

Gradually, as the years go by, we begin to understand better the value of that positive tolerance, united to an intrepid, creative spirit. We recognize the fact that intolerance is nothing but ignorance. Knowledge and experience, free from all prejudice, can alone erect a solid construction.

I am very happy to be able to express in person to the Committee of the French Association of Friends of Roerich Museum my feelings of profound friendship, and to add a few words relating to the future activity of the French Association.

In examining the activities of the Committee of the French Association since its beginning, I perceive immediately a most favorable sign. We have started our common work in the name of the kindly principle of Unity; but the Union can only be established on the basis of an effective sympathy. Now, in observing the results obtained by the French Association, one understands immediately that you have known how to establish a real collaboration always fruitful, and consequently useful.

We have so often recalled our motto: "Art and Science are the pillars of the Evolution of the Future," that at this moment it seems to me unnecessary to reconsider these general ideas. It suffices to affirm the great influence exerted by the currents of exchange between the various countries; these exchanges not only enriching the human spirit, but really ennobling it.

During the course of the last few months, we have had from all sides of the ocean, numerous occasions to collaborate cordially. A French Association of Friends of Roerich Museum has been formed in New York, with the aid of that eminent representative of the Republic, M. Mongendre, the Consul General. Just before my departure from New York I had the honor of inaugurating this group, and I was touched profoundly to see the glorious French flag unite with the starry banner of the United States in a magnificent play of color.

The greetings brought to us by the Consul General, M. Mongendre, Professor Meillet, of the College of France, and the other distinguished speakers, contributed to create, that evening, an atmosphere of real friendship.

The spontaneous ovation which greeted the strains of the Marseillaise showed, once more, how much the citizens of the United States appreciate the great Nation, its friend and associate.

Not long after, several societies affiliated with the Roerich Museum were formed, notably the Society of Saint Francis of Assisi, the Spinoza Association and the Shakespeare Association.

During the course of my recent stay in London, I was very happy to learn of the inauguration at the Roerich

Museum, of a British Group, and also an Hellenic Association, "Origen"; almost simultaneously, a Brazilian Association of Friends of the Roerich Museum was founded at Rio de Janeiro.

Recently the Roerich Museum had the honor to receive a visit from the President of the Republic of Colombia. Following the friendly ties which were formed, one can easily foretell in the near future the formation of a Colombian Association.

It is thus that the union of spirits in the Name of Beauty, of Good and of mutual Comprehension, is formed.

Returning to the activities of the French Association of the Friends of the Roerich Museum, I should like to tell you how broad seem to me the possibilities of all kinds that open before us, certain of them appearing on first glance, unexpectedly.

The American Public enthusiastically hailed the concerts of the Society of Ancient Music, by M. Casadesus, and it is to be expected that the next Representative Exposition of French Modern Art will contribute its part towards reinforcing our friendly ties.

During the course of this year, we have had, at the Roerich Museum more than a hundred artistic and scientific displays of all kinds, destined to explain the creative genius of the various countries.

I hope that the French people who visit the United States with the view of lecturing there, will really be able to enrich the American soul, by explaining there the French doctrines of Art and Literature, and also, by undertaking to make known to the people of the United States the glorious lives of the French heroes, whose feats can give a just idea of French grandeur.

I think that competent authorities in France should consider the possibilities of organizing for American visitors, special trips to the regions where the memory of the national heroes is evoked by the scenes of their magnificent deeds.

In New York, we shall be happy, from time to time, to

be able to show films of French monuments and historical sites, and episodes which will illustrate the glories of this Country.

Following through the same idea, we might propose, on behalf of our American Institutions, the organization of lectures and artistic manifestations in France.

Audience with the President of the French Republic

My present stay in France was marked by manifestations precious to me—of sympathy, friendship and spiritual rapport.

The audience granted to me on the 13th of June, 1930, by the President of the Republic left me with an unforgettable impression.

In eloquent terms, the President expressed his profound knowledge of the role in the world played by art as well as by the activities of our Institutions, so that I could feel this real vibration of spiritual chords, which is so characteristic of glorious France. When the President said that I had "a French heart," it was an expression of sentiment that unites men and nations, and which prepares Humanity for new possibilities. So, when the President declared that there was nothing to oppose the Union of France and the United States I could appreciate his lofty political thought, which actuates the advance towards a fruitful peace.

With broad and friendly strokes the President sketched the situation in Asia, and there again, one felt the precious quality of an action inspired by true culture.

The President charged me to transmit to all our friends his feelings of good-will and respect for our cultural works. I was very much impressed to see how well the President knows and appreciates our Institutions in America and the French Association in Paris.

I was happy to present the President with the American edition of "Himalaya" and the French book published by the *Editions du Vrai et Beau* (with the articles of Madame de Vaux-Phalipau and of Dr. George Chklaver).

Upon leaving this significant audience I thought that it is precisely by similar relations, founded on culture, that the best possibilities are created.

Our essential duty is to bring up a new generation, both vigorous and well-informed. It is due to this broad understanding that the Nations are establishing an efficacious cooperation. Truthfully, this was for me a memorable day, for not only could I appreciate the elevated personality of the President, but also the nobility of the French Nation, with which we are so happy to be able to discuss the principles of true culture.

In reply to my telegram in which I reported to the Trustees of the Roerich Museum the audience which the President of France had just granted me, I received from Mr. Horch, President of the Roerich Museum, the following dispatch: "The President and the Trustees of the Roerich Museum were greatly delighted with the audience which has been granted you by the President of the French Republic. President Doumergue has always maintained the ideal of the great French Nation, and its most lofty aspirations. His enlightened attitude in regard to the peaceful and cultural aims of our Institutions will always remain in the hearts of our numerous American friends, who are striving to create a more intimate union between France and America with the aid of Art and Culture."

Lately, it has been my privilege to meet numerous political and artistic personalities of France.

I am happy to state and to be able to write in our record that the same feelings of reciprocal understanding inspired all these interviews. This will serve, I hope, not only to fortify the present, but also to forge brilliant possibilities for a vast future.

It will be my great happiness to spread this news among our co-workers and the members of the Societies of the Friends of the Roerich Museum in all countries of Europe, North and South America and in Asia.

Personally, I was profoundly touched by the gesture of

the Municipal Council of the City of Paris, who voted to put at my disposal the rooms of the Palais des Beaux Arts with the purpose of installing there an exhibition of my paintings. I have not yet decided on the exact date of this exhibition, because wishing to make it as worthy as possible of the magnificent frame offered it by the "enlightened city," I should like to have, as part of it, some paintings consecrated to those subjects which are particularly dear to me and which are directly related to France. But this will take me some time.

Allow me to entrust to you today two flags; one of them, that of our Museum, and the other the Banner designed to protect art treasures, regarding which you have already expressed your sympathetic feelings. We are at present receiving letters from all quarters of the globe expressing enthusiastic adherence to this plan.

I am happy to inform you that the representatives of the Powers united at Brussels, the 22nd of last May, at the session of the Museum's Office of the Institute of Intellectual Cooperation of the League of Nations, have signed the recommendation of the preliminary plan, as it was presented through the kindness of the Secretariat General of your French Association. This preliminary plan will be examined between the 18th and 22nd of July of this year by the Commission of Intellectual Cooperation of the League of Nations and we are hopeful that it will shortly be ratified by all the interested governments.

But, whatever the final fate of our projects, we can say that, thanks to our combined efforts, this new seed has been sown and it will bear its fruits in due time.

Conforming to the decisions of the Council of Trustees of the Roerich Museum, we have ordered special insignia for the members of our Associations. Let us hope the insignia, this cross of Cultural Work, will bind even closer the members of our Institutions, separated by space, but united in spirit.

Observing the development of the activities of the Committee of the French Association of Friends of Roerich Museum, I think that permanent quarters should be assured them. Faithful to the spirit of union which presides over all our efforts, I thought that we should establish a friendly tie with a French institution pursuing similar aims—the safety and renaissance of Art and of Culture. The League for the Defense of Art, which has united so many eminent persons for the protection of those treasures dear to all of us, would perhaps be an excellent collaborator, because the League, to my knowledge, is an institution whose field of action is limited to France, while our activities spread over many countries; so, our two Associations could complement each other and render mutual service.

Madame de Vaux-Phalipau, who puts all her heart into service for the Association, has asked me to give one of my paintings for the future quarters of our Association; this will be the beginning of a part of the Roerich Museum in France. It was with pleasure that I consented to this request so flattering to me, and during my next voyage in India, where I shall visit our Himalayan Institute in Naggar, I shall be happy to paint a picture for the quarters of the French Association.

I take this occasion to inform you that the Himalayan Research Institute has proposed to M. Mangin, Director of the Museum of Natural History of Paris, a presentation of collections of *flora* of the Himalayan region. M. Mangin with his customary kindness and understanding, has consented to accept this gift. Thus is created a new link in our Franco-American cooperation.

I should like to mention another manifestation of our collaboration—to let you know the proposal which comes to me from the Yugoslavian Academy of Arts and Sciences—which has recently elected me Honorary Member—concerning the organization of an artistic Expedition across the historical sites of Yugoslavia. The letter of the President of the Academy also contained a communication relative to the interest that His Majesty, the King of

Yugoslavia bears towards our institutions. I was delighted to hear the gracious comments on my art that King Alexander made on this occasion.

The fact that this invitation was received during my stay in France created for me an even closer tie with the rest of our activities.

* * *

It is with the greatest satisfaction that we view to what extent the program of events of our various Societies grouped around the Roerich Museum, is free from all shackles and preconceived limitations. This liberty of movement in the vast domain of cultural activities seems to me to be the gage of the development and of the future prosperity of our Associations.

Too often things are complicated by reason of various routine habits. But everything becomes easier when there is a kindly and benevolent enthusiasm, directed towards Science and Beauty.

If, because of ignorance someone criticizes us, we can answer him victoriously: "We are sincere. We are attempting to make everyone's life nobler and more beautiful. We destroy nothing, but we construct. We adopt everywhere a positive attitude, and we avoid all negation. Without being vague pacifists, we should like to see the "Peace Banner" fly as the emblem of a new and magnificent era. I do not think we are abstract idealists. Quite to the contrary, it seems to me that to reflect on the means of beautifying and ennobling life, both individual and collective, is to turn towards the most immediate reality.

This soaring towards the common good, as well as the development of the feeling of the Beautiful, will give us the necessary strength and will assure for our institutions a continual influx of new forces.

France, which seems to me like a precious receptacle of civilization, gives us a glorious example.

Like a Phoenix, rising from its own ashes, always stronger and more beautiful, great and glorious France is always regenerated after each trial which it endures, in the course of its history, evoking from these very trials the impetus towards Progress!

I express my feelings of friendliness and attachment to the French nation, and to all our dear French Friends!

Paris, June 21, 1930.

COOPERATION

To the British Roerich Association

WITH sincere joy I inaugurate the British Association of Roerich Museum.

It is no coincidence that while this association shall be inaugurated here I shall be in London. In this way once more shall be expressed the tides of Anglo-American Friendship. And once more with real enthusiasm we can recollect our reminiscences of Great Britain.

London is especially full of beautiful reminiscences for me. From my childhood, Sir Walter Scott was my beloved author. The best friends of my student days were Shakespeare, Ruskin, Blake, Carlyle and all the romanticists. *Lalla Rookh* planted perhaps one of the first seeds of the East in my imagination. And then, who knows what old reminiscences connected with our Nordic ancestors are flowing around the cliffs of Great Britain? Perhaps some of my ancestors lived at one time in the Hesperides. In any case, London, with its cultured heart—the British Museum—was a true attraction during my entire life.

I have heard the story of how one foreigner, coming to Westminster Abbey for the first time, insisted that somewhere there must be a small room. Every one denied the existence of this room. He insisted, however, and in the records it was found that this room had at one time existed and had subsequently been demolished or connected with others.

In 1920, during my exhibition at the Goupil Galleries, I met many British friends, and I retain forever such happy remembrances of Bishop Bury, Frank Brangwyn, Lord Glenconner, Sir Samuel and Lady Hoare, Albert Coates, Sir Cecil Harcourt-Smith, Sir Bernard Pares, Hagberg

Wright, and other representatives of the official and cultured world. During this time my paintings entered the collections of the Victoria and Albert Museums; and once more the conventional walls in the field of art have been demolished.

During our Expedition in Central Asia, more than once did we feel the cordiality of the British Consuls. I remember how Major Gillan, British Consul in Kashgar, helped us when we were stopped by the Daotai of Khotan. In the same way, we shall never forget the hospitality of Colonel Bailey, the British Resident at Sikkim. We were so pleased to see that he was not only an official representative but also a real scholar knowing the conditions and language of the country.

The name of Queen Victoria is highly revered in Tibet. In northern Tibet, we witnessed a very unusual sign of the popularity of Queen Victoria. In Nagchu, we found a silver coin with an image in a Chinese garment. Upon studying this image, I was surprised to recognize an unquestionable similarity between the Indian Rupee with the image of Queen Victoria. The resemblance was so unexpected, and so complete, that we investigated further, learning that the Indian Rupees bearing the image of Queen Victoria were so highly valued, and so popular in Tibet and China that the Chinese Government of the Unan Province had struck a special coin corresponding to the Victorian-Hindu Rupee, but adding a Chinese garment. This is a sign of true popularity.

I was always closely connected with Shakespearian movements, and knew personally several of the eminent translators of Shakespeare. Thus under great unifying names we can intensify our friendship and work in peaceful enthusiasm for the high ideals of mankind.

My best wishes for your successful work!

New York, 1930.

IN SPITE OF DIFFICULTIES

To the Bulgarian Roerich Society

YOUR last two letters, written in Paris and New York, were communicated to me. Thank you for your sincere lines. Thus, exactly must we act in our service to the Great Light. The entire world is divided now into the destroyers and the builders. And each one, who understands the high significance of Culture, will be among the builders, among those who strain their energy in order to defend the world from the malevolent assaults of darkness. Great must be the ignorance and blindness of those who cannot even distinguish the Light from the Darkness. You understand why the parent of Darkness, from ancient times, has been called the sower of refuse. It is he who so clouds with dust the eyes of the ignorant, that they are entirely unable to distinguish the day from the night.

In sending you my book, "Flowers of Morya's Garden," I have done so in the name of Saint Sergius. Direct your worthiest strivings to this Great Protector, this Builder of the true, spiritual Culture. "Flowers of Morya's Garden" is, as you know, published for the benefit of the famished —for the spiritually famished. Because physical starvation is nought in comparison with starvation of spirit. And for each one who thinks of Bliss, the immediate task is to help. Only in giving do we receive. Then only do we receive that truly great Bliss which the Ancient Wisdom preordains and knows and which is so realistically expressed in true Christianity.

There are two conceptions, Bliss and Heroic Achievement, firmly defined in the Russian words *Blagodat i Podvig*, but which lack adequate expression in other languages. These, one must understand as reality. Clinging to Bliss, one must infuse it actively into daily life. For what else can transform the homely routine of each day into beauty? Only this—Great Bliss! What a wondrous word! Because this realization creates miracles. And the most brutal heart pays homage to the highest Light, which is no less a reality than the sun. But we also, with each torch of ours, evoke the supreme fiery elements; which means that in each heart may also be kindled a purifying flame of all-understanding and all-containment. I am no lover of "mysticism" or "occultism," because both are synonyms of nescience.

As I have so often pointed out in "Paths of Blessing" which you now read, we must strive to clarity, to lucidity, to the truth, in which is revealed the great radiant hierarchy.

From your letters I learn that you are enduring hardships. One must say that now it is difficult for all. Hence we may all rejoice if we have been deemed worthy to be summoned to work, inspired by the example of the great deeds of the most Holy Sergius—the deeds of him, who so often suffered revilement and was abandoned even by his chosen brethren, yet conquered all difficulties only by the power of spirit, continuing unceasingly to build dwellings of Bliss as guiding milestones.

As you know in America, we are building a Chapel in the name of Saint Sergius. Like sentinels of Bliss these signs will stand upon the ways of the gathering of experience. How many of our brothers, now scattered, cull great experiences and knowledge, which will sustain them upon the benevolent ways. I have sent you my address about Culture. Verily, let us all give thought to this great conception, to this step to light. I know that the thought of Culture will benevolently re-echo in your heart and in the rhythm of this sacred tremor, new, invincible forces will suffuse your beings.

Greetings!

1930.

MILESTONES OF CULTURE

To the German Roerich Society

IT was an exceptional joy for me here amidst the white summits of the Himalayas to receive your greetings and invitation.

Between the lines of your message I felt that heartiness which sets aglow all cultural undertakings. It is a great joy to hear that your hearts burn with the thought of culture. And verily, we must gather all the strength of our spirits, if we are to defend the achievements of culture, which are so often overlooked in the vortex of the mechanical life of today.

We must find the best forms of mutual friendly communion and of an interchange of creative achievements. And then—if we know and trust each other, true collaboration will come of itself, illumining our life, which is disturbed through various material crises. If we realize the worth of spiritual values and are conscious of possible useful acquisitions, we will have made an important step towards mutual understanding. The dignity of the creative personality must be defended and the fostering of young shoots of creative work will be one of our brightest tasks.

I shall always be most pleased to receive news from you and to send you my lectures and advice, knowing how sincerely they will be discussed.

Wagner has always been my favorite composer, and since my school days, Goethe and Schiller occupied honored places on my desk.

Durer and Holbein have ever stood for me as witnesses to the magnificent achievements of the spirit, and I remember that my first themes during my school-years were "Undine" and the "Erlkonig."

We must also safeguard and enroot the very same great traditions of Art in contemporary life. Whence otherwise will the nobility of spirit come? How otherwise will grow the dignity of personality? From where will emerge the realization of broad cooperation and mutual trust? From the very same inexhaustible source of radiant, blessed creativeness. Life is transformed by the achievements of Culture. Difficult as these may be during times of narrow materialism, nevertheless we know that these achievements alone will constitute the progressive impetus of humanity. Light is one—and the gates to it are verily international and accessible for all who seek light. Darkness is admitted only during the periods of sleep; but verily it is not for sleep that humanity has been perfecting itself for millions of years.

It is not a truism to think of and to invoke Culture. Through all means, and in all measures, we must bring into the chalice of Culture all the acquisitions of our hearts. It is said that we now approach the epoch of fire. What a wondrous nature-element this is, if we can realize it and apply it with benevolence. Kindling the torches of spirit, is it not beautiful to realize that in other countries the very same torches also radiate? This realization of cooperation will strengthen and uplift our quests. We know not which is more precious: the beholding of these friends with the physical eye or feeling them in the spirit of our heart. It is important to know that the Holy Chalice of Culture is being tirelessly filled and that in hearty cooperation our friends deposit therein their best spiritual values.

In the name of these spiritual works I am sending you from the white summits my sincerest greeting, and I extend to you the assurance of my pleasure in making your personal acquaintance, when the opportunity comes.

1930.

SPELLS OF FINLAND

To the Finnish Roerich Association

I APPRECIATE greatly your kind letter of October 6th, conveying to me the news of my election as Honorary President of the Finnish Roerich Society.

I accept gladly this election so dear to me. Please convey to the Finnish Ambassador and to the Finnish Consul-General in the United States my profound admiration for the great constructiveness which is being achieved by the Finnish Nation. Also please transmit to Dr. Rehlander, to General Mannerheim, and to all my friends in Finland my best feelings. We never forget the time spent on the estate of Dr. Rehlander and the welcome of General Mannerheim, conveyed to me by my friend Mr. Axel Gallen-Kalela on the occasion of the opening of my exhibition in Helsingfors. I always feel that my painting in the Athenaeum is my ambassador of good-will to Finland.

And with heartfelt emotion, I also remember how in America, at a reception luncheon, I gave my greetings to the great Builder of Finland, Saarinen, who created his original style in architecture. I said to him: "Where is that bridge which makes our meetings so friendly? Where is that key which opens our hearts? And where are those wings which carry us over all obstacles in the name of the most noble and most creative? It is the Beautiful which leads us over all bridges! It is the Beautiful which opens even the most difficult lock! It is the Beautiful which weaves the radiant wings and unites the human souls in their striving towards the One Light!"

When I remember the beautiful Museums of Arts, Archeology and Ethnography of Finland, I feel with what care and knowledge the Finns collected their treasures. And we know how deep are the Finnish roots. The esteemed Finnish scholar, Talgren, recalls to us this deeply enrooted ancient Culture. And the word "Culture" is so near and so easily pronounced in Finland.

In my book "Shambhala" I pay tribute to Finland in the following passage of an essay entitled "Guru—the Teacher":

"Once in Finland I sat on the shores of Lake Ladoga with a farm lad. A middle-aged man passed us by and my small companion stood up and with great reverence took off his cap.

"I asked him afterwards, 'Who was this man,' and with special seriousness, the boy answered, 'He is a teacher.'

"I again asked, 'Is it your teacher?'

" 'No,' answered the boy, 'he is the teacher from the neighboring school.'

" 'Then you know him personally,' I persisted.

" 'No,' he answered, with astonishment.

" 'Then why did you greet him with such reverence?'

"Still more seriously, my little companion answered, 'Because he is a teacher.' "

Verily in this little boy, who bared his head before a teacher, is contained the healthy seed of the nation, which knows the past and knows the significance of the word "to build."

When I had to travel across the unforgettable Finnish lakes, visualizing the figures of the wise Vaina moinen, of Aino and Sampo, I saw the ruins of great castles and old temples and became acquainted with ancient customs, I felt so very clearly why Kalevala stands amongst the foremost and unforgettable human creations.

I am quite certain that also you, dear Miss Kettunen, who so heartily care for the welfare of the Finnish Society and you, the Society's President, Mr. Teslof, will bring into the Society's life those healthy creative and heroic elements in which glorious Finland is so rich. Best greetings and wishes.

Himalayas, 1930.

TREASURES OF THE MAYAS

To the South American Roerich Societies

WE may address each other by way of the mind, with all its conventional limitations and separations. But we may approach each other from heart to heart and in this way all superficial structures will be replaced by direct understanding. The entire sphere of constructive life, the realm of future happiness in the entire history of humanity has been built up not so much through intellectual discourses as through the eternal and infallible judgment of the heart.

Happily, all spheres of culture and of beauty are always connected with this language of the heart and only in this way, so many and such lengthy misunderstandings have been solved. While the sophisticated mind is not able to balance the negative and the positive, and like a cripple, is always stepping on the negative side, the heart, in an appreciative and constructive way, can reach and cross all abysses of ignorance and grievance. And it can replace these desolate crevices with the most joyful flowers. In the entire history of humanity, the best ambassadors of goodwill have been the saints, the philosophers and the messengers of beauty. We remember how successful in their humane missions were the great Spaniards, Saint Teresa and Saint Catherine of Sienna. And Apollonius of Tyana and even Peter Paul Rubens, because they used the unconquerable and trustful language of the heart.

The sites of ancient great cultures essentially have their own language. And by the means of this age-old, all-penetrating expression, they can more easily approach each other and visualize the mutual joy and future construction. With inexpressible joy, we regard the constructive, new work of South American countries. And we are happy to feel how the great economical problems are already crowned by the creation of art and knowledge.

In quite an individual and self-expressive way, following its original path, your beautiful country is boldly approaching the new era of the best culture. Without any suppressions, the beautiful wreath grows in its multicolored attainments. And the feeling of human cooperation adds beautiful new flowers to this achievement.

In our Museum, in its many institutions, dedicated to all the creative branches of the Beautiful, from far-off, we regard and value your achievements in the creative fields, sending you our most friendly thoughts of cooperation. We know that, in the same way, you feel in what close unity we strive towards the same constructive and appreciative destiny.

We have dedicated one of the rooms of our building to the artistic and creative expressions of your country. In our spiritual understanding, it is already filled with the best expressions of your highest activity and progress.

But in a physical way, it may be adorned and filled only in the closest cooperation with your best arts. Only the creators and builders of a country can themselves tell us and help us to present the greatness of the essence in the best and most exalting way. So, in full friendship, in deep understanding, help us not only to fill this room with the best and most precious expressions of your country, but also to expand this precious monument most worthily and in the broadest measure. You may be sure that all your suggestions will be accepted with friendly joy and we are sure that our enthusiasm will meet in your hearts the same uplifting feelings.

We feel that there is neither North nor South, nor East nor West, but a mutual feeling, based on the construction of the coming culture which is at hand, and in this way we are all equally united and may meet each other with true brotherly greeting, assured in our heart that such address and such feeling will be accepted in the same enthusiastic and exalted way. We will be happy to hear your response, as from one heart to another.

II

When we begin to think about something constructive, uplifting, and forward-looking, not accidentally to our minds come both the lofty towers of North America and the majestic outlines of South America.

Not occasionally, on the sites of the most ancient culture, are growing the seeds of new peaceful conquests and erection. Pan-America stands as a balance of Asia. It is most instructive to learn how, on the places of the most ancient achievements, are growing the new flowers of human attainments. Even from the cold-blooded scientific point of view, we are already accustomed to speak about currents, rays and emanations. These emanations of culture fertilize the soil, and who knows, perhaps they provide the real enthusiasm of this constructive spirit.

As yet I have never been in South America. But in spirit I feel this physically unseen friendship and mutual understanding. From where does it come? Well, some have asked me if the root of our family comes from Spain, because a branch of our family is in Barcelona. Perhaps, such pan-human feeling of advancing, searching and construction is deep in every human heart. Perhaps the sacred sense of adventure, in search of the great solutions, came into my being from the first years of consciousness, when as hunters, we traveled for days and days through the immense forests of Russia, certainly not with the idea of killing but with the comradeship with nature as our guiding star.

When we studied old structures of India, China and Tibet, our first comparison was with the remains of the Mayan culture. And in my previous article, "Joy of Art," I could not finish this conception with anything other than with some reference to the ancient Mayas. In this way, that which was most ancient and most beautiful came to my mind.

Just now I look upon a ring from Asia, with an inscription of the coming Age of Maitreya. And I cannot forget how one lady, who has studied the remains of Yucatan, recognized the same inscription there, with the meaning of the Union of Fire. Now comes the solution in this formula: Our spiritual, unseen friendship and devotion—does it not come from the all-pervading element of fiery space? In these all-pervading beneficial flames our hearts are enlightened and through them we recognize our sincere friends and co-workers.

Is it not the Union of Fire which now illumines the builders of Pan-America? And Asia when she speaks about the Blessed Shambhala, about Agni Yoga, about the Teaching of Flame, knows that the holy spirit of flame can unite the human hearts in a resplendent evolution.

In March, 1914, I exhibited a series of paintings in which was envisioned the coming war; now I have been happy to bring for the Americas the visions of Asia—the Agni Yoga, the Teaching of Flame, the same conception outlined by the wisdom of the old Yucatan wise-men, the Union of Fire.

Again some of the Great Truth comes to us and this Truth expresses the gathering of all the bearers of fire of the heart, to enlighten the world with peaceful and beautiful labor. The abstract conception of love can again be transmuted into benevolent action, because without constructive action love is dead. But in the New Era nothing is dead, everything lives, uplifted by enlightened labor and enthusiasm. When I hear beautiful songs of Spain and South America, they reveal for me the great East.

Where is East and West? After Asia you come to Greece and you feel the wisdom of the East; you reach Italy and the same wise romance stirs you; Corsica, Spain—in all these places is something still of the Great East. And the Banners of Ferdinand and Isabella are close to Moresque ornaments. You reach New Mexico and in the spaces of this beautiful country again sound for you the anthems of the East; and you know that in Mexico, in Yucatan, in all castles of South America, the same note of great romance, of great vision, of great wisdom, shall be everywhere.

I do not diminish either West, nor South, nor North, nor East—because in practice these divisions are non-existent. And the entire world is divided only in our consciousness. But when, with this consciousness, the fire of space penetrates, then is created the Union of Fire, and the Fire of Enthusiasm is unconquerable.

With this holy banner, we can reach most beautiful lands and we can awaken ancient cultures, for new achievements and for new splendors.

On one of the most ancient Druidic images of far-off Mongolia I have seen in the hands of a stony giant a flaming chalice. These leaders of the great migrations remembered also about the holy spirit of flame. And certainly this inextinguishable torch could bring them through all expanses of Asia, Europe and across all oceans. In the antiquities of Yucatan is inscribed the ancient commandment about fire. In the name of this unifying, great wise symbol, I greet you, my unseen friends of South America.

1930.

HIMALAYAS

To the Himalayan Roerich Society

D EAR Esther:
I thank you for your notification concerning the election of Mme. Roerich and myself as Protectors of the Himalayan Roerich Society founded by you.

In your letter I feel your most worthy strivings. You know that for me the Himalayas are the summit of the World, not only because of their lofty altitude, but because of their benevolent and highly significant traditions. From my books you know that the uplands of the Himalayas and Trans-Himalayas were the most important sites of the migrations of peoples, uniting thus the best styles of the West, emphasizing the importance of Scythia, recalling the Roman style and other unforgettable cultural treasures.

I am certain that you will imbue the life of the Society with the same all-embracing and all-containing beneficent understanding. Let your only enemy be the pitiable homunculus of ignorance. But all who are within the domain of knowledge and glorious creativeness must be friends of Culture. You gather together in the name of Culture. In the name of the great evolutionary foundation you strive to construct a peaceful and radiant future. Culture alone will solve the amassed difficulties of humanity and no one except homunculus will dare to say that it is superfluous or unworthy to consecrate oneself to the service of Culture.

It is long since we worked together, and you of course sense how real and undeferrable are construction and the defense of Culture. Each day's facts prove that this is in no wise exaggeration, but verily a necessity, a Beautiful Necessity. In the name of this Beautiful Necessity act as beneficently and self-sacrificingly as you all, our dear co-workers, have acted in all other constructive work.

Let us not forget that on the very Himalayas the legend of the Fire Blossom was conceived. All thoughts of curative herbs, of wondrous meteoric dust, of magnetic currents and of mighty energies for the welfare of humanity will carry us again to the same snowy giants. A world-depository of spirit. The striving to Bliss and Onward... Where can it be manifested as vitally as upon the heights untrod by human feet!

In the name of these heights, fortify the valor of spirit! Safeguard the treasures of human genius. Indefatigably erect strongholds where the human spirit can strengthen its achievements.

Hold firmly the Banner of Peace!

Greeting! Faith! Success!

1931.

THE STRAIGHT PATH

To the South African Roerich Association

IT is not long since the Colonies of South Africa were far from Art. The construction of life consumed all time and creativeness, and this perpetual friend of progress and florescence could not manifest itself imperatively. How long is it that we know anything at all about the native African Art, which has now taken so important a place not only in the ethnographical departments of museums, but also in the appraisals of Art connoisseurs? Recent decades have considerably precipitated all earthly paths. The abodes of the goddess Cultura have been considerably shifted and new hearths have been created, where creativeness is a welcome guest. Who can pass his life without this glorious guest? What creativeness is possible without the Towers of Beauty, Knowledge—without the treasures of that Bliss which we call Culture.

We have, long since, already understood that civilization, a white collar, golf and the telephone are not the sole pillars of Culture. Without creativeness, without means of evolution, there is no need for us to fly, for we will aspire only to the task of creating a speed record but not of enhancing the quality of the news carried. The signs of progress compel one to think of Culture; otherwise we shall again sink into the chaos of insoluble mechanical problems. The more precious is it, therefore, to note the enlightening initiative of Mr. Jacques Lagrange, inspired with the idea of the Arts of the South African settlers. All creative elements strive to mutual understanding. The language of creativeness is that pan-human tongue, understood by the heart. And what can be more light-bearing, more mutually appealing, than the language of the heart, in comparison with which all dialects of sound are meager and elementary. Only creativeness in all its multifold variety introduces a peaceful all-unifying stream into the entire constructiveness of life. And he, who despite all difficulties which encumber him, strives along the path of light, fulfills the vital task of evolution. We cannot remain inert. Either we move ahead or we retreat in chagrin. To go forward means to create with all means and possibilities, in deed and in thought and to introduce the creative light into all recesses of life.

Each worker of Culture can have but one enemy—verily the dark homunculus of ignorance. Even in antiquity, ignorance was considered, with full deserts, one of the most heinous crimes. Hence it is natural that every enlightened man aspires to live in a country of Culture. But for this every thinking man must indefatigably introduce cultural foundations into his social as well as his personal life. Wealth in itself does not yet predicate Culture. But expansion and refinement of thought and sense of Beauty give that subtlety and nobility of spirit which distinguish the cultured being. Verily he can build the glorious future of his country. He comprehends the sacred responsibility and realizes the Beautiful Necessity in untiring constructiveness. And those who carry the torches of Beauty, will understand the life of their near ones. Culture is in its essence the Service to Light. And Light in its multiple aspects is one.

I accept the election of the South-African Society as Honorary President and send my most sincere greetings and confidence in their successful work.

1931.

SAINT SERGIUS, THE BUILDER

Inauguration of the Chapel of Saint Sergius,
Erected by the Siberian Roerich Association

SAINT SERGIUS,—Builder of the Russian Culture of Spirit! Each mention of this sacred name is an imperative call to incessant spiritual labor, to self-denying construction, and makes Saint Sergius a saint for all ages and nations. I repeat "for all ages and nations," because the culture of the spirit is beyond all boundaries. Truly there is no religion nor teaching whose ministers would not bow before the image of Saint Sergius when they learn of his labors.

Origen ordained: "Behold with the eyes of the heart!" Was it not also the covenant of Saint Sergius himself who in the Flaming Chalice extolled Love and Compassion?

Saint Isaak Syrin says: "When we are at rest, the demons rejoice, but when we are at work, the angels exult." With such angelic works Saint Sergius laid the cornerstone of the Russian Culture of Spirit, bringing it to the treasury of universal worship.

I have had the honor of speaking of Saint Sergius before Buddhists, Moslems, Hebrews, Hindus, Fire-worshipers and venerators of the Great Spirit. And was there ever a denial or a contradiction? No, never—because the all-compassionate and omniscient spiritual culture lies within each human heart. And not through the sword, but at the spiritual repast is disclosed the effulgent cup of benediction.

Is it accidental that upon all destined paths are rising the sacred banners of the Blessed One? It is wondrous to see that even in our time of confusion and darkness, temples and chapels everywhere are being built in the name of Saint Sergius. In Paris, there is a monastery of Saint Sergius; in London there is a group of Saint Sergius students; in South America is the sacred name "San Sergio." Now, near New York, we have the pleasure of consecrating the Chapel of Saint Sergius and in New York, in the home of the Roerich Museum there is a chapel-room to Saint Sergius. In many places of Asia churches and chapels are being constructed in the name of the invincible Leader for good. Numberless books, articles and leaflets are dedicated to this Saint. Everywhere through the world his powerful name is bringing blessings.

When opportunity comes to meet people related in spirit, sooner or later, but unfailingly, you learn from them that, whether in heart or in mind, they carry the Sacred Name which unites and calls us to cross from yesterday into the resplendent tomorrow. Mark that Saint Sergius in his life-time did not waste himself in searching, but constantly striving, ascended and constructed. Beyond a God-seeker he had become a God-bearer. Buddhists called him Bodhisattva; Jews called him Israel; the Hindus, Mahatma.

The Holy Sergius quaffed from the Flaming Chalice. The Saint was served by the Flaming One. In this blessed glow; in this benevolent creative fire, the image of the Saint has come down to us. Flaming, also, were his visions of the Holy Virgin.

He who attains the flame of the heart is always bound with the image of the Saint. This great knowledge, the rarely-descending benevolence, unite forever the name of the Saint with the symbol of omniscience.

"The Saint knows," thus the people remember. "The Saint knows when to redeem." "The Saint knows when to appear." "The Saint knows when to succor." "The Saint knows which hearts are admitted to bliss." "The Saint knows where is unbelief and disloyalty." "The Saint knows where there is sincere offering."

In all contacts with the name of Saint Sergius, we approach the same understanding, the invincibility of his knowledge and the wisdom of his achievement. In this mutual agreement of understanding, of knowledge, of culture we will find salvation for the world. How otherwise can we replace destructive denial, lack of faith, light-mindedness, treason—willful and involuntary? Only in the realization of beautiful benevolence is cooperation possible. Mankind is fatigued with destruction and the conflicts that extinguish the flame of the heart. Wondrously, before us, appears the Great Name of the Leader with whom are inseparably associated the qualities of knowledge, construction, compassion and untiring fortitude. May the Saint help us to become fitting co-workers in his untiring and mighty labor, both visible and invisible, uttered and unuttered—unuttered by the limited human language. Fortunately besides the human language, humanity also has a language of the heart.

In this flaming language, in the fire of the heart, we will come together forgetting the darkness of yesterday, striving together towards the Great Light.

The Light is one, as the darkness is one, and with the bringing of the Light the darkness is dispelled. May the spirit help us to become united with the one Great Light!

1931.

CALL FOR CULTURE

To the Society of Friends of Culture

THE understanding of Culture, according to the meaning of the root itself, directs one's striving towards self-effacing study, perception and accumulation of all searchings which uplift and refine the consciousness. The most crude heart will hesitate to brush aside the noble beauty of culture created by dauntless achievements of spirit. One may differ as to the paths of civilization, one may debate about the signs of progress, but it is impossible not to sense the understanding of culture, the treasure-trove of the towering milestone of true evolution. Each one who lives and thinks also understands his responsibility before the construction of the resplendent future.

In the quiver of searching we reach the living synthesis in order to combine into one the various acquisitions and, after the hostility of ignorance, again to evaluate tolerance, and co-measurement, constructed by knowledge. In the daily unrest and confusion, does it not sometimes seem that among the picayune differences and gray accumulations, the Single Light which leads, condones and rejuvenates, has disappeared? But the hour which blows away the foam, defines the comb of the wave. In various ways one begins to gather the news of how in the most unexpected corners, useful achievements are being created. From afar, comes the call which vigorously resounds the resplendent word, "Culture."

Workers in all fields turn and smile towards this peaceful and responsible call. All forces which create and labor, chastening the voice of unbelief and condemnation, begin mutually to come together, knowing that the dignity of culture will be a shield against insult; knowing that the fire of spirit by which the heart lives, shall help in reaching the consciousness of those near ones and shall vindicate everything, self-sacrificing and constructive.

Destruction is incalculably exhausting. People have begun to gather under the sign of construction and culture. In New York, in March of this year, a Society of Friends of Culture was founded. Immediately, branches in various countries began to join this foundation.

Without special notice, precious information about a work unacclaimed, yet constructive and inspiring, began to pour in. How great and many-faceted an experience is being gathered, how much of irreplaceable labor is being applied contributing to universal understanding.

Varied are the details of the bylaws and regulations of the undivided branches of the Society, which apply to the fundamental aim and striving of each group. But this does not in the least sway the fundamental and all-uniting understanding.

"If we can meet in the name of the values of culture, is this not already a tremendous happiness, impossible not so long ago? Whether it be in extraordinary expressions, or in the convulsions of spirit, let the human heart beat in the name of culture, to which converge all creative discoveries. To think in the correct direction means verily to move on the path towards victory."

It was joyous for me to be able to answer the message of the founders of the Society of Culture of April 4th, as follows:

How joyous it is to unite the precious conception of a Friend with the conception of Culture! Amidst all often unconquerable complexities of modern life the meaning of Culture rises as an invisible power, as that great bridge over which we shall reach the Beautiful Shore.

In various parts of the world, in various conditions and in various strivings we find the very same glad, uniting conception of culture. If something should be forgotten it can be easily forgotten in the name of Culture. If something should be created it can be most easily created in the name of the very same conception of Light. This is not an abstract light, but the Light of Reality, as the Sun itself which warms the human heart, and out of the past directs us or turns us only to the Future.

Studying the foundations of Culture, we see that the dumb, confining "No" is only harmful; whereas the luminous "Yes," alert for achievement and creative labor, creates whole great epochs.

In the new discoveries of the present day, much is bestowed on humanity. People are flying, dissolving arbitrary boundaries. But with what message? People have sent their voices through limitless expanses. But what is thereby expressed? We have the right to perfect these beautiful discoveries, only in the name of Culture. We have the right to think and rejoice, only in the name of Culture. We have the right to create with ease, only in the name of the great future Culture. And there is no human heart so forbidding as not to soften before the concept of Culture.

I am glad to accept your election because every one must bring his drop into the chalice of the achievement of the resplendent future. Gather into cultural working organization in different countries and in different parts of the world in a strong active communion! Stretch over all oceans and over all mountains the valiant hand which knows the joy of labor and cooperation! Once again let us become strong in the realization that the limited "I" gives way to the powerful "We." And this "We"—in the name of enlightened achievement, in the name of the betterment, strengthening and adornment of life—must not fail before the enlightened labor. If the festival of labor lies not in inaction, then during the time of this future festival it will be permitted to ascend the mountain and from there to see the endless threads which are actively uniting humanity in the name of beautiful Culture.

Verily joyous is the consciousness that unity in the name of culture beyond abstractions garbs itself in labor and with its call recalls and inspires the constructive work.

How many are the spiritual unities! How many are the

scientific and artistic undertakings spread over all continents! How many are the working shops and engineering enterprises! How many are the "Sokols" and physical culture groups to be united and strengthened.

How many cooperative and financial undertakings will be conceived by the very same noble and creative call of culture.

How many are the new discoveries! How many are the victories over the chaos of the elements! What a vast unceasing creativeness flashes up there where the vigorous dignity of culture exists!

Long live that which is alive! The Society of Friends of Culture already lives and is being fortified by unexpected, distant friends. It shall live, and this Society shall broadly create bliss, because the hour has come. Greetings.

1930.

PEACE TO ALL BEINGS

To the Maha-Bodhi Society, Calcutta

IT is a great joy to send a welcome to the Maha-Bodhi
Society. With such delicacy and refinement this Society pursues its noble work. All addresses of their Founder
and leader Anagarika Dharmapala are imbued with the
devotion and compassion, which evoke in hearts the most
precious feelings. In touching the heart—that Realm of
Light—we touch the real treasure. A true disciple can be
realized as a result of wide understanding, containment
and compassion.

With the highest feelings I always remember my meetings with representatives of the Buddhist world. I keep
as a precious token the message sent to me by one of the
Leaders of Buddhism in Japan, Archbishop Noguchi. And
the Head Priest of the famous Temple of Kandy writes on
a palm leaf a touching address to the West, full of peaceful calls. Most valuable sound all the Greetings of High
Lamas from Mongolia, Tibet and Sikkim.

Verily, Peace to all beings!

On this great day, so many remarkable and beautiful
texts come to one's memory. With reverence we can imagine how many people pay their respects this day to the
great conception of Lord Buddha.

And after the thousands of volumes dedicated to this
uplifting cause we see once more how simple is the truth:
so simple that it may be inscribed upon the palm of a
hand. Love, labor, self-perfection, and incessant noble
action are the evoking call of the Great Lion.

The Pali Suttras contain many splendid definitions of
Lord Buddha, Who indicates the blessed Golden Path: He
is the Leader of the caravan, the Founder, the Teacher,

the Incomparable Trainer of men. He is the Lord of the Wheel of Benevolent Law. He is the Lion of the law. He is a wondrous doctor; the Venerable Gotama is a Plowman; his Field is Immortality.

"He is the Light of the world. He is the Liberator."

(So speaks the Bodhicharyavatara and Sutta Nipata.)

When an unworthy member deserted the teachings, He wisely said: "Now is the grain divided from the chaff" and incessantly He plowed the field of the human spirit.

In the name of glorious creative labor we send our reverence to this Great Day.

New York, 1930.

LATVIA REBORN

To the Latvian Roerich Society

WHEN I think of Latvia and Riga there appears before me a complete array of unforgettable glowing impressions. I remember that during our visit to the sacred sites of Riga, as we entered the splendid Cathedral of St. Peter, inspiring and majestic music poured from the organ. I was not fortunate enough to learn the name of the gifted organist, who, like Sebastian Bach poured out his divine inspiration, magnificently filling the historic arches with exalted and celestial harmonies.

Very often at this same hour did we attend the Cathedral to listen and become united in this prayer to the Holy Spirit. In our trips around Riga the most impelling impression which has remained with us is of this splendid, inspiring Cathedral. Precisely now, when religion again reaches out from an abstraction to that which is most immediate and most vital, it is especially valuable to recollect the never-fading memory of that Cathedral.

Under the same tokens of cordiality transpired the rest of our encounters in Latvia: with its Past, which is so filled with unusual monuments, beginning with the fine examples of the Stone and Bronze Ages. Several beautiful examples of Antiquity, of the first inhabitants of Latvia, at that time adorned my collection. My grandfather resided in Riga and many of my collaborators in different fields were from Latvia.

With pleasure in my remembrance rises the figure of Yan Rosenthal, of such sincere and vital dramatic gifts. I recall always with warmth William Purvitt, now justly occupying such an outstanding position in the art of Latvia. I am united with him in the memory of our mutual teacher, Kuindji, who possessed the genius of combining and gathering various individuals and nationalities in his hospitable studio, with the aim of serving art.

I also recollect my former pupil, now a prominent promoter of culture in Latvia, Albert Prande.

And now, in the midst of blooming trees and the snowy peaks of Himalaya, we constantly recall Latvia in the token of her language which is so related to the Sanskrit. The Name of God Itself is identical in the Sanskrit and in the Latvian language. How much meaning there is in this illuminating heritage of languages! How imperatively it obliges us to be attentive to these analogies, remembering the roots of languages which guide us from one to another.

After these recollections, you no doubt realize why it gives me such joy to write you all this—and to know that the Center of our Roerich Society has a branch also in Latvia. It is joyful that beneath this new tree are gathering different elements for whom the understanding of real culture is sacred. In the midst of narrow materialistic passions the light of the Spirit often is extinguished, deafening the great national understanding—Culture.

But Culture has two roots: the first one in Druidism and the other in the East. "Cult-Ur" means "Venerating the Light"—and in the name of this inextinguishable great Light, you are cooperating, mutually enlightening each other, carrying spiritual aid to young souls, who are looking for perfection in their daily labor. We will fear neither this work, nor the daily task. In them the Spirit is tempered and the great and unconquerable sense of Light is strengthened. And dedicating ourselves to the creative, indefatigable work, we also reach the wise covenant that in every obstacle is contained also a possibility; with this bright indication we will eliminate every vestige of fear which crushes inspiration.

Let us strive towards the Light, joyfully finding intercourse with the bright accumulations of knowledge and art—these foundations of Culture.

I am convinced that under the enlightening guidance of the President—Dr. F. Lukin, the Roerich Society in Latvia will grow and ever progress.

In spirit with you.

Himalayas, March 24, 1931.

TERRA SLAVONICA

To the Society of Slavonic Culture

"IN what country would you prefer to live?"
"Naturally, in the Country of Culture."
"To what would you dedicate your best thoughts?"
"To Culture."
"To what would you offer your enlightened work?"
"To Culture, of course."
"With what would you restore your consciousness?"
"With the victorious Light of Culture."
"Are you not agitators?"
"In constant labor, we have no time for agitations. We construct. In positive affirmation and realization we aspire to make earthly life more sensitive and more beautiful."

Thus would the Light-bearers of Culture answer the questions of outsiders, or those who are simply unknowing, those fundamentally ignorant, or those who are envious of Light. He who knows the sacred foundation of Culture, evaluates also the Great, the Only, Light. He is convinced of the Hierarchy of Benevolence beyond which there is no created path.

The one who serves Culture ceases to be a dreamer, but becomes incarnate with the greatest and brightest dreams in life. For what can be more resplendent and majestic than the service and realization of the enlightened elements under the shade of which are created great nations? It is necessary, by all means, to strengthen consciousness, that the thoughts of Culture be not abstract, but a constructive affirmation. The one who understands the positive beauty of Culture does not remain asleep, nor does he remain inactive and uncreative. No, he who has immediate perception, will bring his contribution to the harmonious, conscious labor.

The worker of Culture understands real collaboration, that vital cordial cooperation by which even the smallest deed grows. He who has broadened his consciousness by the understanding of Culture, would understand also his co-workers, not coercing them, but wisely transmuting the treasures of human experience. And fearless will be he who perceives Culture, because looking with sensitive and benevolent eyes, he would see that fear is inherent in darkness. Being beyond superstition and prejudice, the servant of Culture understands that the only happiness of thinking man is in ceaseless labor, in creation; for all of existence may be created in beauty. Knowing the value of Culture he would begin to prize the quality of thought and would wisely apply this greatest creative power. From the qualities of the Light-bearers of Culture are eradicated condemnation, slanderous gossip, and speaking about that of which one is ignorant!

What a terrible scourge of ignorance it is to talk of that which one does not know! And how many apparently civilized people err in that regard. The bearer of Culture feels deeply all the divergences between fundamental, spiritual culture and the aggregations of materialistic civilization.

Valuing the luminous cumulations of nations, the servant of Culture would distinguish between the accidental transition and real existence. Understanding this great responsibility of human existence, the Light-bearer of Culture brings to both his thoughts and actions a high quality. He intelligently analyzes the miraculous strength of nature, remembering that without exception, everything that exists may be beneficially utilized for our well-being. In the name of this well-being and Light, you discover in yourself a precious language of the heart—a vocabulary which is fuller and more beautiful than any dictionary. What bright convictions the language of the heart carries with it; and how effectively does its victorious testaments destroy even the darkest gates of lies and ignorance! Certainly we are convinced that lies are foolish and futile, for in the Spirit, a lie finds no refuge. Wisdom rests in reality which renounces neither spiritual nor physical existence. And in the State of Culture lies do not exist. It is impossible to remain static, you must either advance or retreat. The standards of true Culture do not know of retreat. The real bearers of Light do not know disappointment, because the magnet of Light is great.

The great nations—in whose name you are gathered here, and by whose symbols one may discover a creative heritage transmitted in the history of their great migrations—give us instructive examples. We meet here heroism, renunciation and unselfishness, the martyrdom for Light and the noble deeds for creation. These discoveries do not burden those who study them. On the contrary, they inspire them to similar, incessant effort. The great migrations of the nations are not accidental. There can be no accident in the constant phenomena of the world. By these characteristics, is tempered the living strength of nations. With the contact of new neighbors, consciousness widens and develops the forms of new races. Therefore, vital migration is one of the signs of wisdom.

In the steppes of Asia—in this cradle of all spiritual and creative migrations, in ancient times, migrations were considered the completion of education. Even now we meet with remains of traditions of these beginnings of education. In those far-distant lands, the gift of books or sacred objects is considered to be the highest sign of a noble spirit. The great voyagers carried along such remarkable covenants, and on their way created great styles of art and living. We remember the "Alan" heritage and the beautiful "Romanesque style." We also remember the characteristic monasteries both in the Slavic lands and on Asiatic frontiers. Without astonishment we recall that the sword-belts of the Himalayan mountains and their fibulae are found in the Caucasus as well as in Southern Russian steppes and scattered through Europe. On their fibulae, on the breast-plates, we find many images that have become the symbols of whole nations.

Let our breast-plates also bear the word Culture. The same universally evocative symbol. And let every Light-bearer of Culture be reminded of all the enlightened heritages and of the high responsibility for the quality of his creative work. We shall not think about luxury. Culture is found in Beauty and in Knowledge. Immense wealth is not necessary in order to exchange and mutually strengthen the language of the heart.

I believe in the indestructibility of our common creations. In the name of Light and of the Heart, in the name of Beauty and Knowledge, in the name of the vital, fundamental Evolution, I greet you from the snow-white heights of the Himalayas!

1931.

HOLIES OF THE HOME

Address to the Librarian's Convention

EVERY librarian is a friend of the artist and scientist. The librarian is the first messenger of Beauty and Knowledge. It is he who opens the gates and from the dead shelves extracts the hidden word to enlighten the searching mind. No catalogue may replace a librarian. A loving word and experienced hand may produce the miracle of enlightenment. We affirm that Beauty and Knowledge are the bases of the entire culture, and these are changing the complete annals of humanity. This is not a dream. We can prove it through all of history. The immutable facts tell us how from primitive ages all progress, all happiness, all enlightenment of humanity, was led by Beauty and Knowledge.

It is not strange to speak these words at a time when millions of books are printed, and every year a fountain of printed pages forms new snowy mountains. In this labyrinth of paper glaciers, veritable snow blindness can strike the inexperienced traveler. But the librarian, as a true honor-guard of knowledge, is vigilant. Only he knows how to steer the boat through the waves of this ocean of past and future.

The library exists not only to spread knowledge. Each library is an introduction to the bringing of knowledge into the home. Is it possible to imagine a home and a household without books? Again if you will take the most ancient images of the home and household, the finest examples revealed art objects and books. And you can see that these old books, in their beautiful bindings, were held as a true treasure. And not because the library did not exist. Librarians existed through ages and ages. But the human spirit feels that knowledge can be acquired, not only in public places, but also in the calm of the home. We even carry the most sacred books and images with us. They are our unchangeable friends and guides. We know perfectly well that it is not worth while to read a book once. As magic signs, the truth and beauty of the book are absorbed gradually. And we do not know either the day or the hour when we may need the gospel of knowledge. So, the library is the first step of enlightenment. But the true upliftment of knowledge comes in the hour of silence, in solitude, when we can concentrate all our intelligence towards the true meaning of scriptures.

Books are true friends of humanity and each human being is entitled to have these noble possessions. In the East, in the wise East, a book is the most precious gift. And he who gives the gift of a book is regarded as a noble man. During five years of travel in Asia we have seen innumerable libraries in each monastery; in every temple; in every ruined Chinese watch-tower. There was a library with collections of most remarkable books—a collection of famous biographies, dictionaries, history and sciences.

When you see a lonely traveler in the mountains you may be sure that in his knapsack is a book. You may deprive him of everything; he will resign it. But for his real treasure, the book, he will fight.

So, let us remember that books are real treasures and let us collect and cherish them as the noble crest of our home.

New York, 1930.

SACRE

Address at the Wanamaker Auditorium, Under the Auspices of the League of Composers

MANY years ago, I did a painting—the subject of which was woman making her first dress. In this painting were displayed ornaments whose design dated from the most ancient times. But the most amazing thing was to see that these ornaments were closely related to the designs which we see today.

You have no doubt also heard of the ancient Scythian art, now in vogue in Paris, which is considered the forerunner of Cubism.

In 1922, in Chicago, during the production of the "Snow Maiden," The Marshall Field Company tried to create some modern costumes, employing the styles and ornaments taken from old designs and historic figures. It was really remarkable and very significant to see how some of these models came directly from the most ancient sources of design. It was also astonishing to observe how these historic ornaments had been carried out in the most modern way.

In connection with the expression of the old in the new, I am reminded of the time when, in Tibet, I gave some photographs of skyscrapers to the people. They appreciated them most highly because they, in their own country, had had skyscrapers since the Sixteenth Century, in such buildings as the Potala which is seventeen stories in height. And not only were these skyscrapers of a height equal to ours but one should realize that in the character of their design they were in reality the forerunners of our modern skyscrapers. So again, we see that the most ancient and most modern thoughts are united.

In my Diary, I have found a page dedicated to the production of "Le Sacre du Printemps": "Eighteen years have elapsed since with Stravinsky, we sat in the colorful fairy-house, Talashkino in Smolensk, the estate of Princess Tenisheff, working on the scheme of 'Sacre du Printemps.' And Princess Tenisheff asked us to write on the beams of this multi-colored house some excerpts from 'Sacre' as a memento. Probably even now some fragments of Stravinsky's inscriptions remain there still. But who knows if the present inhabitants of this house realize what is written there upon the beams?

"It was a pleasant time when the Temple of the Holy Spirit and my painting, 'Human Forefathers,' were completed. The hills of Smolensk and the white birches and the yellow buttercups and white water-lilies, like ancient lotuses of India, reminded us of the Shepherd *Lel* and *Kupava* or *Krishna* and the *Gopis*. As in these eternal conceptions, was interwoven the wisdom of the East with the best images of the West.

"Then war came and I heard that one of my sketches on Stravinsky's estate as well as the sketches of 'Sacre' were destroyed. Many events have passed by, but the eternal remains."

During these years we have witnessed how in all Asia the eternal rhythm of "Sacre" resounds in the holy mountains and in the deserts where the songs are presented not for human beings but for the great desert itself. When a Mongol refused to repeat his beautiful song to us because "he sang only for the great desert," we remembered Stravinsky and how he embodied in the symphony of "Sacre" the eternal rhythm of human striving and the victory of the spirit. When, in Kashmir, we admired the majestic sight of the festival of Spring, with its gorgeous torch dances, I again recalled the powerful musical concepts of Stravinsky.

When in the mountain monasteries we heard gigantic trumpets and rejoiced before the sacred dances, full of rhythmic symbolic movement, again the names of Stravinsky, Stokowski and Prokofieff come to my mind.

In Sikkim, at the festivals of homage to great Kinchen-junga, we felt the same link with the eternal homage to greatness, which inspired the best poetical images of Siva, who consumed the poison of the world for the sake of Humanity, and of all the great redeemers and heroes, the creators of human ascension.

During this time, I had already heard that "Sacre" was acclaimed everywhere and there no longer exists any conventional prejudice against this expression. And I remember how during the first production in Paris, in 1913, the entire audience whistled and roared so that nothing could even be heard. Who knows, perhaps at this very moment they were enjoying themselves with the same emotions of primitive people. But this savage primitiveness had nothing in common with the refined primitiveness of our ancestors, for whom rhythm, the sacred symbol, and refinement of gesture were great and sacred concepts.

Well, perhaps it was necessary that thousands of years elapse in order that we might witness how humanity could become conventional and how much of prejudice can exist between the listener and the fact. At the same time, it is not so easy to approach the facts honestly. Again, our poor egoism, conceit and conventionality can hinder and shadow reality. But it is so uplifting to feel that in America, during the ten years of activity, I did not sense any cheap chauvinism or bigotry. Perhaps the new combination of nations preserves America from poisonous pettiness, and the heritages of the great culture of the Mayas and Aztecs gave their heroic background to the vast movements of this country. Verily, here in America you do not need to be negative. So many beautiful things are possible if we can keep our positive attitude and open-mindedness. We can feel how the primal energy is electrified in this country; and through this energy in the easiest way you can reach the inner constructive feeling of the nation. This constructive striving of spirit, this joy before the beautiful laws of nature and heroic sacrifice, certainly are the essential feelings of "Sacre du Printemps." We cannot consider

"Sacre" as Russian, nor even Slavic—it is more ancient and pan-human.

This is the natural festival of the soul. This is the joy of love and self-sacrifice, not under the knife of crude conventionality, but in exuberance of spirit, in connecting our earthly existence with a Supreme.

In the multi-colored house of the Tenisheff estate are inscribed fragments of the "Sacre." Princess Tenisheff, the self-sacrificing collector and worker in the art field has already passed away. Nijinsky is no longer with us and already Diaghileff rejoices in higher spheres.

And still "Sacre" is new and the young ones are accepting "Sacre" as a new conception, and perhaps the eternal novelty of the "Sacre" is because spring is eternal, and love is eternal, and sacrifice is eternal. Thus in this new conception, Stravinsky touches the eternal in music. He was modern because he evoked the future; it is the great serpent ring touching the great past.

And the wizard of the Symphony, Stokowski, with his sensitivity for truth and beauty, with his magic baton, like the eternal priest, again evokes to life the sacred tunes that connect the great past and future.

The torch festival in Kashmir is so beautiful! So majestic are the gigantic trumpets in the mountain monasteries! And from beyond Kinchenjunga itself, began the great migration with the *Eternal Sacre!*

We know that growth without refinement is undesirable. Wherever we see expansion without refinement, this growth will express itself in cruelty and rudeness.

Why did the giants perish? Because, no doubt, their growth and strength was unaccompanied by refinement and intelligence.

Another thing which is significant for America: When in 1921, in Arizona, I showed some photographs of the Mongols to some Indians, they said: "Oh, they are Indians! They are our brothers!" And, similarly, when in Mongolia, I showed the Mongols pictures of the American Indians in Santa Fe, they recognized them as their closest relatives. And they told me a beautiful Fairy Tale—how, at one time, there lived two brothers. How the earth on which they lived was split, and since that time these relatives have always been expecting news of one another, and they have always been confident that some time they will receive news of them. Thus from the most ancient times, people look to the future.

When you are in Asia, you see much around you which would here be considered as supernatural. In that country, however, everything is quite natural. We are concerned with the problems which are nearer to life. We dream of having a theater in life. In Asia they have it. During the sacred dances, many sacred designs are seen in Mongolia. Many ancient banners and sacred images are seen in the desert—thousands of people, huge orchestras, beautiful costumes, remarkable designs. Everything there is regarded as an expression of life. If you are admitted to participate in this life you can see no difference between nature and life of today; and this is a splendid realization.

In this way, when you see sacred dances you will remember what kind of beautiful legends are woven around the art and music of the East.

In answer to the question as to why they had such tremendously long trumpets with such powerful sound, a lama in Tibet answered that once upon a time a ruler of Tibet wanted to greet a great Teacher from India. The question arose as to how this Teacher should be greeted. He could not be approached with gold, silver and precious stones. The lama advised the ruler to construct special trumpets, in order to greet the Teacher with new, unprecedented sounds. Again here, the beautiful searching seems so similar to the searching of our days.

Remember the designs of the American Indians in the old pueblos. Before the people were divided into separate nations, they probably had only one language. So in trying to unify the national symbols in one, we can quite easily observe a historic symbol of pure design. In this are collected the perpetual symbols of nature. In the rainbow, the lightning, the clouds, we see the history of the striving of expression toward the beautiful—a striving which is the same everywhere, whether we find that expression in Russia, or in Mongolia or Arizona, it is all the expression of this great human design.

This should be very close to us all because today we are striving toward the next evolution. We are trying to discard old forms and to create something new. But in order to strive for something new we have first to know the old. Only then can we attain the true enhancement of life.

1930.

CREATIVE THOUGHT

Address to the Students of Mr. Howard Giles

WHEN I enter this class during its working hours and see Mr. Giles or Mr. Bisttram inspiring the students, I always rejoice in my innermost being. I know that the students receive fundamental counsel. They hear of basic laws which are at the bottom of the whole of Existence. I feel that creative thought is present. And where creative thought is manifested there can be no fear for the future. I do not mean the tenor, the depicting story, or the dry subject. I visualize the magnificent creative synthesis. Our evolution is inevitably approaching the blessed synthesis. I have precisely in mind unlimited creative thought which impels human wings to spread in beautiful forms and colors. This creative thought adorned by essential laws, beautiful in their constructiveness, uplifts humanity towards its approaching evolution, and from the smallest hearth up to the state and continents, establishes the same sense of the Beautiful, which holds essential kinship with all ages and peoples.

From this sense of the Beautiful is born nobility of spirit, constant creativeness, heroism and attainment. From the same source also springs forth optimism, because every negation is non-creative.

All humanity is divided into "yes" and "no," and we will always be with those who have "yes" in their nature. Beware of the "I" and the "no."

Verily, every one prepares a true certificate for himself. In hidden thoughts he shapes his future actions. A liar is afraid to be betrayed. A traitor in heart is especially afraid of treason. He who is unfaithful in heart shudders with suspicion. An heroic heart knows no fear in life. Verily, thought rules the world. It is a beautiful realization to know that we are, before all, responsible for our thoughts.

Often we repeat the word "thought." We repeat it during our dinners and suppers. We reiterate it in time of suspicion and anathema. We mechanically mumble this word even when we are without defined thought. If we could but realize that in repeating this sacred word we are pronouncing the formula of the greatest power! But how seldom do we realize the dynamic power of thought; how seldom do we control it and direct it in the proper channels! Small and hideous thoughts often fly around our aura like venomous insects. If we could take photographs (and these have been taken) of our auras, we could see that they are filled with small black and grayish insect-like spots. These spots are spots of ignorance—and its breed, darkness.

If we could but realize the unconquerable power of one sharpened benevolent thought and would begin to study the conditions which would help to strengthen such thought, we could gradually eradicate the physical spots of darkness. In one photograph which was taken unexpectedly, two rays of light were seen extending from the shoulders; then an occurrence at this identical moment was verified. It was found that at this moment a beautiful and unselfish thought was generated. Because it was unselfish and creative, it was manifested at once as beautiful rays of light. Who knows but that perhaps before long during elections we will have such photographs of the candidates for our public office, so that we will have real certificates, rather than written ones. Then we shall have facts and only facts.

If we know that there exists only one light, we must follow that light. We would not be discouraged in life because there is only one true ascent and only one descent. Nothing is static. Take the aspect of this ascent. According to the law each ascent is connected with a creative state of mind. History proves that not a single man who had a creative mind was forgotten. Nor do I speak about any definite field such as art, expressed on canvas or in stone or in any other material; but I speak of the sense of the beautiful—that is, the expression of beauty, in the whole of life. Sometimes this expression is transferred to canvas or other materials, but very often it is expressed in thought. Thus we beautify space, we link the planets, for in thought there is no space, nor time. It is said that when a man is highly imbued with a certain thought his weight is altered. It can be proved that in a moment of strong creative thoughts one becomes lighter. We hear that Saint Jean de la Croix and Saint Teresa were at times levitated. This is not an unexplainable miracle. Perhaps you have also witnessed scientific experiments during which in intense thought we lose weight and are even levitated. This is a physical law, a creative law. Thus again cognizant that in touching these constructive laws, you come close to the eternal laws. You express the highest form of thought, and cooperate with the supreme consciousness. Is it not wonderful to bear in your creative mind this beautiful thought that you are in cooperation with the Beautiful, with the Supreme? Therein is your strength, because during this moment of direct cooperation with the Supreme, you create something for the next evolution—for the next life. The aspiration to that life constitutes the eternal goal; it is a beautiful law! No one can limit you as to what way your art can be applied. You cannot create anything without inner sense, form or purpose. Everything has a purpose. But remember that this purpose should be beautiful. Often we hear complaints about insoluble problems in the lives of families, households and states. If you fill your life and that of your closest relatives and friends with the precious sense of the beautiful so that everything ugly gradually fades away, you constantly live in the enthusiasm of the Beautiful. This is for all, not alone for the chosen! We can say that even prisons should be beautified—then we shall have no more prisons! Certainly we do not mean material prisons alone, but the prisons of the spirit. Thus we can dream about a united constructive life.

When we speak about applied arts often the hideous word "commercial art" is used. This is a hideous expression and should be eliminated. What is art? We can have something beautiful and something ugly. A beautiful household object of Benvenuto Cellini, is a work of great art. In art we must use only one principle—the Beautiful! We must remember how to apply art in everyday life. Even floors may be washed beautifully, for there is no true art that is small. In constantly repeating *"the beautiful, the beautiful, the beautiful,"* you begin to be constructive. The ugly negation is the symbol of ignorance, and this ignorance should be eliminated. We should not be afraid to have before us this constant and great thought.

The beginner is often perplexed about how to be creative. He presumes that he must first study the law, then study the colors and create only in the future. But, one must create from the very beginning. Children must be taught to create. The student must state the eternal law of construction for the eternal thought. The laws must saturate the mind and not merely the hand. The study of the basic laws is as an aid in self-expression because we are confident that you are born artists.

Very often we are unprepared to pay attention to every detail of life. Place before yourself a simple object—look at it, close your eyes and imagine it. Tell me sincerely how clear and sharp is the impression? Usually we do not remember the definite color or the definite line, but it is advisable to practice this experiment each day. When you have a few minutes, place before you some article, something simple and colorful, and try to imagine this object and to fix this impression in the third eye. You will see that there is nothing supernatural in it and you will finally notice that it is clear and sharp and has become simple for you. Everybody has heard of Count Saint-Germain who warned France, before the French Revolution. Read his biography. It is told us as an historical fact that he could conduct three conversations and write two different letters, one with each hand. This was not supernatural, but only proof that his consciousness was very refined, very highly developed. In the case of a pianist two hands are used, and each carries a different theme, and besides the pianist is able to conduct a conversation at the same time. Thus if one learns to fix one's consciousness on certain things, one is able to produce so-called "miracles." But, some say this is impossible. Tell them about the "miracle" of the pianist conducting a conversation, perhaps two, while he plays. Here we have the approach to a "miracle" and we must realize how many things purported to be phenomena, or something "supernatural" are in reality very close to life, and they can and should be manifested. When we learn to direct our consciousness, we can fix our mind on something quite definite. We are preparing for the approaching evolution and it is our duty to ponder upon this evolution and the life of the next generation. You are responsible for the next generation and you cannot avoid the responsibility. We can derive great happiness from a beautiful thought.

When next we meet, I want you to tell me of some unusual happening in your life. Let each one view his own life and I am certain that, with sincere and honest attentiveness, each one can find something unusual in it. Recently, addressing a group of young people, I asked them to relate something unusual in their lives; they insisted there was nothing unusual, and spoke of their lives as of a sad routine. They told me that I was going to the mountains where beautiful things occurred, but that there was nothing unusual to be found in the turmoil of the city. I insisted that they think a while and that something would surely come to their minds. Soon one mentioned that, at the moment of her aunt's death, they had heard a strange bell ringing, and had seen something like a cloud passing over their heads. Within half an hour many others remembered wonderful facts and every one was uplifted; and within the next three weeks each member of the group had told me of some beautiful and interesting and amazing facts in their own lives. Hence we have only to collect all the beautiful facts and to relate them directly and honestly. Everybody intends to be honest, but it is seldom that the facts are given impersonally even in the case of some scientists, who have to deal with facts. Many of them do not take the facts without prejudice, without superstition. If some one begins to see wonderful lights, sparks, he is told to wear glasses; in this mechanical way the light of truth is eliminated. But we have to be ready for everything in a direct manner.

Often people complain that their near ones are spoiling their lives. If their consciousness is growing, they will realize that their relatives and friends are human beings and that they should try to open their hearts. Sometimes this is easy, sometimes difficult. But if your key does not work, be assured it is not beautiful. But every human being has a heart; and the heart remains a heart. Thus, if we are not able to open this heart, probably our keys do not fit this sacred casket; and certainly such a key is not beautiful enough. We often hear that in some homes art cannot be introduced. That their owners think art is unnecessary. In such cases, how can it be shown to them that the Beautiful has value? During revolutions, when property and money were destroyed, objects of art were preserved and during some periods a country was able to exist on the income from its art objects. Keep this fact in mind, and some time you may be able to prove by it how much the value of these objects increases in times of war and revolution. Ask someone to give you the exact value of a share—it is impossible. So much depends upon the demand. So, often an object which seems to have little value, proves to be of great worth, and is practically priceless. Often bankers and business men have been wiped out during a revolution, while artists and art collectors have survived. Thus creative production survives, scientific inventions survive and thought survives! So let us learn to direct all our thoughts in the direction of the Beautiful.

I hope next year to find you here again, a step more advanced in creative power. I shall feel in your work the manifestations of your consciousness. I am certain that you are constantly growing and creating.

In all Fairy Tales we read of bolted doors with hidden treasures, which open only to a magic key. Within ourselves the poison of anger and irritation collects in harmful strata and in order to overcome its power we must eradicate it as something destructive and impractical. In the same way cancers form, holding and gathering poisons which destroy us if they are not eliminated. There have been cases of cancer cured by psychic power. Learn to eradicate all poisonous thoughts—see the sparks and lights and study these lights. Then you will create something for the future of humanity.

Help to grow the wings of humanity.

1930.

SEVEN SAINTS

Preface to the Book "Flambeaux"

IT is truly beautiful, if amidst the turmoil of life, in the waves of unsolved social problems, we still may hold up before us the glowing Flambeaux of all ages. It is truly beautiful, to study the lives of these great seekers and attainers, as charts for valor, inexhaustible energy and tolerance. It is beautiful, through the depthless well of love and tolerance to understand the great movements of refined souls which connected the highest knowledge with the highest aspirations. Thus, in studying biographies, we are becoming real cooperators with the supreme evolution and in the brilliant rays of supreme light, may emerge true knowledge. This refined knowledge is based on real comprehension and tolerance. From this source comes the great understanding. And from the great understanding rises the Supremely Beautiful, the enlightening and refining enthusiasm of life.

Contemporary life is changing rapidly; the signs of the new evolution are knocking at all doors. Magnificent energics, powerful rays, countless discoveries abolishing con ventional boundaries and conceptions are poured through the brains of the great scientists. Antiquity is disclosing to us the secrets of its hoary past and the future is extending the mighty hand of ascent. In this true, unconventional science, we feel the splendid responsibility before the coming generations. We gradually comprehend the harm of everything negative. We begin to value enlightened positiveness and constructiveness, and in this measure, in merciful tolerance, we can prepare for our next generation a vital happiness, turning vague abstractions into beneficent realities.

In this glorious Seven we have great educators, great messengers, great peace-makers, great builders, great arbiters, and they evoked the same earthly path. They worked endlessly. They were here, they were confronted with the same obstacles, the same ignorance, superstition and intolerance. And through their knowledge they conquered this darkness. They knew the Eternal Law that only in giving we receive. In this knowledge, in this constructive work, they became real lights. And when we use the title *Flambeaux*, it is not an abstraction, because nothing is abstract. It is a real expression of beautiful, wise attainment.

1931.

HAIL—ARTISTS!

Preface to the Book, "American Artists"

A RENAISSANCE of art is the evidence of the renaissance of a nation. In a declining country, art becomes only an abstract luxury. But when a country is in its full prowess, art becomes the real motive power of its people. Let us imagine the history of humanity without the treasures of beauty. We will then readily realize that the epochs are left meaningless, denuded of their soul. Without a manifestation of the spirit of the Beautiful, we shall remain amid the ugliness of death. And when we proclaim that beauty, art, is life, we speak about the coming evolution of beauty. Everything accomplished for art is an attainment for evolution. Every co-worker in this field is already a hero.

Is it not our superb duty to reveal these true heroes of the nation to America? The coming generation should know precisely to whom it is indebted for its upliftment, and why it has been privileged to have for its uses all attainments and discoveries.

The life of an artist is not an easy one. But because of this very eternal struggle this life is always beautiful. Thirty years ago it was my privilege to introduce American art to Russia. Then, long before I had adopted this country as my own, I already felt the virility and essential strength of its growing self-expression. And now, observing the fruitful development of American art, so multicolored, so manifold, I see how true was my first impression.

From the pure-hearted colonial expression, through such great masters as Sargent, Whistler, Ryder, Thayer, Homer, Bellows, Henri, Hawthorne, Chanler, to the present brilliant host of creative builders of the coming era of

America, I feel how fundamental and dynamic has been the unfoldment of American art life.

Admiring the work of living American artists, we see such an astounding variety of potentialities. Let us remember such outstanding names as Leon Kroll, Rockwell Kent, Eugene Speicher, Gari Melchers, Eugene Higgins, Leon Dabo, John E. Costigan, Howard Giles, Alfeo Faggi, Robert Edmond Jones, Gaston Lachaise, Cecilia Beaux, Abram Poole, Paul Manship, Malvina Hoffman, Hunt Diederich, Norman Bel Geddes, Frederick Frieseke, Maurice Stern, August Vincent Tack, Emil Bisttram, Gutzon Borglum, Robert Laurent, William Auerbach Levy, Lee Simonson, Jacob Epstein, Edward Redfield, Raymond Jonson. What an endless roll of varied and virile talents! I do not name them alphabetically but even sometimes place near each other complete opposites. It is impossible to mention the whole roll of names which constitute the history of arts of a growing country. And many there are, still young, but who have already conquered an honored place. The list of names alone would make a vast chapter of an encyclopedia. Beginning a sequel of appreciative volumes dedicated to the pride of a nation, we know that this sequel will be voluminous and these future dimensions can verily bring joy, for these are true testimonies of the flourishing of Culture.

It is great praise to this country that the roll of its creative workers cannot be expressed in one volume, but merits an entire great series, even with the briefest appreciations. As a beginning of this series of heroic builders of the future—the artists—we are happy to feel what a vast material is still before us and what a joy it is to show to the young generations the brilliant legion which has constructed the most beautiful achievements. Wherever art and knowledge flourish we may be enthusiasts. And in this joyful enthusiasm we may greet the true creative forces of our nation. A biography is not only a monument to the creator and the worker, but it is the best evocation for the youth to come. I am happy to greet the brilliant artists, to hail the essence of beautiful creative thought and to salute the young generation to which this creative thought shall bring its coming happiness.

1930.

LOVE UNCONQUERABLE

*To the Saint Francis of Assisi Association of
Roerich Society*

PERUGINO, Giotto, Zurbaran, Costa, Murillo, Ribera, Schiavone, Filippo Lippi, Hans Fries, Margaritone, Sassetta, Taddeo Gaddi, Vivarini, Moretto da Brescia, Cimabue ... Who could have gathered and united spiritually these manifold and even opposite artists? Who could have inspired such a multitude of great poets? Who could have imbued with such exalted thoughts such a legion of illustrious authors? During whose prayer did the monastery become aglow as a resplendent dome? Who was levitated in ecstasy of spirit? Who has strewn the treasures of benevolence as the natural sparks of his earthly existence?

He—the very one, immortal and radiant, in the very essence of spirit. Saint Francis, who attracted adults as well as children. The safe haven for animals, as well as for birds. Only he could converse with and convert the wolf. And upon his hand the birds found safest refuge.

Let us see wherein lies the power of this world-wide magnet of Saint Francis. Certainly in his highest ecstasy he approached the Supreme. In an unusual power of consciousness he merged with the Lord. He knew of the high quality of the prayer of heart, which alone can teach vital Love. For him Love was not an abstraction but the daily nurture of his spirit. And one more remarkable quality makes the image of Saint Francis sacred to us: He never condemned.

Even if some of his actions were interpreted by his followers as protests against the imperfect customs of his contemporaries, yet these actions were so gentle and so saturated with benevolent symbols, that the protest ascended on the same wings of all-conquering Love.

If each of us cannot with equal success follow him in the power of ecstasy, then each one must imitate at least two qualities of Saint Francis: incessant activity and non-condemnation.

In His victorious non-condemnation, Saint Francis gave the summons to the greatest wisdom of life, which is easily achieved. Every worker, after sufficient experience, begins inevitably to realize how deadening are denial and condemnation and how creative and constructive is every understanding. To love means to forgive; to forgive means to understand; to understand means to know; to know means to approach the threshold of wisdom.

Every worker, sooner or later, feels that condemnation and negation are but the signs of non-success. Every real creator, imitating the Lord in his inner essence does not even have the spare time for condemnation in his constantly growing creativeness. Glance at a condemner and you will at once be convinced that he is not a creator. Through experience you will likewise be easily convinced that the garden of negation is a gloomy and a meager one.

How, then, will you face and conquer the difficulties of life? In sad experience you will soon learn that the shield of negation and condemnation is an unworthy one. Furthermore, you will be convinced that such shield is harmful. As a magnet of darkness, it will attract everything negative to you. What a sad old-age and future you will prepare for yourselves, spitting the bile of condemnation, unsuccessfully crossing the steps of life and criminally distorting the sacred understanding of Love!

Hence, following the covenants of Saint Francis, filled with Love, create, create ... and create!

In this constant creation you shall attain the wisdom of Joy. You will find the day too short to express that to which your spirit prompts you. In the name of broad understanding you will begin to approach the realization of synthesis. The conquest of Beauty and Knowledge will be consummated for you not as dry details, but as sacred signs of the synthesis of evolution. In your creation you will always realize the highest responsibility before the great infinite. This responsibility will be the healing corrective in the transformation of your entire life. This realization of responsibility will help you once more to abstain from condemnation. Verily, you shall find no time for condemnation and negation.

To create, to help and to give—this will saturate all your being and, in spite of all difficulties of darkness and ignorance, will transform your life into constant joy. This creative joy will bring you the daily bread for the morrow.

It was a great joy to me, when you so enthusiastically accepted my plan for the inauguration of the Saint Francis Society. It is impossible to learn of such a Society without a smile of joy. We search for the highest Culture, Beauty, Science, Peace. Will not the smile of Saint Francis be the mighty Shield in these noble strivings?

When I paint the Image of Saint Francis I shall choose the moment when the birds gathered around him. This is prompted by an old reminiscence. I was happy to have as my first Teacher an extraordinary man: the eminent Master Kuindji was not only a remarkable artist, but also a great Teacher of life. His personal life was a secluded one and only his closest disciples knew the depth of his soul. At noon he climbed out on the roof of his house and after the daily noon signal of the cannon shot, thousands of birds gathered around him and he fed them from his hands—doves, sparrows, swallows and flocks of other city birds crowded around him, covering his shoulders, hands and head. He used to say to me: "Come closer, I will tell them they should not fear you." We called Kuindji "Saint Francis," and the vision of this powerful gray-haired and smiling figure, covered by the birds in joyous twittering, shall forever remain one of my most cherished memories. I myself witnessed how crows and other birds of prey sat there without harming their small brothers.

One of Kuindji's usual delights was to help the poor

without their knowing whence the bliss came. His career was an extraordinary one. A simple shepherd boy in the Crimea, he became one of the most illustrious painters, due to his talent and work. And the same smile, which nurtured the birds, made him the possessor of three houses. Needless to say, he willed his entire fortune to the nation for artistic aims and purposes. This "Saint Francis" of my youth is inseparably linked with the Image of Saint Francis whom I later admired during my pilgrimages to the sanctuaries of Italy.

The sacred permeation of Assisi is sensed even by casual visitors. How much deeper is it felt by one who is on the quest! You, who have united in the name of Saint Francis, let his smile abide with you! Let his ineffable spiritual refinement strengthen you! In the inspiration of Saint Francis you will find an ever new and inexhaustible creativeness. You will remember that even a genius must perform his daily labor untiringly. In the name of Saint Francis, you will find that radiant affirmation, which will protect you from deadly negation and destructive condemnation. In the name of Saint Francis you will find inexhaustible strength against all evils. You will understand the meaning of blessed cooperation and union. Create, create ... and create!

Glory to Saint Francis!

1931.

VITAL WISDOM

To the Spinoza Center of Roerich Society

THE remembrance of the Spinoza Center of the Roerich Museum will forever remain one of the most precious impressions for me. In our times of unrest and commotion, in these days of the crumbling of mechanical civilization, each sign of spiritual upliftment is especially valuable.

I always remember with what eagerness and perseverance Dr. Frederick Kettner came to me and what ardor I felt in his approach in the name of the great philosopher, Spinoza. No less precious was it for me to see the group of striving young workers united in the great ideas of Spinoza and the ardent spirit of Dr. Kettner. I do not exaggerate, but wish to express that which I witnessed.

It is impossible that one should not be aroused to great spiritual joy at the sight of youth, working without great means, striving and self-supporting, religiously gathering around a great name and using all its leisure time for the study of a high philosophy. And they do not study for abstract purposes. Nay, they transform their lives through it, and within their hearts high ideals begin to live. These self-sacrificing torches illumine the surrounding darkness and form one more stronghold against ignorance. And we know how militant is ignorance and how contagious is darkness.

The leader of the group, Dr. Kettner, is a true teacher, for he not only guides the meetings and gives the lectures, but he is consulted in vital matters of life. He arms the young warriors with the most unfailing armor. He tells them how practical is the Good and how shameful and self-destructive is evil. And the Good is there, where are creation, constructiveness and spiritualization. The Good is there where are containment, devotion and love. The highest is in the light of sacrifice and the basest is in the darkness of treason.

The conceptions of evolution and attainment, abstract for the average brain, become the vital cornerstones of everyday life. Such foundations are affirmed there, where life is so difficult; there where the struggle often withers away the best forces.

Is it not remarkable to see that a numerous group of youth has chosen as its weapon so high a philosophy? They have evoked and surrounded themselves with the name of a sage, who so fearlessly and self-sacrificingly brought into life the regenerated conception of Be-ness. Under his perspicacious understanding, matter occupied its befitting place and was uplifted. To uplift is a noble action. In uplifting we unavoidably uplift ourselves, because in creating the energy upward—everything from beginning to end, moves in this direction. With this noble upliftment comes also the quality of tolerance, so much needed. If we introduce tolerance only conventionally and superficially, nothing but hypocrisy can be created. Only through noble upliftment of the spirit, through incessantly realized labor comes this wonderful guest—tolerance. Precisely this quality when introduced naturally, creates the smile of Wisdom. I am speaking of that smile of Wisdom with which the Sage listens to the seeker. In his caressing eyes and the silent nod is expressed: "Try, my son! Never mind if thou walkest now by the side road. Only walk without looking back, not fearing the stones, nor the thorns. Remember, if the steep slope would be too smooth, the ascent would be still more difficult for thee. The stones not only do not hinder thee, but support thee. Do not forget it and bless these stones, for they may be used as steps.

I recollect how once in the East a learned Rabbi said: "You also are Israel, for each one in the quest of light is Israel." Thus was expressed the Wisdom of the immemorial ages. In it resounds upliftment as well as tolerance.

When you, the participants of our Spinoza Center, gather for a meeting, you garb yourselves in the festive cloth, because as I know, this meeting is a festival for you. Such an attitude is already a pledge for this upliftment, and the consequence is tolerance and containment. You know how the great Spinoza suffered in his life only because he selflessly expressed true knowledge. But we know that martyrdom is but the tension of energies. In this tension you receive the right to knock at all gates where useful construction can be strengthened. I repeat, you have transferred the philosophy from abstraction into life. In this you follow the beginnings of true evolution, for all Teachings and all philosophies are given for life. After all there is no high Teaching which is not also practical in the highest sense of the word. We can solve numberless problems of the contemporary disturbances only by the beautiful and highest consciousness. Only the Bridge of Beauty will be strong enough for crossing from the bank of darkness to the side of light. You know what great significance is allotted in the sacred Teachings to the symbol of the bridge. Upon this bridge will come the Highest in glory!

I know that the Spinoza Center will grow, because it began upon sane principles, vital in tangible reality. Not mist, but light lies at the foundation of evolution. If we are capable of understanding that light is color and sound, we shall also realize that everything beautiful is also needed for the construction of the Temple of evolution. The Djinns helped King Solomon build the Temple. Invoking the Light and the Beautiful, we shall force even the Djinns to help in the great construction. In the name of great knowledge and beautiful achievement, I welcome you!

1931.

ADAMANTIUS

To the Origen Roerich Association

ADAMANTIUS. This remarkable by-name character-izes best of all the great name under whose protection you have assembled. Very often by-names are given only after death, but sometimes a definite quality is so vividly pronounced that even during his life, a man is linked with a definite symbol. Adamant, the hardest diamond, unbreakable, even cutting that which is itself hard. Origen, Adamantius! Does not this express the Teacher's entire devotion to Truth? A devotion which could not be shaken by privations, nor by temptations nor by customs? Origen is considered officially the Teacher of the Church; but he could also be officially recognized as a Saint, as a Father of the Church, and could have enjoyed the highest ecclesiastic distinctions and privileges during his life.

Instead of being an Archbishop, Origen is found with prisoners or perhaps in the home for criminals. The Church incriminates him with:

"Origen, the wonder of his age by reason of his prodigious mind and the profundity of his erudition, was accused by two Alexandrian Councils, and, after his death, in the Council of Constantinople. Origen did not think correctly about many truths of the Christian Church. Expounding the non-gentile teachings of the preexistence of the soul, he did not reflect properly upon Christ, believing that a certain number of spiritual beings of equal worth were created, of whom one strove with such flaming love that he became united with the highest Word and became its bearer upon earth. Holding to the belief in the incarnation of the God-Word and the creation of the world, Origen did not rightly comprehend the death of Christ by crucifixion, representing it as something which had its spiritual counterpart in a spiritual world. He attributed too much to the acts of natural forces, with which our nature is gifted. ..."

From the viewpoint of contemporary understanding it is even incomprehensible to us, how incriminations could have been made which resulted in imprisonment. For in the image of Origen is expressed so ardently the quest for Truth, which not only did not belittle, but on the contrary, opened limitless vistas for the sacred union with the Supreme.

The numerous works written by Origen—of which not all have reached us, and of these, not all have been translated and published—show his astounding erudition and luminous ever-striving intelligence. But the enemies of Origen, in order to seal forever his importance, had recourse to the measure customary to them—persecution.

Forgetting the still-recent Golgotha, they decided in the name of the Great Martyr of Golgotha, to make a martyr also of Origen, overlooking the fact that the crown of thorns is the highest guaranty of glory. Let us remember the history of various martyrdoms. In their variety, this sorrowful history will manifest to us one and the same law—the consequence of self-sacrifice. If it is possible to connect anything else with the conception of true glory, it will necessarily be linked with self-sacrifice in the quality of Adamant.

When speaking of martyrdom, one recalls the pictures of remarkable artists who depicted the outrages inflicted upon the great Martyrs. Turn to the paintings of Hieronimus Bosch, Peter Breughel, Durer, Orcagna and other equally great creators, and study the types of persecutors depicted by them. Does it not seem to you that in these realistic living types you will find faces familiar to you even now? Verily, dark and negative types still live. But just they, amidst other causes, prompt us to turn with especial intensity to those symbols from which emanates the great Light. You have turned to that source which is inseparably linked with the strong conception of Adamantius. Let this quality become your own distinction.

Around this quality you will find ceaseless creative labor. You will find all-contentment, the non-belittling and the unquenchable striving to light.

The study of the works of Origen will be for you the impulse for the study of the Principles—"De Principii." The luminous and high logic of the author shall bring to you across the ages the very same perseverance, freedom, valiance, perspicacity. Briefly you will be armed for your best work and creations.

Without these qualities it will be difficult for you to realize that creativeness is, above all, our way of imitating the Supreme.

We remember how we began the Master Institute of United Arts ten years ago in the house of the Greek Orthodox Cathedral. The Honorable Reverend Father Lazaris was the first to welcome our Educational beginning, in which we set forth our belief that only Beauty and Knowledge can unite and lead humanity to real prosperity and happiness. Father Lazaris understood so well that Beauty and Wisdom are the pillars of Religion. For if we sincerely write the history of the Beautiful, we must write along with it the history of Religion. And conversely, beginning with Religion, we must inevitably reach the Beautiful.

Beautiful thoughts! These creators of the future have embodied that which is most precious to us: the Image of Origen. His was the foresight to perceive a vision of the Almighty's creativeness. Among the reverenced icons there is an Image of deepest significance: "Sophia, the Almighty's Wisdom." At the hours of your highest exaltation, this Wisdom will whisper to you: "Create, do not be idle. Know how to give; only in giving do we receive." Upon a fiery steed with flaming wings, soaring through space, is represented—"Sophia, the Almighty's Wisdom."

Origen ordained: "With the eyes of the heart shalt thou see." In the name of this all-reaching language of the heart, in the name of the all-penetrating eyes of the spirit, I welcome you who gather around the immortal name of Origen!

1931.

GLORY OF SAMURAI

To the Japanese Bearers of Culture

KOMIO, the beautiful Queen of Nara, sang: "I shall not pluck thee, oh flower! but shall dedicate thee to the Buddhas of the past, present and future."

In this invocation of the past and the future is contained the entire power of the Japanese genius. Why does one's memory so ineffaceably retain the pictures of old Japanese Masters? Why do we remember the gestures and the unrepeatable mimicry of the Japanese actors? And why does the spirit of the Japanese Samurai remain in the history of humanity as an image of heroism, of true patriotism and courage? It was necessary to imbue these concepts with such persuasion that friends as well as enemies, near and distant ones, would have no doubt in applying these epithets.

Beyond the obvious limits is constructed a special language. An unutterable feeling-knowledge is created there where we contact the realm of Spirit. In this realm we understand each other by unexpected rules of life. There we begin to cognize with a vision close to the eternal miracle of Truth.

The miracle of life, all-conquering and majestic! That miracle which fills all depths of Be-ness. Seldom is it manifested by the human hand. From ancient times its radiant sparks have reached us, but its substance is usually already disintegrated. But, still alive is the web of this miraculous life embodied by the old Japanese Masters. The fragrance of the benevolent fairy-tale still streams from the leaves guarded by lime from the unbreakable patina of the varnish. Unlimited is the horizon of the living eye and heart—that, which had been created by the old Japanese, teaches and amazes. An astounding life is depicted; even in the minute is expressed the great truth. In the finest hieroglyphs of life is given the entire character of the synthesis. In daily striving is realized the highest lawfulness. The phantasmagoria of life has become filled with highest persuasion. In a beautiful harmony of colors is expressed a mighty song which can uplift our restless consciousness. Many summits of art are culminated in the creations of the Japanese Masters. Many problems so difficult for manhood have been boldly solved by the Japanese creators. The aristocracy of art, popularity, attainment—all these, so very precious to human nature, and so frequently rejected by prejudice—all these gems, correlated by Japanese Masters, are clad in the Beautiful.

In speaking of Japan—we may use the word, *beautiful.* To this people belongs this concept; a people which in spring comes forth to salute awakening nature; a people, which, delving daily into its treasury of art, selects the painting for every day; a people unable to appraise a work of art in ordinary terms. Where else, besides Japan, are there so many private collections of art? In what other country is it so honorable to be called an art collector? In what country, other than Japan, as in the school test "Fujiyama," is a prize awarded for the most selfless description? A multitude of such facts will be evident if in an affirmative way we study the life of Japan; and yet we are unaware of many touching and heroic details. Our measurements are, no doubt, insensible to a great deal which is perfectly evident to the Japanese themselves. But we recollect Japan in the blossoms of its cherry orchards, and we feel that that sacred flower, of which Komio, the divine Queen of Nara, sang so beautifully, still lives.

And the Japanese nation, vitally realizing its rich traditions, will carry further the high culture which, in its time, uniquely helped this nation to occupy such a prominent place.

The supreme human stronghold and treasure consists in the possibility of our meeting in the name of the highest culture. In this great conception we shall all bring together all conquests of the highest cults, of all-conquering Beauty and uplifting Knowledge. In our time of earthly upheavals it is not a truism to pronounce an invocation to high Culture. It is more than timely to strengthen each other, so that the Conception of high Culture be not neglected, and individual, family, and state be affirmed on this strong basis; for beyond these noble gates no vulgarity, nor deterioration can intrude.

We are searching for mutual understanding. Prizes for peace are awarded. We aspire to the Banner of Peace, which will protect all cultural treasures against vandalism and brutality in time of war as well as in time of peace. We understand that in time of peace very often vandalism pursues its ravages no less than in time of war. We know that sometimes war in spirit is not less dangerous than a war in the field. A spiritual murder is also more dangerous than a physical one. All the latest inventions and discoveries offer so many still unrealized possibilities, that the duty of all the devotees to Culture is to apply the given possibilities to the highest. Each fire can be extinguished. In the twilight of daily life, people can involuntarily decline in spirit and unnoticeably effect cruelty, vulgarity and egoism. The spiritual garden is still more in need of watering than the material one, and in the name of the beautiful gardens of Japan, in the name of reverence of the great ancestors, in the name of the eternally blossoming flower of Komio, the Queen of Nara, I welcome you, invisible friends! I firmly believe that since the ideals of highest Culture are everywhere similar, no oceans nor mountains can impede the friendly intentions of humanity.

Those who live in aspiring ascent will unavoidably meet on the crossroads of the great Infinity. In mutual creative work I welcome you!

Naggar, February 3, 1931.

FIRM PATHS

To the Colombian Cultural Roerich Association

YOUR message about my election as Honorary President of the Colombian Roerich Society has reached me in the Himalayas. I can tell you heartily what joy your message gave to me. I know the President of your Society, General De Leon, and I know your enthusiastic work for the Common Good. I have the best feelings for the President of Colombia, Dr. Enrique Olaya Herrera. All that I have heard about his enlightened activity proves how strong a man he is and how great a statesman. Countries are in need of great spirits and a strong hand, which can lead them to prosperity and towards real evolution. I know that the principle of cooperation is close to you and that you realize firmly how much humanity needs the spreading of enlightening knowledge and beauty, which are the only vital factors of Life and Ascension.

You know that we cannot remain standing on one place. We are either retrograding or ascending. In the name of this constant ascension, in the name of the constant fight against all evils of ignorance, I am sending to you all my message of unbreakable courage, of patience and joy of labor, and of the victory of true Progress and the Coming Golden Age of Humanity.

At present in many lands serious crises occur. But in their essence they are not only financial crises—more often they are crises of dying hearts. The formula of fine Culture is not in need of luxury. Verily for the flaming hearts, for those inspired by the high conceptions of culture, not money itself is essential but a constant growth and refinement of Spirit is wanted. The necessary means also come from the same source of the growing sacred

Fire. There, where are laboring hands, where are devotion and the burning of the heart, there these qualities will also give success to activities. This sacred Fire gives strength to overcome all obstacles. Really what special means would be needed in order that a handful of faithful devotees could assemble from time to time, and in hearty exchange kindle the torch of true Culture? For enthusiasts even a cup of tea is unnecessary, because for them it is not the teapot which boils, but the heart.

Spiritual understanding and harmony weave the radiant garment of the Mother of the World—the sacred Culture. By this creative path you shall ascend.

Let us join our hands and give our earnest oath, that we will all, by all means, strengthen and broaden the noble work of enlightenment and betterment of Life.

Himalayas, January, 1931.

ON THE THRESHOLD OF THE TENTH ANNIVERSARY

To the Board of Trustees of Roerich Museum,
New York, 1931

IT gave me great pleasure to read in your last reports that in spite of the general financial crisis our activities are not only not curtailed but expanding widely. During so unusual a crisis, we must prepare our minds as to how to meet it. As I penetrate the very roots of each question, there come to my mind the pioneers with their covered wagons. When they began their new life, they could expect only poisoned arrows instead of help or loans. Nevertheless only by their incessant labor and spreading of activities they created that brilliant civilization to which we are witness. In the work of culture during this difficult time, we are equally pioneers; and the same poisoned arrows await us from behind corners. But in our hands are the same creative labor and the very same unwavering realization of the righteousness and necessity of our works. No one, not even a slightly civilized man, could tell us that our activities are not needed or are even harmful. Hence the direct conclusion that only by strengthening of our activities will we overcome all poisoned arrows, as well as the financial crisis.

Certainly we can and we must introduce vital economy in all those details where the essential and moral side of our activities is not diminished. The questions of expenditures and all other financial problems must be solved, first of all, in a justly economic way. As you understand we can not shrink and diminish in our essential activities.

If we became like pigmies, we could easily be carried away by the torrent which has broken the dams. We cannot say that any of the Departments may be without workers—this would mean that it has to become silent and close. But we must give so much work to these workers that even the most short-sighted eye will be amazed by this created light.

Each of our departments in its program must create possibilities for self-support. Various campaigns for special funds are of course also needed. Amidst these campaigns, those for small sums among the masses, should occupy a special place. Perhaps campaigns of one dollar, or there where millions of people will be approached, there can be a campaign of a quarter. We work for the culture of the masses and thus have the right to appeal to masses. Even for a quarter we can give a small pamphlet of use for each one or a reproduction which would convey to them the essence of these strivings.

Another condition entitles us to this broad cooperation; our primary calculations and budgets were absolutely correct, applicable to the time when made. It is not our fault that since then, the general financial situation has completely changed. How can we then bar the torrent of this misfortune? We can overflow this torrent by a still more powerful torrent of work, watchfulness and creativeness.

Already if we honestly take the facts of our activities alone, not overlooking nor diminishing anything light-mindedly, we shall see an unrepeated scope of activities which resounded and awakened sympathy in more than twenty countries.

For example, our Annuals—in which, because of their size, much that is essential is omitted—also there is manifested and formulated an activity which even those who are envious, do not consider small. All the strange legends about the "unusual powers," strengthened by the envious, prove how generously they give us credit. One of the last legends says that we even coin our own money. Let our signs of culture be these true banknotes. Let the true list of facts about our activities grow limitlessly, so that we may say even to the most cruel persecutor: "Shame! Are you so daring as to oppress such a useful and speedily growing cultural work from whose roots your own children will benefit?"

I have recently written to you about the martyrdom of Creation, Science and Culture and therefore I do not touch now on this subject. At present I wish to stress only that which stands in contrast to all who extinguish Culture. Truly we can already in full right show them the list of facts of our activities. Let us remember the past year of 1930 when our activities were so heavily impeded. Let us remember the hundreds of meetings of our Societies in the name of Culture. Let us remember the numerous concerts and lectures. Let us remember the valuable exhibitions in which not only individuals but governments of countries cooperated. Let us remember the apparent growth of the School. Let us remember the publications of our Press which are gradually covering a vast field. Let us remember the completion of the Building. Let us remember all Foreign Societies and our European Center in Paris. Let us remember how much that is useful we offer to our co-members. Let us remember the two hundred thousand visitors to the Museum during this term alone. Let us remember the thousands of expressions of sympathy for our Peace Pact and that the proposed Banner of Peace is already waving on some Museums. Let us remember all the results and all the publications of the Roerich Central Asiatic Expedition. Let us remember the foundation of the Himalayan Research Institute, the first *Journal* of which has already presented many valuable results; also the lectures of Dr. George Roerich in America. Let us remember that Miss Frances R. Grant's visit to South America for cultural aims would make up a whole volume of highly useful facts. Let us remember that the Expeditions of Dr. Walter Koelz from the Himalayan Research Institute have brought back a vast scientific material through which we could already enrich American and Foreign Museums and Universities. Let us remember my declaration made at the meeting of our French Society in Paris about those contacts which we succeeded in making. Verily each of the named facts can be justly developed into an entire book. And we can in full realization affirm that our work, so useful for general culture, cannot be forgotten in the history of America. And our main privilege is, that we need neither to exaggerate extravagantly nor to enhance.

We have only to show honestly all facts, knowing inwardly that we all have verily given ourselves to the service of Social progress and Culture. And we are no longer novices; we are already celebrating the decade of our unceasing labors in America. And if upon this scale we lay also my forty years of cultural activities and experiences appreciated in the literature of many countries, then in full sincerity we can say that we are creating and building; and we summon others to the cultural work, truly needed by humanity.

Multitudes of unknown friends in different continents appreciate our efforts and often we receive signs of appreciation of our work from where we least expected it. Without exaggeration we may say we have these invisible friends of ours even in deserts and beyond the seas and mountains.

We have been called enthusiasts; and I shall never forget how inspiringly and with such certainty Miss Grant said in her speech to a large audience: "Yes, we are enthusiasts and nothing can break our enthusiasm." I was happy to hear this unwaveringness because only by unfailing achievement can we avoid all poisoned arrows and continue the structure of the Abode, where the spirit of future humanity can come to regenerate and nurture itself. Verily we are enthusiasts and this enthusiasm is based not on blind fanaticism but on open-heartedness, on the synthesis of knowledge, strengthened by the wisdom of ages.

When we made up the austere charter of our Institutions, in no way did we exaggerate, for all of us have offered all our possessions for this work of Culture. The ignorant, impelled by malice, may presume that something was concealed from them, but we may justly be proud because the facts are eloquent. Thus we can meet the new decade of our Institutions in full consciousness of untiring labor and useful results in spite of all difficulties. We are not at all dreamers or idealists; on the contrary, looking at the results, we have the right to consider ourselves practical realists. We dislike clouds and mists and everything connected with the idea of "Mist." We like the light. We like the tangible—not in the material but in the spiritual meaning. If we are in need of means for the educational fund, we know how each penny will be used and again in confidence we can realize the usefulness of all that will be accomplished, securing the most immediate tangible results. I am aware that I pronounce these words at a moment of the greatest financial crisis, but I also know that all crises are cured by spiritual values.

Culture (Cult-Ur) is the cult of Light, as I recently wrote to you; and in the name of this Light we have the right to summon our known and unknown friends to creative labor, to glorious cooperation, during which, as in a megaphone, human forces are magnified.

After all we know that in the Universe nothing is final, because everything faces the great Infinity. We know of the great Hierarchy of Bliss and we are confident in the Victory of Light!

The laws of Light are unbreakable!

Himalayas, 1931.

PEACE AND CULTURE

To the Young Men's Buddhist Association, Colombo

ON this memorable day we must remember each other with especial vividness, and mutually strengthen each other by the basic conceptions of true evolution. The Great Gotama Buddha ordained in manifold ways the conception of Peace and Culture. *Peace* signifies an unceasing construction. *Culture* means an eternal cognizance and betterment of life through the foundations of glorious progress.

Everything created by hostility is impractical and perishable. The history of mankind has given us remarkable examples of how necessary for progress is peaceful creativeness. The hand tires from the sword, but the creating hand, sustained by the might of the spirit, is untiring and unconquerable. No sword can destroy the heritage of culture. The human mind may temporarily deviate from the primary sources, but at the predestined hour it will have to recur to them with renewed powers of the spirit.

The subtlest energies which were preordained are already proven to be not an abstraction; and true scientists already apply them for the betterment of life. The life upon the far-off worlds, foreseen ages ago, as well as the new possibilities for humanity, cease to be fairy tales; we already use these possibilities, finding new hours for uplifting meditations. And these very meditations also renew. They can become shorter and more intense. The Teaching about pure food has already entered convincingly into life, for even limited minds already know of the most powerful vitamins. All which is vital, in its glorious prognosis, will not disappear, but like every truth will appear in an ever-broadening conception. Humanity begins to understand that the hand of Peace is the mightiest. There never can be such indefatigable tenacity in the hand of War as in the hand of Peace. He who is the bearer of Peace and Culture does not have to coerce others, for in his constructive enthusiasm he will be imbued with radiant creativeness and the greatest understanding of true cooperation.

The foundations of Peace and Culture make man verily invincible and realizing all spiritual conditions, he becomes tolerant and all-embracing. Each tolerance is but a sign of weakness. If we understand that each lie, each fallacy must be exposed, it means that, first of all, a lie is stupid and impractical. But what has he to hide who has consecrated himself to Peace and Culture? Studying the foundations of the Teachings, he can do nothing that would violate what is noble, because knowledge is needed for evolution. Helping his near ones, he helps the general welfare, which in all ages has been appreciated. Striving to Peace, he becomes a pillar of a progressing State. By not slandering the near ones, we increase the productiveness of the common creation. By not quarreling, we prove that we possess the knowledge of the foundations. By not Wasting time in idleness, we prove that we are true co-workers of the limitless cosmic energies. Finding joy in the daily labor we show that the conception of Infinity is not alien to us. In not harming others, we do no harm to ourselves, and by eternally giving, we realize that in giving we receive. And this blessed receiving is not the secret hoard of a miser. And we understand how creative is affirmation and how destructive is negation. Among the basic conceptions, not even a complete ignoramus would dare to attack those of Peace and Culture.

The mentioning of Lalitavistara upon the pages of the "Legende Doree" is one of the benevolent signs through which true understanding is being formed. The border between Light and Darkness crosses the whole world and disclosing it, we become defenders of the Culture of Light. There cannot be any culture of darkness. If we can visualize the stronghold of Light, then as a counterbalance there will be the abyss of darkness of ignorance. But, on days of commemoration at least, every trace of darkness should be annihilated.

On such memorable days we must bring great spiritual offerings. And if today we bring our true striving to Peace and Culture and vow not to deviate from these high principles, then we will deserve to have our work adjudged as noble actions. Verily ordained are the deeds of nobility —the deeds of Peace and Culture.

Himalayas, May, 1931.

HEALTH OF SPIRIT

To the Washington Roerich Society

"Resplendently flowered, Thou, Queen Omnipotent, Beloved of all!
"Harken, O Hygeia, Blessed Mother of all, Thou, Who bringest
    happiness!
"Thy Grace saves the sick bodies of mortals,
"Thy Grace adorns each hearth with joy inexhaustible
"And regenerates science. Oh Queen Omnipotent, all Cosmos is
    Thine.
"Hades itself, the destroyer of souls, shudders before Thee.
"Oh, Most Benevolent, Eternally Young, Thou, the Refuge of
    Mortals!
"Free art Thou from turmoil and all that is needless for man-
    kind.
"For Thou, Queen Omnipotent, rulest all and Thine is the
    World.
"Oh Goddess, Thy devotees await Thee. Thou art their Eternal
    Protector.
"Oh, Thou Benevolent, smite all pestilent germs of ravaging
    scourges."

THUS during the fire offerings of manna resounds the Orphic Hymn to the Goddess of Health, Hygeia. Verily divinely the ancients understood the conception of health. The sublime Goddess Hygeia is not head of a medical department, but she bestows health in its full conception—the health of body and spirit. How precious it is that in mutual understanding we can speak about the health of the spirit without which the health of the body would be but monstrosity.

Our spirit strives again to the light of Apollo and the sun-like Mithra and the fiery life-giver, Zoroaster. Do we become pagans in pronouncing these conceptions? Those who think of light, will come unavoidably to the one Light. In whatever form we shall perceive light, the heart is always aware that in light we find the life-giver.

"This is the day of the testimony of the manifestation of the Word and the fulfillment of the affirmation."

"God ordains for you that which is benevolent and commands for you that which shall bring you to Him, the Lord of all Teachings."

Were not these words pronounced by the New Testament, were they not pronounced by the Bible, or are these words perhaps from the Book of Authenticity, "Kitjab El Igan"? These words direct one to the one Light that makes us gather all our best experiences and accumulations in order to approach it more closely. And how shall we name this mighty treasury of all that is best and most precious for our spirit? We shall agree honestly and sincerely upon the conception—Culture. Was there not in antiquity a Goddess Cultura? Was there not an Angel Cultur, whose service consisted in the opening of the wondrous Gates?

There is no sacrilege in bringing everything pertaining to Culture closer to the highest conceptions. At times the decline of the human spirit reached such abysses that each manifestation of the Highest Spiritual Inspiration was already considered as something not timely, shameful and irrelevant with the conception of a contemporary "serious" man. Numerous have been the senseless destructions, resulting from this distortion of the foundations. We know of Bliss, we know of psychic energy, we know of vitamines. It seems that from the orange and lemon itself filled with vitamines, from the seed which begins to germinate through its basic substance, there opens a path upward even for the most limited trend of thought. Verily upward, for there is no seed which grows downward. Even the smallest blade of grass or each little leaf knows the direction of the light and stretches toward it. And wars and earthquakes and sicknesses and the horrors of rebellions of the human spirit sufficiently impel humanity to raise its head and search for new paths. Let these paths lead not through the caves of hermits. They can be found in life.

The towers of spirit can be erected there where rise the towers built by hands. And if it be whispered to you once more that it is superfluous to remind any one of Culture, or that sufficient has been done for Culture, you can boldly call the whisperer ignorant. Besides, he will probably not be able to understand the difference between Culture and civilization. And for him civilization will be but the standard of vulgarity. And you will easily witness how resourceful such a whisperer becomes when he finds himself in the ill atmosphere of slander, gossip and other ulcers of vulgarity, so dear to him.

No measures are sufficient to cover the needs of true Culture. Culture is as sublime as Infinity. And when the human spirit realizes Infinity, it places man under the obligation of unceasing perfection. Thus Infinity becomes for us a reality. Nobody can hide his head from reality like an ostrich. It means that reality is unavoidable, hence one must become its worthy co-worker.

Those who cognize the significance of Culture uproot from their hearts above all every conception of fear, the fear of death, the fear of enemies. When in the innermost heart one firmly knows that one proceeds unwaveringly to the light, his sole enemy then will be darkness alone. But darkness is dispelled by light. Thus it means that an inspired heart which carries light is the dispeller of darkness.

Culture rests upon Beauty and Knowledge. It grows through the realization of the blessed Hierarchy of Light. Thus to the mechanical knowledge the fire of the heart must be added. In this will be the cardinal distinction of Culture from civilization.

We assemble for the sake of the restoration of the language of the heart. We gather for exchange and mutual strength through the tokens of the heart, recurring to the Primary Sources without prejudice or superstition. The human being who reflects in himself the entire radiance of Cosmos cannot be content with meanness, spiritual poverty and falsehood, because of the corruptibility of the present day. Sooner or later psychic energy rises in rebellion, if refused a broad channel for its wondrous ascent. The history of mankind has given enough examples of this rebellion of psychic energy. These experiences ought to suffice as reminders to humanity of how urgent it is to recur consciously to creative thought, to light-bearing creativeness, understanding it not as a far-off abstraction but as an undeferrable vital necessity.

Let these qualities of undeferrability and vitality be our immediate stimulus. For we are responsible for the coming generation. As a gardener is responsible for his garden, thus humanity bears the responsibility for the planet entrusted to it. Humanity has no right to stain, to obscure and to pervert the glorious sublime creation. Who of the thinking ones will dare then to belittle and darken creative thought?

At our meetings we shall not quarrel, leaving this to dark ignorance. It is said: "The first sign of lack of culture is a quarrel." Let us not belittle each other, because out of the small is generated the small. Let us feel ourselves as hearty co-workers for the enhancement of life and the deepening of knowledge. Before us lies an immeasurable field of work and to each are given unlimited possibilities, for the approach to light is boundless. Our thought will abandon rivalry for there is enough room in Infinity. Besides, containment and tolerance are the first adornments of Culture. Let us eradicate all germs of mean thoughts, because each laboring one has verily no time to preoccupy himself with these. Our meetings shall be the source of vital interchange of inspiration and strengthening but not a burden of false trifles.

When drawing from the Primary Sources, how beautiful are the examples of creativeness with which we can inspire each other! From the Churches of the Roman Middle Age to the great covenants of the ancient East, to the monuments of Egypt, China, India, Maya, Persia and Japan—how limitless, benevolent and real are they all! Let us also not forget our contemporary Arts and Sciences remembering that these will serve as foundations for the future styles of life.

At our meetings, let the scientist, the artist and all builders of life greet each other in friendship, for essentially they all are the very same carriers of evolution, the very same initiates of thought—creativeness. Let our meetings be blessed by the radiance of the Madonna and the quick-helping, hundred-armed Heavenly Mother and the many-eyed Dukkar and the many-handed Kwan Yin and Lakshmi in her creative Image. The Moslems reverence Miriam—the Mother of Christ; the Bible gives us touching Images of self-sacrifice of womanhood; in the most ancient places of Asia were found cults of adoration of the Mother of the World. Under this benevolent sign let us remember that with which we began. Let us remember how inspiringly the Hellenes glorified Hygeia, the Mother of all; thus the ancients realized that the strength of the spirit was the health of the body. In the name of this invisible strength, in the name of the eternal snows of the Himalayas, the Guardians of the precious meteoric dust—these messengers of the far-off worlds—I trust you will find within yourself the inexhaustible vigor, patience and good-will to serve Culture—the glorious Culture of the Future!

Himalayas, 1931.

BLESSED HIERARCHY

To the Youngest Friends

"How do you do, Dr. Lukin:

"You do not know me, but I know you, although I have not seen you. Auntie told me that you are President of the Latvian Roerich Society. I too am his friend; he did not see me either. I am Serge Vitol and I am seven-and-a-half years old. And I wish you should make a society for children only not to babble, but to learn how to live better and to be good. I wanted to come to you but I cannot because I am going to Lithuania. I live there. I will come back in March and shall come to see you and then I shall tell you a great secret.

"Yours respectfully, Serge Vitol."

THUS writes our young friend, Serge Vitol, to the President of our Latvian Society, Dr. Lukin. And Dr. Lukin with his usual all-embracingness and goodness remarks that we must also be prepared for such requirements. When I recollect the multitude of statements of similar nature from known and unknown friends, then verily, we must without delay fulfill this noble desire of the young seekers for the betterment of life. Let us then pay firm attention to the words pronounced by Serge Vitol "not to babble but to live better." This is the same vital formula of which we adults always dream and which again and again is dissolved in aimless and sterile babbling, prattle and gossip. How wonderful it will be if our young friends manifest firm striving in quest of "how to live better." Notice, our friend does not speak of entertainment, of having a good time, but he speaks of the betterment of life. He comes thus simply to the question of the necessity for betterment of life. And this simplicity is permeated with the vitality which can revivify any arid desert. Although I do not know personally this young friend, I feel that he will not be satisfied with games nor with our vulgar conception of a kindergarten, where, instead of a positive prognosis, the germs of prejudice are so often being enrooted. Our friend and all other young friends whom we know, aspire to have a real Society for the betterment of life. He wishes to have serious work, for as I have already mentioned before, the young ones try to execute with especial care, the work entrusted to them by the elder. Even in the household, the young ones participate deeply and seriously in the commissions given to them. We remember with what unusual care five-year-old Olaf set the table, even getting up on a chair in order from above better to see whether everything was in its place. And what zeal seven-year-old Vladimir manifested in cleaning a rifle, because he was entrusted not with a toy gun, but with a real gun. And how Alien loved the paintings and had long conversations with them about matters most serious. And how little Jerome tried to introduce in his preparatory class the principle of lawful statesmanship. An endless number of examples can be quoted showing true and thoughtful cooperation of young friends. I do not forget that my painting for the Kansas City Museum was acquired through a subscription of school-children, and that the painting itself was chosen by their vote. And the painting selected was "The Lord" —the expectation of the arrival of the Supreme Lord.

Does this not reflect the inner realization of Hierarchy among our young friends—this most precious conception of creativeness, which later on so often becomes sullied and disintegrates?

In one assembly of young friends the project for a City of the Future was discussed. One of the participants of the assembly stated that his city would have no prisons; another said that his city would begin with the erection of a hospital; the third aspired to have a Temple in the center of his city; a fourth had roof-gardens in mind; another made a project of special roofs for the landing of airplanes.

None of those present at this assembly thought of vaude-villes and vulgar entertainments, so dear to the hearts of adults. Have in mind, however, that these participants were not at all anemic pessimists but were strong, happy and joyous. But neither golf, nor fistic smashing of jaws, nor vulgar beaches were included in the dreams of the young.

I have seen innumerable children's designs. Except a few, which were obviously the results of the influences of family surroundings, I never saw one malicious caricature or one mean subject. I recollect how little Stefani depicted the story of Joan of Arc; I recollect fantastic cities, flowers, and animals. I remember various collections, I recollect essays of five and six-year-old children about expeditions and their observations in the field of Natural History; about the discovery of new lands, stars and a new sun. I recollect whole books which were written during the first school years, on ornithology, dendrology and mineralogy. I remember very artistic and instructive postcard collections, which in contrast to those of adults, did not include the vulgar subjects which often are published in such profusion as though at the demand of the masses. Let us remember the theaters arranged by young friends with all adaptations, in order that they should be like a real theater. I remember how once a young friend, having invited his playmates to visit him, distributed among them his toy soldiers, but set himself down with a book to read. In answer to everyone's astonishment, he said: "Let them be busy if they are interested and I will read in the meanwhile." During the construction of a model fleet, the ships with their many sails are not always directed to war, but on the contrary, they carry important news, discover new lands, transport new machinery or defend their own shores.

Penetrating into the self-development of conscious-ness of our young friends, we find an endless multitude of facts and comparisons which give deep joy. If the distorted conceptions of life would not obscure the development of these consciousnesses, how many true possibilities of progress would be created and how much of the vulgar and mean would disappear from life.

Many a time an adult through a light-minded and foolish attitude toward the foundations of life and religion, diverts forever the worthy striving instinct of the younger generation. Sometimes, in an unjust accusation, a child's mother makes pretense of consulting God, and Oh horror! this God gives an unjust verdict, and, under the eyes of the young ones, the church is transformed into a club. As though it would pass unnoticed by the young eyes! But vigilant are the eyes of the young and they notice much which later on perhaps might slip attention. The absorption of the first years is more intense than that of the following years.

Dear Serge Vitol, you have a kind Aunt who gave you the address of Dr. Lukin. Dear Serge—and all of you—have variously manifested your hearty and serious intentions! We shall in every way encourage your Societies with the aim of "how to live better." We shall consider it our joy when our friends learn to open the glorious Gates. We shall rejoice with you if you find the joy of creative labor and if you realize the power of thought.

You speak about your secrets but the secret of your heart is not destructive. It is constructive and benevolent. You desire to know of the good and you intend to go towards it by the shortest and straightest way. This good will be vouchsafed to you, if you will reach it in full and radiant faith, this immutable knowledge will lead you to the Good, to the Beautiful, which is crowned by the one, all-conquering Light! It shall be a day of joy to receive news from your Societies that strive to the Good! Thus shall we enrich the store of our joys. Let us affirm ourselves in the joy of creative labor, in the joy of cooperation, in the joy of cognizance and in all joys, which will lead us to the great realization of Culture.

Himalayas, 1931.

SACRED PRINCIPLES

To the Academy of Creative Arts of
Roerich Society, New York

DEAR Mr. Schrack and Friends,
Together with the fragrance of the flowers that now cover the slopes of the Himalayas, came your hearty messages. With equal heartiness I may tell you that from the very beginning of your Academy I sympathized with your aim and helped you invisibly. In your foundation are contained many most valuable conceptions, which bring us closer together.

You did not fear the conception of "Academy" which so often is understood in the sense of fossilization and conventionalism. You were unafraid because, to the usual conception of Academy, you added the all-enlivening conception of creativeness. First of all you thought of the great creative principle. You understood creativeness as the leading principle of life; otherwise speaking, you thought of the stamina which lies at the very base of the future evolution. Hail to you!

There was another conception of which you were unafraid, yet which is a terrifying one to mediocre souls. You were not afraid to pronounce the conception "Teacher." There are many who are without individuality and creative thought, yet who are horrified at the conception of the great Hierarchy. For the mediocre, the word "Teacher" is a synonym of "enslaver" and "strangler"; they regard it as identical with the clutch of conventionality from which the young heart seemingly strives to liberate itself. But these hearts are verily no longer young. They are already withered and poisoned by the venom of impotency.

Turning to biographies, we see that for the mighty creators the Teacher remained unforgettable; for to them, he was the bestower not of fetters but of wings. It was he who knew the cipher to the magic key, which taught them to open the complex locks of the heart. He stimulated them to think creatively and to create, create, create untiringly by day and by night. For creativeness does not demand time or space. It is beyond these dimensions and its language is primarily expressed by the language of the heart which exceeds in wealth and beauty all other languages. Not without cause did the Ancient Wisdom of the East regard him who asserted that he spoke only from himself, as a dead tree bereft of its roots. In this synthesis of the conception of Hierarchy are comprised the covenants of creative life. A tree without roots is condemned to decay; only the roots that penetrate deeply into the primary essence of the minerals can maintain balance, can nurture the stem and adorn it with the exquisite creation of branches and fragrant blossoms. Thus, you did not fear the conception of a Teacher, hence your hearts are free; hence there is no slavery within you; hence within you abides the creativeness of life. Hail to you!

In giving we receive. You were not afraid to assemble and manifest your aspirations of creativeness, enhancement and betterment of life, of cooperation, of mutual help. Small souls, who perhaps but recently have emerged from the animal kingdom always apprehend cooperation. To them the bestial "I" excels all evolution and the entire Cosmos. This bestial "I" prompts them to hide, to conceal, to slander and to quarrel, with the same inhuman screeching and spitting displayed by enraged monkeys and other animals. But let us not excessively offend the monkeys, for often the malicious venom of certain human brutes is more hideous than the leaps of irritated animals. For they are deprived of our consciousness, but the consciousness obscured by hatred and envy is the most horrid substance. Will not an enlightened consciousness first of all prompt us to realize that "we" is more powerful than "I"? Verily the light-bearing armor of achievement is infinitely more firm than the rusty scales of meanness, wrathful vulgarity and envy. You were not afraid of cooperation. Thus you have once again joined forces with the knights of evolution; you have, so to speak, given a most sacred oath to create daily, to labor and not to quarrel, leaving clashes and quarrels to those insignificant ones who are destined to be ejected into cosmic refuse. Verily it is not timely to continue disunion and disintegration. The world's situation does not permit any one to indulge in the abomination of destructive sport. In everything is decidedly felt the turning of the lever of evolution. There is possible either a speedy regress to savagery or the wondrous transfiguration of life. Amidst daily labor, through conquering personal difficulties, you found time and energy for cooperation and unity to manifest the most precious, the most noble and the most beautiful. Hail to you!

In the very name of your venture, in the mentioning of the sacred word *creativeness* is already contained the pledge that you will not proceed by the dead and usual ways. You will broadly set aside the limits of possibilities. You will understand and kindle each individuality; every heart pained by expressed emotion will be warmed by you. For in these sacred pains grows the seed of wondrous achievement. You firmly remember that creativeness, art, are expressible in all possible forms—as in the intellectual and physical, so in those of spirit. One expresses the conviction of creativeness in sound, another in color, a third in form, a fourth in creative thought, which imbues the space of the worlds in the same splendor as all other expressions. Pronouncing the word *creativeness,* you did not hesitate before the crowning conception of Infinity. Only certain animals have the skeleton so constructed that it prevents them from looking upwards. You did not hesitate to take upon yourself the responsibility of carrying the sacred concept of creativeness. You feared not to appear as enthusiasts before the mediocre, for you know that the enthusiasm of creative thought is invincible. Hail to you!

The mentioned foundations, the covenant of existence

chosen by you shall safeguard you from ruin, so long as you will sacredly preserve them. Truly shameful and humiliating are disintegration and decay; these two conceptions, degrading to humanity, are linked with retrogression and downfall. Verily it would be disgraceful to imitate these two horrors.

You call me Teacher and Leader and we all know what responsibility these two conceptions lay upon one. You also give me the attribute "Adamantius." Certainly thus you wish to express the invincibility which must be manifested in the defense of Culture and Light. In this struggle against darkness you will encounter all monsters of ignorance and treacherous slanders. With each passing year of creative work you will realize more and more how indispensable is the quality "Adamantius," in helping withstand the bottomless darkness of ignorance. In return, I too wish to express my certitude that the hour will strike when I shall be able to apply to you and the Academy of Creative Arts the same attribute, "Adamantius." Besides, the word "Adamantius" evokes some precious memories for me. When next we meet we shall speak of them.

Thus, let us be united in the name of Creativeness, in the name of the conception of Teacher, in the name of Cooperation, in the name of Infinity, in the name of Light, in the name of Culture.

With my entire experience and all my best thoughts, I will rejoice in helping you.

Himalayas, 1931.

VIJAYA TAGORE!

Address on the Seventieth Anniversary of
Dr. Rabindranath Tagore, May 8th, 1931
(For Tagore's Golden Book)

IT may seem to some that the questions of Culture which have preoccupied the human mind since times immemorial, are already strongholds. It may seem as if entire cities and countries have accepted Culture or that our times can, in self-content, look back upon those far, far removed ones—poor ones, who had neither telephones nor radio and were even deprived of moving pictures. What an error of conceit! And how few understand that Culture as such dwells upon the summits; and the ways to these strongholds of human spiritual ascent are, as before, unusually difficult, even perhaps still more difficult than in some previous epochs.

Our ships are very swift. Someone has expressed his intention of constructing a ship of one hundred thousand tons. It would be instructive to know what were his intentions as to the quality of cargo for shipment. Was it intended for opium, in the hope of profit?

Our houses rise high—already we have structures one hundred stories high—much higher than the Tower of Babel. However, often in our living quarters, room is lacking either for a desk or a bookcase. Very roomy are our slaughter houses. Thanks to an unusual technique a hundred thousand animals may be slaughtered. But at the same time modestly and almost unknown, the researches of scientists about vegetable vitamines continue.

With all our so-called education, few will agree that a lemon or orange may replace a bloody beefsteak. Only recently, even seemingly learned physicians sent their patients to slaughter houses that they should be able to drink the warm blood. The very same physicians advised as the most curative means the devouring of raw bloody meat like beasts. But even in those countries, where since ancient times conditions of nature compel the aborigines to use only raw meat, they act judiciously, eating it either dried by the air or, in an extreme case they use it smoked.

Our mechanical technique has applied all efforts to produce as many robots as possible. True, even robots were overcome with mechanical madness and disturbed the traffic of the world. Somebody has invented a mechanical salesman for shops and the next inventor has livened the lips of the machine with a mechanical "Thank you!" But, in the wake of mechanization are born armies of unemployed. Is this the achievement of Culture?

Only recently cannons were brought into churches to be blessed. Nevertheless discussions on peace and religion in society have become something unbefitting and shameful. Should some one dare, in place of ugly one-sided sport, or instead of slander and calumny, to speak of the uplifting principles of Culture, the well-brought up people, with a shrug of their shoulders, whisper "How dull he is." And if some one on entering a drawing-room dares to express the sacred sign of his own religion, he is simply considered not only badly bred, but a crass bigot as well.

The questions of religion and spirit, the questions of Culture are, for the appeasing of ignorance, transformed into abstraction. If everything uplifting is made abstract, it means that we are evidently not responsible for it.

In the best case people excuse themselves because of the routine, the daily work, which would seem to hinder them from turning to the uplifting foundations of the spirit. So often it is forgotten that the daily labor is a benevolent *pranayama.* It creates energy, it brings us nearer to the cosmic rhythm, it helps us kindle the inner fires: these benevolent links with the spacial Agni. So often we find causes of self-vindication! We go afar in avoiding the responsibility, forgetting that the great responsibility for the condition of the entire planet is un-escapable wherever human distinction is attained. Does not this distinction demand the application of all powers in searching the corresponding rhythm of evolution?

It obliges one to think how to avoid finding oneself in the cosmic refuse.

This is not an abstraction. Verily this is vivid reality as true as Existence itself! And do not we ourselves willfully choose either disintegration or creation, negation or affirmation, creativeness or death? Does not the entire history of humanity indicate the highest bliss of creative thought in whatever form it be expressed and wherever manifested? The great examples of history display to us unusual creators of thought who either clothed it in matter or broadly proclaimed it through the spacial megaphone.

If all is one, then is not all interrelated, as was expressed long since in the ancient wisdom? We repeat the sacred hymns of the Bhagavad Gita and the Psalms about indestructibility, about all-conquering spirit; but often in chanting we lose our comprehension that the expressed wisdom is given for immediate application.

Does not Culture imperatively demand the immediate application to life of all the beautiful which we ourselves have dismissed into the exile of abstraction? The condition of the planet is such that either a true approach to evolution will have to be found or we are threatened with spiritual savagery. The great Agni will either awaken the most blissful force or will turn to the ashes of destruction the illusory Maya which we in conceit mistake for a basic stronghold. Either we once again realize the grandeur and immutable necessity of the Hierarchy of Bliss; or in barbarism we will reject every conception of Teacher and of the noble leadership of the Guru.

If the strongholds of Culture, as always, crown the heights, withstanding all the difficulties of a thorny and stormy path, how then must we be grateful to all those who have assumed the strain of the leadership of Culture.

And with what care must we safeguard the walls of these strongholds created by untiring daily labor. How we must bless those who kindle and sustain our enthusiasm. When we think of invincible energy, blessed enthusiasm, pure Culture, before me always rises the image of Rabindranath Tagore, so dear to me. Great must be the potentiality of that spirit, which prompts him untiringly to apply in life the foundations of true Culture. The songs of Tagore are inspirational calls to Culture; they are his prayers about great Culture, his blessings to the seekers of the paths of ascent. Synthesizing his immense activities—which ascend the very same mountain of Bliss, and which penetrate into the narrowest alleys of life—could any one abstain from the feeling of inspiring joy? So blissful, so beautiful is the essence of the hymns, the calls and works of Tagore.

Verily Shanti-Niketan is growing like the tree of Culture. We cannot judge how a powerful tree grows, why its branches are spreading in one form or another. By the conditions of winds or other conditions of nature, we would find an explanation. What is important is for our spirit to realize that this tree is growing; or in the language of a stronghold, it is important that the walls are being strengthened. And we know that these walls are constructed in the name of Culture and exist only because of Culture.

Is it not sacredly-joyous, this feeling which overwhelms us, as we look at the eternal snows of the Himalayas saturated with the miracle-working dust from far-off worlds, in realizing that now in our midst lives Rabindranath Tagore; that for seven decades he has untiringly glorified and praised the Beautiful and ceaselessly accumulated the eternal stones of Culture, erecting the stronghold of joy of the human spirit. This is so urgent! This is so undeferrably needed! Let us repeat untiringly about the necessity of the strongholds of Culture. Let us without end proclaim this true pride of a nation and of the entire world.

The strongholds of Culture as magnets gather all which

pertains to Culture and like anchors, they hold the ships of spirit, which toss in the stormy ocean of the elements.

Tagore lives for the glory of Culture. Let Shanti-Niketan stand as a guiding milestone for the growth of the human spirit, as a construction of the most needed, the most noble and most beautiful.

Vijaya Tagore! Vijaya Shanti-Niketan!

Himalayas, May, 1931.

THE GUARD OF THE MOTHER
OF THE WORLD

To the New York State Federation of Women's Clubs

VERITABLY beautiful was the address of Mrs. William Dick Sporborg in speaking for the four hundred thousand women whom she represents at the meeting of the Peace Banner on March 24th, in the Roerich Museum. This enlightened leader, in giving utterance to the powerful spirit of American Womanhood said: "We believe that mutual interests upon which nations can come together are the things to emphasize—the cultural needs, the artistic and scientific aspects. Because Nicholas Roerich realizes ... that until such time as a peace machine may really be substituted for the war system, he has devised this marvelous idea of protecting educational, artistic and religious institutions so that they may survive even such horrible conflagrations as world war. But I am quite sure that this is only a challenge on his part to make us realize that the thing towards which we must work is an education of the people of all nations toward the abject futility of warfare of any kind... We have carefully studied the situation with the intent that we are going to lend our spirits and all of our influence to such movements as this very great man, Nicholas Roerich, has initiated. ... I want you to know that we stand foursquare back of your organization, and we feel it a great honor to be permitted to-night to add our great tribute to Nicholas Roerich."

The words of Mrs. Sporborg must remain inscribed forever upon the tablets of Woman's achievements—those tablets which rise high under the eternal symbol of the Great Mother of the World. It is veritably inspiring to perceive with what broad vision Mrs. Sporborg has embraced the plan of preserving the treasures of culture. As is necessary to our time, Mrs. Sporborg sees its application not only in times of war, but with each hour when the creations of the human spirit are so imperative to universal progress.

Truly, the "education of the people of all nations" in the direction of true culture will be accomplished under a Banner of Peace, for Peace and Culture are indivisible! Who, if not woman, can infuse into the human spirit its highest concept of Culture! It is she who, beginning from the cradle through all phases of life up to the highest aspect of statesmanship, patiently and untiringly inculcates the concept of culture as life's contribution to a sublime evolution.

Much has been spoken of the lofty mission of Womanhood. Now the time has come for action. It is but natural that the hearts of women should vibrate to the calls of Culture and Peace. It is deeply gratifying to me that women have understood that my challenge is aimed at the foundations of a cultural transfiguration of life. To this end, we may pronounce our solemn oath, to serve this great cause. We know that the ignorant will sneer at this, because the concept of culture is as unbearable to ignorance as light is to darkness. But we also know that the very hostility of ignorance constitutes a stepping-stone to attainment; and history has taught us that this very stepping-stone may be utilized as a foundation for the construction of treasuries of Beauty and Knowledge. History again teaches us that ignorance has opposed every genuine, every creative force. Hence, the attacks of ignorance must not hinder us, but on the contrary, inspire us. We all know that each moment of tension creates energy, and we must be sufficiently enlightened to cull its benefits. Is there not deep satisfaction in the realization that our opponents are the groundlings of ignorance? Who, other than the ignorant, can oppose the aspirations of Culture? Who else would become wrathful over another's dream of a country of culture? Who else would be embittered over another's protection of the treasures of human genius? And who else would dare to pronounce the statement that further efforts were not needed for culture, that it had already been sufficiently served? Truly, only those who are deeply obscured and deeply ignorant could thus impede the aspirations of culture.

The Banner of Peace has aroused the sympathies of many statesmen, leaders and representatives of countries. The Museums' Committee of the League of Nations, under the Presidency of M. Jules Destree, has unanimously accepted our Peace Pact. We have heard expressions of sympathy from the Tribunal at The Hague. The representatives of numberless museums and cultural institutions have enthusiastically endorsed this idea. A special Conference is being organized in Belgium under the inspiring initiative of M. Tulpinck; and a League of Cities for the Protection of Cultural Treasures has been formed. As we anticipated and foresaw, this idea reaches outside of the limits of war; the human heart is resounding to a call for Universal Culture. It is gratifying to realize that during our complex and restless times the idea of culture can have such an impelling significance. Thus is erected a superb milestone on the path of human ascent.

Recalling the participation of women in this great cultural cause, we cannot forget the words of ancient wisdom: "To enumerate the achievements of Womanhood, is to write the history of the world. To enumerate the ecstasies of illumination, is to enumerate the visions of Womanhood. To study cooperation is to perceive the hand of Womanhood." Achievement, inspiration, cooperation—those true treasures, woman now brings to Culture: therein lies the assurance that the roots of the tree of culture will penetrate deeply in all directions and will grow mightily, nourished by the rays of cosmic conception.

Culture cannot flourish without enthusiasm. Culture fossilizes if deprived of the fire of loyalty and devotion. Culture becomes impoverished without the daily effort of conscious contribution. Culture is silenced there where the heart is inarticulate. For what is more beautiful than the peaceful, all-comprehensive language of the heart!

At this moment, I am by no means a visionary. When

we speak of culture, we are all realists, constructive positivists, for whom the progress of humanity is most precious and undeferrable. We have no right to regard our daily routine as an impediment to cultural striving. On the contrary, daily routine may become transfigured and ennobled if performed in full consciousness of culture.

I feel that Mrs. Sporborg is truly the voice of the vast legion of women in those towering spires of America. Those spires whose very heights sound out their summons to an ascent of the human spirit and impel us to sacred vigilance over the foundations of true progress. Humanity is already aware of the differences between culture and civilization. The elect among humanity know how civilization may sometimes expire; but the seeds of culture eternally guard their immortal vitality. And the towers of culture stand as beacon-lights for mankind.

If each member of the Federation of Women's Clubs would inspire only ten friends with the expressed idea of culture, one can already have many millions of couriers of culture. The omnipotent magnet of culture will inspire them undelayingly to infuse the principles of culture in their consummate power into the lives of their families, their communities, their organizations. What a superb crusade in the name of culture can be visualized thus simply. And our objective is not a tower of Babel—that symbol of dissolution and dissension—but an all-unifying Tower of Light, wherein we may be united by the one language-omnipotent of the heart.

In this language of the heart, we greet you, Legion of Women and Light-bearers! Honor to your invincible enthusiasm! Voicing the name of the Himalayas, symbol of the most lofty summits, we offer you our full-hearted cooperation. We greet you in the joy of our mutual striving towards that most sublime and most imperative destiny of humanity. With you we shall attain!

1931.

THE REALM OF CULTURE

Declaration to the Committee of the French Roerich Society and the Russian Section

FRIENDS:
Last year I had the joy of greeting you and, together with you, of remarking a succession of happy signs beneath which our work progressed. A year has now passed and in full justice we may say that the time has not gone aimlessly. Many splendid seeds were sown in our common labors.

In line with our basic principle of beginning everything with a small seed, we may see how the potential energy of this seed, from the sacred tree of Culture, is growing—growing even faster than may be expected. In my Declaration last year, I said to you: "Each cultural worker can say, 'We construct culture.' " He will be right, because wherein does the structure of Culture lie, if not in self-sacrificing, enlightened, beautiful labor? Let there be one more distinction of your cultural work: let there disappear from it all divisions, conventionally created by prejudice and ignorance. Many efforts upon the field of Culture have been destroyed and become hideous, precisely because of these living conventionalities. The sacred flame of Culture does not tolerate ignorant limitations. Whether we notice the life-creating torch in a hut or illuminating the halls of a palace, it is equally valuable to us, because this torch has become kindled with the very same all-exalting light. Let this condition stand as the cornerstone of our structure and preserve us from the gashing claws of ignorance.

In addition to the call of Culture, we already have above us the Banner of Peace, the luminous covenants of which should not be extinguished in human hearts. We must not only grant our faith to this Banner, but also desire to uplift it through the entire activity of enlightened labor. How many beautiful manifestations this staff of culture affords us! Each creator, each worker, without hindrances and coercion, can find application for his knowledge and his abilities. I have already had opportunity to speak of the League of Culture, of a Universal Day of Culture. Will it not be now one of the most beautiful tasks ahead of us to strive undelayingly in this direction; to begin work without delay in this limitless field, where there is no impediment, where there can be no human hatred and where the pettiness of malice and envy will be dispersed as is darkness before light?

The mission of our Committee may be beautiful not only in giving lectures, concerts, exhibitions in the name of Culture, but also in sending out representatives, fine messengers of Righteousness and Knowledge, to the schools, enlightened societies, factories, cottages and prisons where in beautiful, enlightened expression, they can acquaint others with the highest values of humanity. Poets, artists, musicians, scientists, entrusted by the committee, may become welcome guests at the varied repasts of the human spirit. And how easy is this fulfilled, if only it be begun in the potentiality of the seed.

In the Fund already inaugurated by us for the Banner of Peace and for popular education, one of the first appropriations must be in the name of this enlightened and luminous creative movement. I speak of the necessity of appropriations from the Fund, because it would be unenlightened to believe that the designated carriers of Light have their own means to fulfill this benevolent aim. Verily it would again be cruel to demand that someone without his own means should spend his very last pittance for the manifestations of Knowledge and Beauty. Let us express it more simply—of course, our messengers must be definitely paid; there is nothing unacceptable in this. It would be difficult to demand payment from the listeners, because a Luminous word or sound cannot be bought. But the universal fund into which everyone will bring his voluntary mite will be the sign that humanity has already become sufficiently matured to carry the Banner of Culture. Besides, we are aware that each Luminous thought ripens in space, and that the great realistic conception of the highest justice verily exists. It means that if we direct all the forces of our spirit in this direction, the material shell of the work will also naturally mold itself, as countless examples indicate. But one thing is necessary for success—one must shoot an arrow of complete, invincible, absolute striving. If we are unsuccessful, it means that in some instance the heart faltered; it means that in some instance, someone retreated and did not stretch forth his hands to the key of the gates. Then it is of no use to cast blame, of no use to malign; one must blame only oneself for nullity, for featurelessness, for the betrayal of the most Luminous and most Resplendent.

But one should not presuppose any possibility of retreat. We must walk as firmly and closely as we began. Let us set into the soil the seed of our decided wish. Now, without delay, let us organize small committees which will create the program of our call to Culture. Let everyone who can manifest a cultural gesture, express what he is ready to share. Let everyone also name his friends, each of whom, in his province, can call to mind the greatest cultural values of humanity. I already feel these hours of mutual understanding, when passages of the beautiful classics and the best of modern attainments are read. I already hear the sounds of the great festival of the past and the victorious syntheses of the future. Everything must have some means of beginning. I beg you to accept from me the sum of three thousand francs towards the Banner of Peace Fund as an honorarium to three lecturers, poets or artists, who bring the glad tidings of that which is so undelayingly necessary for the human heart. You may decide as to where it is best to inaugurate this—under our own roof or in some institution of a similarly progressive character. Let two of the events apply to France and one to the Russian Section. Decide among yourselves who can most significantly inaugurate this and when. With this, we shall lay the foundation of the new traditions of Culture, when Knowledge will be transmitted not merely for information, but also for ennobling the heart, for the enlightenment and unification of the human spirit.

The first number of the Annual, dedicated to the Banner of Peace, has already appeared. It is time to think of the second one. In this second one, will not poets, writers and artists ring the sacred bells? The Annuals of the Banner of Peace, as well as the Journal devoted to cataloguing the treasures of humanity, must enter into the immediate program of the Banner of Peace Fund.

In my previous Declaration our future home was mentioned, the home of Culture in Paris. Let us strengthen this thought in space, just as for several years we have strengthened the Institutions in America, which already have branches in more than seventeen countries. Primarily, it is necessary for one to know with absolute precision in what cause he acts and creates. Cementing the Banner of Peace and Culture with all its Beauty and Knowledge into the foundation, and sustained by this concept, we can heartily embrace each other; and in sending out our messengers of Light, we can say: *"You shall be conquerors!"*

I will end with my poem "With a Smile?" written in 1921.

> Messenger, my Messenger!
> Thou standest and smilest
> And thou dost not know what thou hast brought
> Me. Thou hast brought me the gift
> Of healing. Each tear of mine
> Shall heal the wounds of the world.
>
> But, Ruler, whence shall I
> Take so many tears and to which
> Of the wounds of the world shall I give
> My first torrent?
> Messenger,

O my Messenger, thou standest
And smilest. Dost thou not have
A command to heal sorrow
    With a smile?

Kyelang, 1931.

TEREM OF ICONS

IT is in Moscow, at the Czar Alexis' Palace of Iconography, and a skillful and beautiful work is being created.

The painting in the Palace is not being created at random, in one way or another, but according to statutes, according to strict command, known to the great Monarch, the Czar himself, and to the sovereign patriarchs. In the Palace are worked out the charts of cities, leaves of manuscripts; the needs of the treasury are being executed; blockheads, chimneys, stores are being decorated, accounts are being made; but the chief work, the true iconographical work, is being conducted according to the various ancient orders. All forms of icon-customs started long ago, during the time of the Czar Ivan Vasilevitch, since the Stoglav Council and even further back also, from the statutes of Athon.

The icon is created according to established rule. The designer sets the first and chief foundation, and outlines the drawing on a linden or an oak board. On this, the image-painter paints the figure, and his apprentices do everything else; sacred vestments and other attires. The master of flower work finishes the icon; around the saints, he paints the sky, the mountains, caves, trees; into the fissures he lays the golden stars on the sky or rays. The gold painters outline the edges and the surface of the icon with gold paint. The younger masters, *levkas*-workers and grinders, prepare the *levkas*—in other words, the plaster and glue for the covering of the icon canvas. They wet the glue, grind the colors and do all this most secretly; for these secret instructions of the elder people are being sacredly guarded in a family and the elder will only reveal to a son his secret of making *levkas* or preparing the gold. Sometimes he will give him written instructions about it, but the paper will be written in some cunning code. The apprentices prepare the wooden boards for the icons, glue them over, iron them with licerose leaf; there is plenty of all sorts of work in the Palace of Iconography for the younger master-grinder, enough also for the secretary and for the clerk who is. in charge of the office in the Palace.

The work in the Palace moves along briskly. And the work moves briskly because the great Czar of all the Russias, Alexis Michailovitch, has granted the icon-masters a charter. He himself used to come to the Palace and often favors the diligent masters with the Czarist brew and rum, with beautiful garments and with all other favors. But not only because of the Czar's kindness is the artistic work progressing with such diligence, but because this work is sacred and pleasing to God; it has received honor from the Lord Christ, Himself. Did He not "also deign to inscribe His Image upon a veil for the Czar Avgar, miraculously"? This work is revered also by the saintly apostles; and hence the people perform this task of painting always in love and not because of command or coercion.

In the morning, at the rise of the fair sun, from China-town on Icon Street, where many of the icon-painters live, the masters walk in friendly groups to the work, crossing themselves by the gilt domes of the Kremlin's temples, and begin their labor. They put on their aprons stained in color and glue, they tie their foreheads with a leather or hemp gear, so that oily locks of hair should not creep into their eyes; and they prepare the colors on nails or on a plank. One works silently, knitting his brows; another mournfully and drawlingly sings his canticles, befitting the meaning of the image; still another babbles at work, flinging across to his comrade a word of kindness or a challenge. But the painting does not suffer from such talk, because the hand knows its work; if however, it is necessary to make a subtle line or diligently draw a design, then not only does the din cease, but the head even helps the elbow and shoulder to carry on the line, and the tongue itself assiduously works on the lips in the same direction.

And the icon-painters carry on not only religious conversations, but worldly ones as well; and they have their fun too, but the jests are good ones, without profanity, without blasphemy against the name of the Lord or of honest art.

Various masters are gathered in the Palace; those who receive wages and those who receive board and those from the town who are of all three grades: in the first grade they are divided according to their art—icon-painters of the first grade who receive a *grivna* each, the masters from the second grade receive two *altyns* and five *denga,* the third grade icon-painters receive two *altyns* and two *denga.* Besides money, the icon-painters receive wine from the nobility and brew and filtered mead, and viands and pies from the food and bread house.

Some of the famous image-painters: Simon Ushakoff, Bogdan Saltanoff and others do not come into the Palace but go to the administration of the Palace of Arms. There they are to witness the art of a young icon-painter, just arrived from Vologda. And these image-painters will say whether he has sufficient experience to paint an icon image solidly and excellently. But if he is still inexperienced, then the clerk will announce to the unsuccessful master, that by the command of the great Monarch, he is dismissed from Moscow; henceforth he cannot be sent to the icon works, but he is to live in Vologda as heretofore.

II

While they work, they converse about the newly circulated edict. A bald-headed old image-painter with a hump and a tuberous nose, weightily raising his finger, looks around at the masters in a pompous way and repeats that part of the edict which he apparently likes very much:

" 'And be it pronounced that in our Czarist orthodox-Christian Empire, the image-painters of holy icons are diligent and honest; as true ecclesiastic vessels of the Church's munificence, the artists should be respected; and all others should accept the precedence of the artists and the brush, which exceeds in a multi-colored way the reed or pen of a writer.' Not every man will the great Monarch favor with such a kind word!

"And so it has been in all times. Already the Stoglav gives the command to respect the artist more than ordinary people..."

"And what does 'more' mean? Before an ordinary man one takes off one hat; then does one have to take off two hats before an icon-painter? ..."

"And who is a plain man? I will say, that a boyar himself is an ordinary man, next to a painter, because God did not reveal to him the craft of art..."

"If a thing be not the work of thy brain, do not talk of it with pride: every one knows what reverence is due to icon-painters and honest masters. They are revered also by spiritual fathers and by the chiefs of armies and by boyars and by all people."

An old man joins in. He proudly asserts that the Patriarch of Antioch, Makary himself, begged the Monarch to send him icons... "—such is the fame of Russian icon-painting!"

But the old man does not remember that the Patriarch could not have been accommodated with icons in any other place. However, this is not said as a reproach to the art-craft of the Moscovite image-painters.

The masters talk and wonder how it is that the emigrant from the land of the Shah, the image-painter Bogdan Saltanoff, is placed on equal rank with the lists of Moscovite nobles; such a thing—that an icon-painter be made nobleman—has never as yet occurred. Concerning Saltanoff, opinions are divided; some think that it was granted to him for his fine art, others because he accepted the Russian-Orthodox faith. After speaking of the Shah's emigrant Saltanoff, they begin to talk of other foreigners; they remember how irreverently some of the foreigners acted in regard to the blessing of the Patriarch and how the Patriarch became angry and ordered them to be differently garbed from the Russian people. Some are for the foreigners and some are against.

"Why is it that often the great Monarch gives greater privileges to the masters beyond the sea than to our own? For, as regards the craftsmanship, our own is just as bold..."

"And, look here, the Loputzky master was praised and overpraised, and he taught in such a manner that his own pupils wrote a petition stating that the master did not teach them true craftsmanship. And this was not an invention, but the truth. Afterwards all the pupils were taken away from him and given to Danilo Vuchters."

The foreign masters are especially attacked by a tall icon-painter with a leather band around his head, on his straight flaxen hair. According to his words it is not necessary to favor foreigners, when there is not enough money to pay wages to our native artists. He cites Ivashka Solovei, an icon-painter of the Palace of Arms, reduced by sorrow and old age, who now tramps with his wife from house to house, day and night, naked and barefooted, and about whom he wrote a petition to the Monarch, begging permission for him to enter a monastery.

They argue at length and recall how the Monarch and the patriarch investigate even the smallest need of the icon-painters, if it reaches them...

"Even thus wrote the Patriarch: 'Artem beat up the peasant Panka defending himself from thieves; even if he would have stabbed them defending himself from them, still his guilt is little.' "...

"What is to be said? It is a sin for the Monarch to take more care of foreigners than of our own people! And yet some of our own people watch so zealously the Czar's interest: for instance Ushakoff, who spoke so frankly, telling the boyars that the Granovitaya Palace of the Kremlin should be decorated anew, with a solid design much better than before; especially since the frost was coming and the fresco design would not be strong, and would not last for ever. All thought that they would redecorate in the Autumn, but because Simon spoke so bluntly, they postponed it."

III

The doors of the Palace hang on heavy wrought-iron hinges; the long plates of the hinges lie along the entire width of the door, and are hollowed out with a pattern. The hinges begin to squeak—the door opens and admits into the Palace the old image-painters and with them the boyar and the clerk. These eminent people have come from a trial; especially for this occasion the image-painters have dressed themselves in the rich garb bestowed upon them: single-breasted garments with silver buttons, caftans of damask with interwoven gold bands, cloaks, decorated cloth trousers, boots of morocco leather —thus elegantly are attired the image-painters. Their beards are combed and their hair greased, so that it is impossible to distinguish them from the boyars.

The son of a peasant from Vologda, Sergushko Rojkoff, who painted an icon of his imagination, is on trial; on a wooden board is the image of the All-Merciful Saviour, the Holy Mother and John the Precursor. And, according to the evidence of the Moscow image-painters, Simon Ushakoff and others, Sergushko appears to be a good master. The icon-painters surround the new comrade and ask who has vouched for him, because a new member must be vouched for by experienced icon-painters. They must vouch for him, in case Sergushko will not be present at the work of the Czar's icon-painting, or lest he stay away or begin to drink, in which case the vouchers have to bear the fine of the Czar. They are finding out from where Sergushko comes, what is the present condition of art in Vologda, how the masters live in Vologda. And they listen to Sergushko's tales.

Sergushko relates that Matvei Guryeff, the icon-painter, has stolen away from the Swamensky Monastery in Vologda and lives in Totma; that Agei Avtomakoff and

Dmitri Klokoff have become old; that Sergei Anisimoff is now obscure. And that some other icon-painters do neither the Czar's work nor murals, nor any other painting, because they are old and cannot see any craft-work, and they wander amongst the people, begging alms in Christ's Name since they are aged, maimed, poor and in debt. The icon-painters listen to the sad tales from Vologda, look at Sergushko's old caftan; out of place is such a caftan in the bright Palace, and patches seem absurd next to the golden woven attire. They become confused and downcast and again they ask Sergushko with what art the icons are painted in the villages and woods of Vologda. Are not the icons painted carelessly, merely to barter them among the ignorant peasants? Do they preserve the old versions? ... "The Czar issued a severe edict about this when the news reached him of the unskilled painters from Kholuisk!"

With the courtier speaks Danilo Vouchters, the foreign master from Caezar's land, who has just entered the Palace. He approaches the boyar with low bows, cunningly bending his thinly clad feet. He speaks with the aid of a translator, and the substance of his speech is that, only because of the resplendent inexpressible mercy of the Czar, and because of the very generous and excellent salary, did he decide upon the difficult journey to Moscovia. Vouchters makes an agreement with the boyar as to how much salary he will receive. They decide that Vouchters will receive twenty roubles in money, twenty *tchetvort* (about eight bushels) of rye, ten *tchetvort* of wheat, one *tchetvort* of buck-wheat barley, a quart of peas, ten quarts of malt, ten *polots* of meat, ten buckets of wine. Vouchters grumbles, and asks that five sturgeon and five salmon be added, and that an agreement shall be written, that Vouchters teach the Russian masters to paint in the wisest craft.

The boyar leaves Vouchters, and now discusses with the clerk and the favorite masters as to where it is best to obtain icon-painters for the time when the Ouspensky Cathedral is to be decorated; because for this work the number of Moscow masters from the Palace and city will not be sufficient.

In a dignified way the boyar gives orders to the clerk,

"Prepare, Artamon, an edict for the people of Pscov, that they should search for icon-painters who do decorative and other work; men from the suburbs, men who belong to boyar and princes and merchants and other people, in order that the mural decoration of the church shall not suffer."

To find and procure such masters, one must proceed cautiously and with the observance of great impartiality; otherwise there will be complaints, that some of the icon-painters are suffering distant losses and ruination, or that others of them are not hired for mural decorative work. Good masters have work everywhere; every one values a good master; only very reluctantly are they permitted to leave for insatiable Moscow.

In order to keep an icon-painter, the voyevods and even the Church fathers, abbots, and archbishops go so far as to dissemble; they are ready to send false information to the Czar's Palace, notwithstanding the danger that they may be discovered acting in crafty self-interest; that soldiers, with strict orders, will come. But the holy fathers and the servants of the Czar will nevertheless pretend that the good masters are unknown to them, or are absent, and they will conceal them in monastery cells, so great is the need for real icon-painters.

IV

"Have pity, resplendent boyar, do not let us be utterly ruined!" A ragged peasant is fighting his way to the boyar and, reaching him, bows to the floor.

"I appeal to thee, boyar, for my little son, a pupil of the icon-school. Have pity on my son! The master will ruin him because of personal interest, and there is now a threat over him, because he could not even run away from him. The fine is awfully big. Here is the copy of the agreement."

The clerk accepts the agreement, silently looks it over

and through his teeth murmurs: "after reaching said age, not to run away, neither to steal!" Then *sotto voce* he reads to the boyar: "... And in case his son Larionoff, not awaiting the prescribed time, will run away from me by stealth, then I shall take from Larion twenty roubles as agreed."

"Yes, the fine is not a small one; fifteen roubles is a pretty big fine, but twenty is still more inconsiderate."

"And what is the matter?" asks the clerk, displeased that the trial is before everyone—before the boyar—so that he, the clerk, must deal with the petition according to the law, and thus have no profit.

"I ask for justice from the icon-master, Terenti Agafonoff," the peasant begins quickly, "because he took my little boy into the school and it is already the third year, and he has not taught him the craft of painting, but only how to gild wood and canvas. Besides, the teaching of this master is no good; he does not teach the student to profit, but only wishes to profit himself; the body measurements given by him are not correct; neither has the master taught him to draw, nor skillfully to design. And whatever the boy paints well, according to his understanding, then the master disapproves of it, or compares it with the work of another pupil, his nephew. And there is neither benefit nor honor for my little boy. Have mercy upon me, boyar, and grant me permission to take home my little boy, Larivonka, without the fine."

The peasant bows down, and from behind him comes forward a thin man in a dark caftan, who puts his hand on his breast, clears his throat and hesitatingly begins:

"And it is said in the teaching of the Stoglav Council, Chapter 43: 'If the Lord shall not grant one such skill, and he shall begin to paint badly or begin to live not in accordance with the correct covenants and yet the master will point him out as better and more worthy and shall exhibit the paintings of such a one and not the other, then the holy man, after such teaching will place this master under indictment, so that the rest shall fear and not dare to act similarly.' It has thus been said in Stoglav, and therefore the master Agafonoff is guilty in that he favors his nephew and therefore he has a wrong conception of his guardianship of the Czar's work. God did not reveal the craft to his nephew and if Agafonoff, through his absurd cunning, will place his nephew in the Palace, then it will be a detriment to the Czar's work."

"And what kind of a man art thou?" the clerk interrupts him.

"He is my brother-in-law, Filipko; he pities my little boy. He is a good little boy, but he has hard luck with the master, forgive me! But that Agafonoff is twisting his soul, for the sake of his nephew—that is the truth, because his nephew lives idly and immorally, and my little boy suffers because of him."

"Thy petition is important and complicated." The boyar wrinkles his brows (not because he is sorry for the Czar's work, but because he will not be able to leave the Palace for home so soon).

"It is not right to try this case before the people. Go to the clerk's house; call Terenti there; where does he work?"

"Here," said the boyar.

"Terenti does not paint in the Palace now, but in the catacombs of the Red Wing."

"Send for him; let him not delay, let him stop his work and hurry to the clerk's office." The boyar goes away, and with him go the clerk and petitioners.

The icon-painters become quiet; they know something has happened to their comrade, but they also know that this hard luck is deserved, although Terenti alone is not threatened, but some of the other masters as well are destined for a similar storm because of their friendship and favor towards their relatives.

"Yes," decides Simon Ushakoff, (and every one knows that Simon does not speak casually). "That is all self-interest. But real love for the work is not in evidence. Terenti sells his skill, the one accorded him by God, but he only thinks of himself, and it will serve him right if they indict him and let him sit without work. Do not envy; direct your pupil honestly, do not resort to subterfuge in your soul; do not conceal one who is talented. It is no wonder that the youngsters did not love Terenti!"

The icon-painters are silent; many bend their heads; they look at their work, without raising their eyes. They think: "It is easy for Ushakoff to speak; not everybody is like him." And within their souls they already hate Ushakoff because he is so renowned for his art, because every one listens to him, because he pronounces the truth. But, thank God, not all of them think thus, and more than half of them sincerely nod their heads to Simon for his frank words. With such masters as Simon, art is being uplifted. Not for some time will the hum of conversation again be heard, nor will any one smile. In midday they dine, then have supper and then the end of their work is near.

In the corner, an old icon-painter, with his beard falling upon his breast in great locks, with a dry hooked nose, his eyes deep in their sockets, teaches a youngster, emphasizing the accent on the letter "O."

"—And they gave him sacred water and sacred relics, so that mixing the sacred water and sacred relics with colors, he should paint an holy and hallowed icon. And he painted this holy icon, and only on Saturdays and Sundays did he partake of food, and with great zeal and vigilance in great silence did he create it..."

"I wonder what Olenka is doing?"—is the earthly thought passing in the mind of the young one. And the image-painter already guesses his thoughts and still more austerely pierces him through with his steely eyes and repeats imposingly:

"God help the present masters! Many of them paint saints the same as themselves: with big stomachs, with fat faces and hands and feet, like blocks of wood. And they themselves do not live purely, they do not remember that it befits an icon-painter to be modest, benignant, pious but not a babbler, a fun-maker, not quarrelsome, not envious, not a robber, not a murderer, but above all, to guard the purity of the soul and body with greatest care. And if you can remain like that to the end, then marry in lawful wedlock, and come to the Church fathers and confess to them, and live according to their command, fasting and praying, in temperance and with humility, away from all sorts of mischief; and with the greatest care, paint the Image of the Lord. Let people be shaken by bodily passions, but spiritually and zealously working for the glory of honest art, strive with the brush and the good word. Not to everyone does God grant the ability to paint His Image and likeness, and to whomsoever He does not so grant—let him abstain from poor work. Nor should he boast, in God's name, of his craft. And if any one begins to say that he lives and supports himself by this or that—do not listen to such talk. Not every human being can be an icon-painter; there is plenty of handicraft bestowed by the Lord, which can support and keep alive a human being outside of icon-painting"—so teaches the master.

The sunset cannot penetrate the tiny windows of mica. The Palace becomes darker. The icon-painters disperse. The tiny halos and designs on the icons no longer glow. The dark outlines of the images tremble and the big, white eyes of the Saints glimmer sharply. Twilight creeps from out the corners, folds in a gray cover the supply stock of icon boards and canvases, and softens the shadows of the benches. Diligently and rhythmically resound the precepts concerning this fine art.

A beautiful, serene and intricate work is created in the Terem of Icons.

1899.

ANCIENT TEMPLES OF FINLAND

IN Finland the sorceresses still brew their potions from the heads of snakes. Over the hills of Finland spread out the labyrinths—ingenious, impenetrable mazes—mute witnesses of immemorial rites. There, giants are still buried in long kurgans. The canticle is still sounding. Olafsberg remembers even up to now the wandering knights of the Northlands. The ancient temples know them. Wooden churches still stand, linking Norway with our own Northern Russia. Such a church is in Keuruu.

The great northern crossroad in Finland is of great significance to us. The fantastic legends of the people live on in the strange beauty of the countryside—in endless mountains and sudden lakes, in shaggy boulders and rock-filled rapids.

* * *

Scandinavia offers one of the most beautiful aspects of historical-artistic questions. Only the mystery of Eastern movements may be compared to it in profundity. Strange were the people who transfixed with their boundless power the most ancient lands, infusing them with their own strong and vital culture. Everywhere the Scandinavians left behind them the best and healthiest influences. That precious quality—the sense of personal dignity—penetrated the sovereignty of nations, after the coming of the Northerners. Their relics are full of this deep dignity.

The results of the Scandinavian migrations are most significant in Russia. Upsala gave us anthropomorphous deities. The fiords permitted navigation; the Varengians supplied military order. Through several centuries we habitually received strength and support from the North.

Although we have valuable research records of the North, the Varengian question is still counted among the tasks of the future. Slowly, as with a spade, archeology uproots a varied mass of inventions and facts. Thus far this history is still in the process of being compiled. Often one can go back only two centuries in discussing the beginning of the present age. However, that will suffice.

All the data in the Scandinavian question is of interest and value to us. That which is interesting by itself becomes more significant when it takes its place as a link of one great whole. The importance of the ancient Finnish temples is but a detail of the question at large, as we shall see. However, their history promises us some very interesting conclusions in the future.

First of all it is necessary to understand fully the earliest migrations of the Scandinavians towards the East. This is of greater moment than the contrary movement of the Novgorodians. One must be aware of the settlement of the Scandinavians in the western corner of Finland in the Tenth Century. Thus, if one follows the facts, the wide stone Catholic churches will not seem strange when found in the bushes of the fiords, even in the Twelfth and Thirteenth Centuries. Then let us turn quickly to the steps of the Scandinavian movement Eastwards. We may trace the colonization to quite recent centuries, embracing the culture of Konigsberg; in evidence, the rich bronze and silver antiques of Curland; the Gnesdor culture and that of Luzinsk; the discoveries of Chernigoff and Kieff; the discoveries in the upper Volga districts, in Volkhoff and in Mistinsk. All these tell us not of a temporary culture emanating from the North, but of a deep and lasting gift.

If one speaks about Russia in this manner, then it can be clearly understood why the nation nearest to Scandinavia—Finland—a land thickly inhabited by small tribes —was permeated with the customs of the Viking explorers, by the beginning of the Tenth Century. While admitting that the Ladogians were receiving tribute at that time from the Tovasts, it is necessary to acknowledge that the traces of Russian migrations in that era remained very modest in Finland. There were a few mounds, a few crosses of the Novgorod type; no more than the discovery of Kufi coins! But in western Finland the mounds near the sea and on the islands speak of the explorations of the Scandinavians.

It is a catastrophe for the Krivitchi! It is quite pitiful that a long time ago we learned to love the nearest to our hearts—the Slavs. Their historical importance is being undermined. The Finnish data abbreviates the ranges of the activities of the northern Slavic tribes. That most important study of A. Spitzyn dealing with the long kurgans of the upper and lower Dnjepr district, attributes these monuments not to the Slavs but to the Finns. G. Neovius, in his latest book about the Scandinavian migrations to Russia, based upon records furnished by the Stockholm archives, points out that in the district near Ladoga, in the locality of Kensholm, there is a lake called Rourin—the Swedish pronunciation of Rurin. This historian also disproves the deductions of Nestor concerning who taught the Slavs the custom of inviting foreigners to become colonists of their lands. He claims that this was a Scandinavian characteristic, not a Slavic one; also that Scandinavians had settled upon the shores of Volkhor and Dnjepr a long time before the Slavs came there. Thus this invitation—utterly foreign to the Slavic nature—is quite habitual and natural to the Scandinavian. What is more reasonable than that colonists should invite the nearest Freiherr into their own settlement which was in need of order for the defense of their trading roads? A clever move! And there seems to be no more simple or practical fashion of explaining these facts. These courageous Northern people would be lured by the abundance of fur-bearing animals that filled the forests in those days and even flourish today—and by the beauty of the region north of Lake Ladoga. The article by Neovius is called "Om Spar af Forhistorian Skandinavian Kolonisation in Karden." (*Museum* N-2, 1907.)

Many historians, apparently unknown to each other, are studying these Northern migrations. Not theories but actual facts are being uprooted. We are in need of all possible data as to the Scandinavian movement to the East. All the material leads to the belief that there was an ancient domination of Scandinavians in western Finland. All the facts of this migration are significant and I repeat, they are more important because only recently there was a movement, in spite of historical evidence, to emphasize only the Novgorod influence among the Finns.

The sea passage through the fiords was calm. The harbors were easily accessible. The shores were high. There were easy means of defense. Forest districts abound with game and fowl. Rivers and lakes were filled with fish. All these advantages undoubtedly led the Scandinavians to settle upon the shores within Poiro-Uusikirkko. The primitive influences of these peoples may be presumed to have penetrated into the interior as far as Tavastgus. From the West also there entered the influence of Catholic Christianity. This bore no great consequences except upon separate little villages of Korelia. There remained only the foundation of a monastery from Valaam and Konertz, notwithstanding the founding of Valaam in 992. It is not strange that towards the Thirteenth Century, even before the known campaigns upon Korelia by Tornel Knudson there were stone temples already on the western shore. Gradually, however, thanks to the efforts of Catholicism, the temples were decorated and painted. The solid construction of the edifices and the strength of the granite and cobblestones have preserved these most ancient temples of Finland up to our own days.

Let us not look for the "non-existent" in the simple constructions of temples, in their high facades—adorned by many crosses—in the long windows and low doors, now practically all widened. We shall not find revelation in them. We see many similarities in the churches of Sweden, Denmark and picturesque Pomeranian Norway, Scotland, Ireland. Similar sources inspired the artists—

the same northern legends of the Middle Ages, and their various interpretations prompted the treatment of the subjects. Sometimes the same bishops who came from beyond the sea, organized their own workmen for this work. And thus, the group of Finnish temples with their mural decorations, stand out among the extraordinary manifestations of these influences in the northern lands. After all, the same influences may be spoken of in regard to Russian churches. Shall we then fear comparison with Athos, Caucasia, Byzantium or the primitives of Italy? Of course not! The local influence, the individual understanding of the sources is outspoken everywhere. In the early mural decorations of Novgorod, Pscov and Lake Ladoga is the reinterpretation of the Byzantine; in Moscow and Yaroslavl as dimly as a distant cloud of smoke, one feels the influence of the Italian primitives. And, ascertaining the origin of the murals, one cannot imagine why the derivation of our monuments should not be clear. If it be proven, however, that the temples in Vladimir and in Nerli were constructed not by Russians but by the hands of Alans, would this make them less interesting? The order of succession always was and will be everywhere. That which is beautiful, interesting and curious, remains thus in spite of everything. And it is necessary to guard this principle of art with all our strength. Only prejudiced eyes refuse to see the similarities to something long-before established, although it may be in some other name. I reply to this argument, that the churches of Finland are not Finnish, but absolutely Swedish, and hence are not of real Finnish origin. But opinions differ.

In the murals of Finnish churches there are undoubted peculiarities. The stamp of the North, the stamp of an earlier Christianity is clearly present in the Western-Finnish temples. One should pay attention to them. They are in peril. The majority of these churches are in modest village parishes. There the interest in the beauty of antiquity is of course of a very different character, especially with respect to Catholic beauty. For many Protestant ministers, mural decorations are an unnecessary luxury. As relics of near-by foreign (Swedish) influence, the most ancient temples in principle cannot be dear to the important, influential part of the population. Many of the murals still remain covered by the austere Protestant over-painting. I had an opportunity to see white walls with a reddish dark stain where some of the covered images were imperfectly painted over. In view of the great number of churches in Western Finland, one may expect discoveries of widely interesting phases of Northern decorations.

Cases are also known where a painting already discovered was plastered over again. A joy for vandals! To plaster up that which justly attracted the attention of English and Scandinavian scientists. This barbarity took place by the way in Nousiainen in the second oldest church known. It is believed that the oldest is Mariankirko which, up to the year of 1300 was a cathedral. Regarding the mural decoration of Nousiainen, practically nothing is published except the very old articles by Mr. Nervander. ("Kirkollilesta taiteesta Suomesta Keskiaikana." Kirjoittus E. Nervander. *Kelsingissa* 1887-8.) The text of these leaflets is in Finnish and Swedish. The illustrations, which are in the form of sketches are poor, but because of the dearth of other sources, one has to search in these articles for these ancient images of Nousiainen. These murals were never reproduced in an artistic manner. Another edition exists about the ancient temples in Finland, but only two hundred copies of this book were printed and they could not have been of great value because book dealers do not even attempt to get them.

The character of the images in Nousiainen was never fully described—part of the superimposed layers have not fallen off. Now the whole church is whitewashed. Only upon the sarcophagus of Heinrich the Bishop—for the relics of Heinrich were transferred on June the eighteenth in the year thirteen hundred from Nousiainen to Twinu—is there an interesting series of sketches on copper of the life of the bishop. It is quite evident from the character of this sketch that it comes from the same remarkable church for which so many miles of difficult road were traversed.

Of the murals in Nousiainen, let us see Mr. Nervander's own description. Although he saw the murals in the church, he did not come to their defense. He preferred to diminish their significance rather than to stress their importance. Let us hear his old-fashioned language and interpretations:

"Absolutely unique murals were discovered in Nousiainen, in the year eighteen hundred and eighty under many layers of plaster. Never have such things been found before in Christian temples. The entire mural decoration was in two tones—brick-red and gray. In the very year of their discovery these murals were plastered over. The sight of these images was too strange, too repulsive, to those who wanted to see within a temple, pictures which elevated religious emotions. High upon the walls, on the pillars and vaults, were ornaments, sometimes conventionalized, sometimes fantastic, depicting gigantic birds. Further down, the ornaments were painted in the likeness of various animals, elks, unicorns, foxes, horses, wolves, and fantastic beings and nymphs. Besides these were seen images of shields, a few heads of Saints surrounded by carefully executed aureoles. There were images which seemed to depict the arrival of the Scandinavian conquerors in Finland.

"Although the plaster had been carefully removed, nevertheless the paintings suffered in some places. Thus the greater part of the head was lost from the Image of Christ. The next part of the mural illustrated an ancient boat guided by a tall helmsman. Still further on, in a very damaged part of the painting were seen two figures, preparing for a duel. One man was mounted upon a horse; before him was a little dog; the other man, clad in a sharp-pointed Lapland hat, was sitting on an animal with many feet and near him was a creature resembling a wolf. This duel may be symbolic of the duel between Christianity and paganism. Another strange image might have the same meaning—to the left stood a tree with birds on its branches, while a lone bird, in the act of flying away is attacked by two foxes; to the right a large animal, possibly an elk or a unicorn, stands with tongue outstretched. Christ was apparently painted in the symbol of these animals. Lower down, there was an executioner with his weapon raised, seizing the head of a small human being. The executioner was apparently about to cut off this head as he has numerous other heads which are lying on the other side of a cross. If one were to attempt an explanation of this very strange and hardly visible picture, one might say that it represents the happiness of those who stand by the Tree of Life, and the tragic destruction of others who are enticed by the foxy cunning of the Vain World. Then there was Christ—Lord of life and death and the fate of martyrs.

"These fresco-painters appeared to like the ancient pictures of Ireland and Scotland and have made a rather belated application of them here in a Christian church. The path of these drawings was laid through Gotland with whose inhabitants the people of Finland had had close relationships from ancient times." (P. 32.)

According to the illustrations of Mr. Nervander's article, the pictures in Nousiainen resemble the drawings and niches on the Northern rocks, Hallristningaz. One feels in them a borderline of Palatin Capilla and the figures of Chud—at the time when Christianity placed its hand upon sacred Shamanism. One must agree with Nervander that such an adornment in a church is absolutely unique!

How remarkably impressive must have been these tall, spacious, white temples, covered on vault, pillars and walls with reddish and grayish hieroglyphs of Northern life! What a noble combination of colors! A knowledge of a few characteristics of the drawing, might have avoided whole pages of presumptions. Some detail left by the artist, even unconsciously, could have thrown light upon the entire question of Northern habitation and, of course, of Russia. The significance of such a temple might have been greater than the Ring of Mathilde. And now there remain only white surfaces and the fear that this precious art is not only plastered over, but forever lost!

It is vitally necessary to try to save these murals. I believe that if this article reaches Professors Aspelin, Ivar Hemel, I. Ailio, M. Appelgren, the most noted Finnish archaeologists, with the cultural ideals they possess, they will immediately try to correct the mistake of the past. And they shall do even better than in the restorations in Lohja, although there the impression of antiquity is very carefully preserved. The Senate will not fail to appropriate the necessary funds for so important an enterprise. According to Neovius, the frescoes in Narantal, Porvoo and Sjondea have met with the same fate. Everything was whitewashed over!

There still remain murals in Kemio, Lohja, Hattula (1520) Kumlinge, Rauma (this mural decoration was done in 1510-1522), Lieto and Pohja; in 1903 frescoes were discovered in Sauvo, and in 1904 the stucco was broken off in Pernio. It is interesting to note that besides the year, the name of the artist Petrus Heinricson is inscribed, and he is known to have finished this work in 1470.

A very faded fresco on the outer wall in Hattula is attributed to the same era as the Nousiainen Murals—that is, about the end of the Twelfth, and beginning of the Thirteenth Centuries. This fresco represents the Crucified One surrounded by Mary and John. The beautiful, simple interpretation vividly transfers the spectator to the Twelfth Century. The flower ornamentation, executed with great subtlety, is exquisitely arranged around this fresco.

As a link between the most ancient paintings *al'secco* and later ones of the Fifteenth Century, one may point out the ornaments in Hattula. Rich are the combinations of fruits and flowers. The colors are green, white, blue, red and gray. In the frescoes of the Fifteenth Century, one must note, first of all, the ornaments in Tevsala. Their epoch is attributed to the period of the Bishop, Olaf Manguson (1450-1460); his coat of arms is painted on the walls of the church. These ancient pictures in Tevsala must have been considered among the best in Finland, and hence it is more provoking that part of them are still covered, still hidden under the stucco.

Most of the mural decorations of the temples are only partly preserved; therefore it is difficult to speak of the entire impression.

One of the most complete effects is given in the church in Lohja. In 1886 the murals in Lohja and in Hattula were rescued from the stucco with comparative success. And now a quarter of a century that has passed has partly evened and blended the rough scars due to renovation. This church was known as far back as 1290 when Lohja was one of the most important parishes in Finland. The structure of the temple is like that of a large, enlongated ship with two side entrances. Upon a high facade, stands a white cross which guards the structure. On both sides are the symbols of the two Substances of the Lord. Next to the temple is the belfry. The lower floor is laid with large cobblestones; the top is of wood. One may presume the general effect of the belfry to be of the Sixteenth Century. The painting of the temple is attributed to the years 1489-1500—the middle period for the Finnish temples. There are indications that the temple was adorned by an unknown woman artist from the convent in Naantal, near Sho. Parts of these paintings have much in common with the pictures in the *Breviarium Upsalense* (1496). From other substantial data, we recognize the coat of arms in the hands of one of the angels to be that of the first Catholic bishop, Arvin Kurk, who died in 1523. Sections of these murals naturally suffered during the widening of the windows and doors. An organ which was set over the main entrance has also covered other parts. The entrance of the temple is adorned with scenes depicting the murder of Abel and the pranks of the devil upon the people. One devil in the figure of a dog, is drinking milk from a milk-pail under a cow, in order to bring this milk to a man who has sold himself to him. Others are sitting on prancing horses; still others are helping an executioner in torturing a martyr. Devils help their servants at their labors in the fields.

Within the temple the paintings begin at the height of a man's shoulder and continue up through the vaults and walls. On the double row of pillars, holding up the vaults in the center of the church, are great paintings of saints and apostles. Large surfaces and vaults are decorated with paintings of Eden, the Exodus from Hell, the Stoning of the Adulteress, Genealogy of Christ, Christopher and the Child, the Holy Virgin and a few scenes from the Passion. Amongst the pictures of saints that are specially beloved are Saint Catherine of Sweden (canonized in 1479) Saint Heinrich and Lalli. The colors are laid in great flat surfaces, sharply traced around the fold.

Among the figures are ornaments. Empty places are filled with small stars. The background is white. It is clear to me that vivid and expressive painting is needed on so light a surface. Likewise, because of the primitive type of low, narrow windows and because of the height of the temple, a definite decoration is necessary. Within a temple, the light must also be soft and shaded. A temple as a spiritual fortress, a temple as a refuge from the enemy must reflect the suggestive glow of an intimate twilight.

For the revelations of the soul the light of a public square is not needed. Within the walls of a temple, people do not give in to or implicitly follow the letter of Catholicism. The men of the past valued that which is now destroyed through our own indifference and stupid errors. The people who enlarged the windows and doors erred greatly and destroyed much. For it is only in the evening twilight that one can really perceive the primitive impression of the decoration. The walls and vaults of the temple, as I said before, are constructed of large and small polished pebbles. The sides of the stones protrude from the wall and create sudden designs in the surface, some merely small sharp corners, others seeming to continue in a sinuous line. Did the builders attempt to create this effect or did the kind and gentle caress of Time transform these plain walls, lending them the artistic, complex beauty that they possess today? The dust, deposited on all the convexities of the stones, has changed the harsh outlines of a cold wall into the soft folds of a delicately blended, silvery Gobelin. The white surfaces have been adorned by the palette of Time, with warm soft colors. The figures no longer stand out with sharp contours but merge in mellow folds; the ornaments softly glow in the background. Time has given a beauty common to all ages and to all peoples.

Finns! Love your most ancient temples and learn how to preserve them!

1909.

TALASHKINO

WE have become poor in beauty. We have lost all beauty from our homes, from our surroundings, from within ourselves, from our problems. Only fragments of the beauty of former times strangely remain in our lives and do not serve to transform anything. It is hard to believe, but it is so. It is even out of fashion to talk of it.

Dead, dead is the great Pan!

Infused with visions of beauty, numberless publications are issued; they live a few decades, and die with the same aspiration. As before, our self-satisfied consciousness keeps silent. As before, with surprised raillery, we observe the sincere attempts for the adornment of our existence, and on opportunity, treat miserably the restless searchers. Slowly the ranks of the lovers of art are increasing.

Such is the case with us in Russia.

It is not easy to speak thus. It is necessary to feel a new impulse—without fear of realizing that the ancient Russia in its artistic conception was closer than we to the contemporary West. It is necessary. But is it possible?

It is shameful! During the Stone Age there was finer feeling for the importance of decoration, with its originality and endless variety. Not for our indifference blossomed the beauty of the old Oriental arts. The delightful currents of the Renaissance are far from our hectic din. Sadness grips our hearts while we look in the museums at the beautiful dead forms of the not-distant ages. Better let us not ponder on the ornaments of antiquity! It is simpler to pity the savage days of long ago and boast of our "progress." How absurd that word often sounds! What can one expect from us? In celebrating a thousand years of our Empire, we did not learn to revere worthily even the beauty of our ancient periods; to appreciate them, even historically, if otherwise the paths of art are unattainable for us.

It is difficult in Russia to get an idea of antiquity; the new ways are hard, unyielding.

For us, beauty is an empty sound, incomprehensible and shameful, something unfit. Beauty is useless where exists the great depression of our age—all-powerful vulgarity; where one sees and feels things through vulgarity; where the unusual is depressed by a thousand hands. Need we give examples?

We cannot expect beauty in the rush of the metropolis, nor from its poor museums, nor from its commercial arts.

Every aspect of beauty is a rare guest there.

In such springs the living water is polluted as it flows from silence and peace—the very earth. Summit and base. The crown and the origin will illumine the light of beauty, so that the mediocre should perish.

Action is needed. New steps and achievements are needed regardless of how difficult they are.

In recent days we have attempted to lay the way for new springs. All regenerators of life are worthy of great honor. For several years already, I have observed such sources. As in every vital venture, there is no coercion. The ancient period deserves the best attention: in it is to be found the living power, the power of beauty aspiring towards the new; and its origins have woven for the crystals of all ageless ornament, all kingdoms of nature: wild animals, birds, rocks, flowers. How many enchanting colors, how many new incomparable lines!

The beautifier of life does not need to search any materials. All he needs is to search new ideas, new views and to penetrate into the nobility of the old forms.

And how far is the inspiring example of antiquity from the perverted style which, due to our short-sightedness, we call modern?

From the source—as I think of it—work the friends of art, filled with the best ideas.

To this source come our worthiest artists. Vrubel, the most delicate master—went to the source. From the same source started Maliutin, Stelletzky and others equally interesting. Close to the source is the work of the late artists Polenova and Yakunchikova. The source creates new powers. It strengthens Sinoviev and Beketov—our talented youth. Borstchevsky, who contributed so much to the lovers of Russian antiquity with his sketches, and who has not been sufficiently studied by our academic artists, was inspired by the source.

Such a venture makes us joyful.

* * *

In the Smolensky Krivitchi, on the great highway to Greece, is such a source. There is much of originality. The undertaking is wide open to every gifted, every sincere searcher. One hears talk not only about favorites of the moment, but of many others, whose names are not at present on the crest of the wave. Princess Tenisheff—Maria Klaudievna—is striving ardently to establish such a venture on her estate, Talashkino, near Smolensk. From the proximity of such a center of art, interest is being revived also for the ancient city of Smolensk.

The late Mr. Sisov, an old friend of Talashkino, always responsive to every living idea, spoke cordially to me of the beginning of the new movement, S. P. Diaghileff, the editor of *Mir Iskustva*, writing of the results of the workshops of the Princess, sensitively described his impressions, "Talashkino has a great future," said M. V. Nesterov recently to me.

The main thing: Talashkino lacks the oppression of the conjured circle. Even if one cannot avoid the exaggerations and abstractions, which always exist in art, one feels how flexible is this venture, how able to accept all that is worthy, finding fermentation—growth.

True love of art is needed in order to arouse and establish such an artistic menage. The building of workshops, schools and museums is complicated and full of difficulties. But Maria Klaudievna possesses such love. She lived long with art. She has already succeeded in many great undertakings.

In the Russian Museum in Petersburg she has a department of Russian Water-Color art. Only due to the efforts of the Princess, the Museum did not close its doors to such artists as Vrubel, Somov and a whole line of excellent Finns. It is an excellent collection. It is rapidly increasing with new acquisitions. Her original idea was still broader. She thought of a complete collection of the water-color art of the entire history of the Occident. Plans were made for its realization, but the means of the Museum were not sufficient to undertake it. Thus collapsed the idea of a broadly planned and necessary work in the capital.

The appearance of *Mir Iskustva* was the first help to the Princess. How much care was expressed in helping the creations of so many artists!

At last now is completed the collection of the superb museum of our ethnographic art and art-crafts. And again the museum is presented for public use. Smolensk will have this joy. The museum has already been transported from Talashkino to the city. Many excellent objects have been carefully collected. Remarkable are the embroideries, the carvings, the icons and the yarn and metal objects. They are united by a personal taste, not only by literal science. The subjective side always gives an impression of appropriateness to such collections. Besides the old objects the works of the latest masters will occupy a conspicuous position, such as the incomparable ingenuities of Lalique, Fallize, Gallays, Colonna, Tiffany and other superb creators. As was to be expected, Smolensk has looked askance and preferred to dig sand just from out the walls and towers, from out its famous necklace of buildings but to save one of them for its museum seemed too much! But it is just as well. It is safer for the museum to stand on its own site, fortified by clear-cut statutes against all eventualities, than to depend on the mercy of our "culture."

To arouse tirelessly so many ventures precious to art

is unprecedented in our age; it is only possible through special love of art and long preparation. And when you see at Talashkino the joy over the kurgans' enamel, the combs of Lalique, the latest samples of bookbinding, miniatures, Limoge, Cloisonne, carved triptychs, embroideries—the most beautiful things imaginable, you rejoice inwardly over the work itself.

It means that it will endure.

* * *

In Talashkino the broad home-like spirit is unexpectedly combined with the freedom of art; a country house with ornate chambers; a hand-written chronicle with the latest utterances of the Occident. Much is conflicting. But in this conflict is a special pulse which reflects our many-sided life.

This pulse beats with a special force in Talashkino. A special aspect is acquired by the agricultural school and art work shops. It develops in the students and young masters a specially penetrating mien. In the surrounding population—always close to the art movement of Talashkino— is impressed an eternal stamp of the everlasting sense of life. Thousands of surrounding workmen and women go to Talashkino, so that it has a tremendous influence on the whole neighborhood; thus stretches out the endless web of the better life to come.

On the sacred hearth, away from the contamination of the city, the people create again newly conceived objects, without servility, without the trade marks of factories— creating lovingly and freely. We are reminded of the covenants of our forefathers and of the beauty and solidity of ancient works. In our youth are born new demands, strengthened by fine example. There is no need to run to the wine-shop—we can celebrate our holy days without it when there is so much around to keep one's mind busy and to carry one out of the daily monotony.

Even *Mikula* digs the beauty of life out of the soil. The beauty is impressed on the life of the village, and is transmitted unto many generations. Again all details of work may arouse the consciousness to something pure and good. Much also can be discovered in efforts of this kind.

We need it all. From the big life of art, from the latest vigorous circles to the solitude of the village—everywhere is needed the foundation of desire and aspiration. Yet there are difficulties without end.

The visions of a clear approach to life's aspects, inborn with the secrets of nature, subconscious, are beautiful as nature, and are depthlessly great in the meaning of beauty. In order to see, one has to bathe one's eyes with pure art, without methods, boundaries and conditions. Whoever sees thus will not return to the commonplace.

I look at Talashkino.

It is evident that an inner necessity combined with consciousness of solid foundation developed the venture of the schools and museum in Talashkino.

After knowing the creative ways of the best masters of all ages, after the jubilee dates of the teaching of Ruskin, it is ridiculous to speak of the worth of technique in developed creations. But with us, where the industrialist and artist are so often divided, when the very combination of these words is endless in syllables and dark in meaning; where those who bear this long title are multiplying, but whose names are not yet recorded in the history of art; with us, one can still praise the conscious creation of our applied art. In this Talashkino deserves great praise.

Here lie no secrets of austere augurs. All phases of art are clear to the workers in the art shops. The domestic hearth fully attentive to the best contemporary publications, to the works of new artists, to the excited discussions of exhibitions—is close to all of us. Every student creates his Holy of Holies in the execution of the selected craft; albums, designs, copies and compositions.

Besides the natural ability of the carver or the embroiderer, in the works of the students is felt the natural creator of a style, who understands and appreciates the quality of his material. Thus the students hear of the unity of craft and creation not only verbally, but they acquire the consciousness by practice. The Princess herself gives an example by applying the ornaments to various materials. Artists who have been in the work-shops, do not remain indifferent to the various productions. And the students in technical practice, remember the creative principles. It is evident that the work for them is not a soulless ideal, "without blemish," but closely conscious in the very details of spontaneity, which make the art objects so supreme. Working in nature leads to the same point.

The degrees of higher and lower become more pliable. It is plain to the students that above all and of most value is the artistic spark, which alone contains the true perfection of technique. There are many misunderstandings on this plane. I remember that A. I. Kuindji also told me the very same thing, seemingly familiar to all—the same A. I. Kuindji, whom, for some reason or other they failed to understand, speaking of him as an enemy of applied art. But he, like an artist, of course valued creation too highly to admit the label of commercialism. Undoubtedly the Princess also prefers the creative feature of the work rather than orders from stores for the repetition of sold objects. Instead of an answer in some cases, she prefers, as the only proper thing, to give objects with new designs. The mere atmosphere of the work for sale in stores apparently does not satisfy her, so she is endeavoring to establish better conditions through exhibitions. Such a fear of cheapening the work is a splendid guarantee. In aspiring to perfection and variety the students acquire a solid barricade against the future temptations of life.

With the years the graduates of Talashkino will heartily remember the period of their schooling.

* * *

A procession of keen memories:
Gates and posts designed with figures, animals and flowers; Fairy-like chambers... Embroideries. ... A profusion of patterns; sharp festoons, padded *nastebka*, transpar-

ent weaves, "Moscow weaves," back-stitch crosses, woolens, open sack-cloths, checked linens, hooked cloth ... plain textiles, velvety and soft to the sight. Dye-shops, with the mystery of colors; tufts of grass and roots; the ancient witch of Mordva, in antiquated garb of cotton thistle—the witch of the combination of fast colors.

Choruses. Music. Village life—a theater. A theater really ingenious. I remember the preparations for the "Tale of Seven Giants." I, a visitor, see the whole ant-hill of action. Music is written. The text is prepared. What work on the costumes! The ones newly made should be splendid and equal to the old ones taken from the museum. Staging. Dances. And it is difficult to believe that they are students! How they hurry, after working at the carpenter's bench, the scythe, and the rake, to get into ancient garments; how they rehearse their parts; how they move in their dances and play in the orchestra! Unwillingly they meet the night. And it is over.

Last summer I enjoyed a similar presentation. I was a member of the noisy joy!

Thus I witnessed the beginning of the temple of this life. Its end lies far away. They are adding to it all that is best. In this construction can be happily realized all the miracle-working traditions of ancient Russia, with its refined feeling for decoration. And the unusual, unrestrained sweep of designs of the out-walls of the cathedral of Yuriev-Polsky, the phantasmagoria of the temples of Rostov and Yaroslavl and the impressiveness of the Prophets of the Novgorod Sophia—all these divine treasures of ours should not be forgotten. Even the temples of Ajanta and Lhassa. Years may pass in quiet labor! May the covenants of beauty be fully realized in this venture!

Where else could we wish more the apotheosis of beauty than in a temple, that highest creation of our spirit?

* * *

One wonders at the success of Talashkino. One wonders why the objects of its work-shops are disposed of so fast. These are the clefts in the solid order of the past which give hope for the future. Not without reason do they naturally appreciate abroad the value of what Princess Tenisheva is doing, and speak benevolently of her work. Not without reason the young people are enthusiastic in applying their efforts to such an undertaking. There is always goodness in the ideals of the youth, not oppressed by the prejudices of the age.

While speaking now of the work, we can say only something of its current development. It is hard to prophesy how it will develop; what kind of difficulties it will meet, and what kind of traces it will leave on Russian life. One can merely guess that its future will be just as remarkable as its beginning. The roots of the undertaking are not far from the "unity" of style in the aspirations of the young Occident. The difference in approach does not obscure the ends—the triumph of the austere form and line, and the merging with the "oneness" of the Western style, not in its blind imitation, but in the unity of the profundity of beauty. Some consider the products of Talashkino impeccable. Others deny this, forgetting that the one main feature of the creation of Talashkino is—the absence of a boring conclusive limit.

There is the usual discussion, as of everything than can be placed in the customary measures.

One hears different views of the character of the products of Talashkino. One calls this style new, sophisticated and impractical. It is said that it is a direct heritage from the ancient Russian traditions. One finds in it a path towards the renovation of Russia's entire domestic life. One sees in it almost an entire national inheritance. There are reproaches for the crudeness of material and technique; Maliutin is arraigned for this ... I do not know what is right. I do not want to think of it. It is superfluous. It does not help, either the creators or the consumers. With such thoughts one merely limits a venture which is free in spirit. The peasant's embroideries, with their agreeable vegetable colors and traditional stitches and patterns, crystallized by centuries; the mellow carvings and pottery in the completed objects—what does it matter to them to whom, or how they appeal? It does not matter whose eye will be caressed and calmed by them.

It is important if such ventures are but growing and developing. It is important, since in that way, art becomes a necessity.

We smile at it bitterly. "It is not forbidden to despise art." Nobody is compelled to love it. It is just that art should not demand any more from a government than what Diogenes asked of Alexander: "Stand aside. Do not obscure the sun." This modest request of art is addressed to the masses, the academies, often to the critics, and to many artists.

It is at present, and in the immediate future that art will be remote from us, as we will be absorbed by other developments of life. Perhaps never was Russian thought as removed from art as it is now. Nevertheless, it is agreeable to meditate on art. It is agreeable to realize that perhaps by the path of temporary removal, we will approach its vital substance. Very likely... And our half-closed eyes will open to something much more lasting.

Towards that we must work. Efforts are needed, not only of isolated individuals, deprived of work, or departing for the mountains, or depressed in their best aspirations; powerful manifestations, broad in sweep are needed. Such is the work of Princess Tenisheva—powerful in its unexpected fusion of the core of earth and the best words of culture.

Away from the marts, from profits and calculations, develops a great, noble and beautiful enterprise.

Thus I think of Talashkino.

1908.

PRINCESS TENISHEFF

For the Kondakov Institute's Commemorative Volume,
Prague

THROUGHOUT the history of mankind, periods of destruction and denial have always been succeeded by those of construction. In these latter the "constructors" of all ages and nations have found themselves on the same side.

Men destroyed, squandered, with nothing to substitute for what they laid waste. But it is said: "Do not destroy the temple unless you can erect a new one in its place."

The names of the squanderers and of the destroyers have either been swallowed in the darkness of oblivion or have become dreadful phantoms, terrifying new generations.

But in times of reconstruction the names of those who took up the task of building anew, mindful of the future, will be linked together in one endless chain. And humanity will always look back at them with a sigh of refuge in the hope for evolution. Varied are their names, far divided are they by countless centuries, diverse are the fields on which they wielded their invincible weapons for the progress of humanity; yet in spite of all these differences, they possess the same qualities.

Indefatigability, fearlessness, thirst for knowledge, tolerance and a capacity for enlightened labor—such are the qualities of the seekers for truth. There is still another quality which unites more closely these varied phenomena —that difficulty of attainment, inherent in all progressive movements, falls to the lot of these toilers whose aim is to bring spiritual light to the universe.

It is a custom to speak lightly of the "martyrs of science,

the martyrs of creative work, the martyrs of constructive work, the martyrs of the seeking spirit." These words are uttered as calmly as a discussion of one's daily diet or conventional habits, as though this martyrdom had become indispensable and immutable. The adherents of coarseness and vulgarity warn their children, "Why should you become martyrs, when, thanks to our efforts, we can offer you an easy life, and an appetite unspoiled by burdensome thoughts. See how hard it is for the seekers for truth: only a very few of them walk unwounded along the precipice of life. You are our children and therefore you must assume the same undisturbed position in the cemetery which we have earned by our desire for tranquility."

Yet, beyond all question, it is this very tranquility which comprises the most terrible death, because that which lives never demands quiescence, but on the contrary lives in an eternal pulsation of self-perfection.

Maria Klaudievna Tenisheva—a "constructor" and a collector—has left us.

Her life could have been calm and untroubled. Conforming to the established standards, she could have safely invested her capital in various countries and found herself, in the end, among those who take no part in the violent commotions of humanity and live peacefully until a natural death overtakes them.

But a longing for knowledge and for beauty, an irresistible urge to create and to build, kept Maria Tenisheva away from the still waters. She never experienced the deadly tranquility. She yearned to know, to create, to go forward.

Perhaps those who only met Maria Tenisheva amidst the conventional smiles of social life, would disagree with me. For the spirit of seeking was so tense and so deeply rooted within her that its essence came to the surface only on rare occasions. To know that side of her character one had to meet her at work and even then in the bright moments of creative work. Then Maria Tenisheva would irresistibly blaze forth with the sacred fire of creating, building, collecting and preserving the treasures by which the Spirit of man endures.

Indeed, she strove whole-heartedly and untiringly to safeguard the valuable shoots of art and knowledge. Every collector knows how zealously one should protect all constructive effort against the vise-like grasp of those who aim to destroy it.

Let us sum up all that Maria Tenisheva has accomplished!

To the city of Smolensk she gave a splendid museum, many canvases which would arouse the envy of any metropolitan museum.

To the Russian Museum she donated a marvelous collection of water-colors where, side by side with the Russian painters, were represented some of the best foreign masters. But the Museum Administration of that time did not comprehend the wide reach of such a gesture and refused to accept the foreign masterpieces. It appears as though we were unable to think beyond dead molds.

Let us remember another case of rank injustice. The diocese of Smolensk—with the benediction of its bishop—had placed and sold at auction sacred utensils from the Smolensk Cathedral Sacristy. Maria Tenisheva, wishing to preserve these valuable artistic pieces for the city of Smolensk, commissioned the curator of her museum, Mr. Borstchevsky, to purchase them at the auction. But instead of gratitude for an action which benefited the city of Smolensk, Maria Tenisheva was attacked in the papers by a certain General V. for "pillaging the Smolensk Sacristy." The affair went to court and the slanderer was put to shame. But this goes to show the state of affairs in Russia of that time and the manner of attacks that the collector had to suffer in the interests of the people.

Many museums are indebted to Maria Tenisheva.

The Museum of the Society for the Encouragement of Fine Arts, the Museum of the Stieglitz School Society, the Museum of the Moscow Archaeological Institute and many others contain donations from Maria Tenisheva.

Many schools were founded by her and others supported by her. And finally there was the art nucleus at Talashkino where Maria Tenisheva tried to assemble the best men of art for the revival of artistic principles.

Let us remember the artistic work-shops organized in Talashkino. Let us remember the inspiring plays. Let us remember the art students who were sent abroad to study —to that same studio where later Maria Tenisheva herself found refuge. Let us remember all the measures taken by Maria Tenisheva to increase the production of artistic handicraft and embroidery among the peasants of the Smolensk province. Let us remember "Rodnik"—the art-craft store in Moscow. Let us remember the exceptional care with which Maria Tenisheva surrounded painters. Let us remember the fairy-like "teremki"[2] of Maliutin. Let us remember the excavations in the Kremlin of Novgorod made possible through the support of Maria Tenisheva. Let us remember the archaeologists Prachov, Borstchevsky, Ouspensky... Let us remember the exhibitions organized by this remarkable woman to show the importance of Russian art. Let us remember the musicians and the writers, both Russian and foreign, who came to Talashkino. Stravinsky wrote a passage from his "Sacred Spring" upon the balustrade of one of Maliutin's "teremki" Let us remember that it was Maria Tenisheva again who came to Diaghilev's aid and helped to organize the splendid magazine Mir Iskustva (The World ot Art) which proved to be the domain of new conquests of art.

One must keep in mind that it was not an easy task, in the end of the nineties of the last century, to break the bonds of "academism" and enter the ranks of the new art. Such a deed was never crowned by official laurels. On the contrary every movement in that direction brought forth an avalanche of enmity and slander. But Maria Tenisheva had no fear of it. Besides, indifference to calumny also

---

[2] *"Terem"* (or *"teremok"*) in ancient Russia was the most secluded part of a house whore women lived in complete privacy.

proves to be one of the characteristics of selfless seeking for truth. There is no doubt that a weaker spirit than that of Maria Tenisheva could have found many reasons to give up the fight and to justify a withdrawal. Tenisheva, instead, turned into new spheres of activity. During the last years spent by her in Talashkino, she was attracted by the thought of building a church. We decided to call this church "The Temple of the Spirit." The central place in it was to be occupied by the painting of the Mother of the World.

Our common work, which had bound us previously, was now more crystallized by our common thoughts about the temple. All ideas about the synthesis of iconographic presentations gave great joy to Maria Tenisheva. Many things were planned for the church in our intimate conversations.

The first tidings of the war reached us while we were at work in the church. The plans came to a stop and were never completed. But if the greater part of the temple's walls has remained unpainted, the fundamental thought of this undertaking, nevertheless, has been expressed, and this crowning bequest of Maria Tenisheva in Talashkino showed how true she has remained to her original tendency to build and believe in the future and in new ideas.

Later years held new wanderings for Maria Tenisheva, a complete change of her outward life and a revaluation of many people. I am sorry that I haven't with me, here in the Himalayas, one of her last letters, which should be quoted fully whenever an attempt to characterize her is made. In this remarkable letter she expresses the fullness of her understanding of contemporary events. Leaving aside her personal feelings, passing by national and other considerations, Maria Tenisheva without the slightest bitterness transports her thought into the future, speaking in still more unifying tones.

Having only her working table, a small studio and a tiny villa in the environs of Paris (I used to call it "Small Talashkino") Maria Tenisheva found herself again free in her thoughts. She took no time for the appraisal of men's characters but spoke of the future—the future that is Knowledge. The problems of art's heritage, expressed in the traditions and ornaments of the Far East not only had not faded in her eyes but had acquired an added brilliancy. Yet she did not become a theorist. No shocks could tear her away from life. She was working, filled as before with the desire to give people the joys of art.

Of the various kinds of art, Maria Tenisheva had chosen for herself the most difficult and the most monumental. Her enamels, founded upon the principles of the ancient, age-old industry, are spread widely throughout the world. Her symbolic birds, *Syrin*, her white cities, her flowery glazes, her images of recluses indicate clearly the direction of her thoughts and creative work. The Fire Bird —of the enchanted country of the future—captivated and lifted her above everyday life. Here lay the source of her inviolable buoyancy of spirit and devotion to knowledge.

The enamels of Maria Tenisheva in French museums and in various private collections will be a living memory to her remarkable life and her strivings toward the Fire Flower—Creative Work.

At a time when great masses of people were in the tumult of contemporary questions, forgetting the future in the froth of current events, Maria Tenisheva was interested in the migration of peoples and the Gothic heritage and asked me to find, in the depths of Asia, the necessary data for her problems, repeating: "It is absolutely necessary to find it. These enamels and this flowery ornament must be confirmed."

Maria Tenisheva learned about our departure for Central Asia when she was lying sick in her Small Talashkino.

"Well, Father Nicholas," she greeted me at our last meeting, "it seems as though you have really decided to build a temple." Her face bore an austere expression and she reminded one of an Old Believer as she lay in bed, covered with a shawl. As we were leaving Small Talashkino my wife said to me: "She is a true Martha Possadnitza.[3] What strength, what austerity!"

I can imagine how glad Maria Tenisheva would have been to learn now, after our expedition, that her conjecture about the migration of peoples was entirely correct. And her joy would have been boundless could she have seen some of the ornaments, ascertained the analogy between Tibetan antiquities and those of Scythia and of Alan, seen Tibetan swords and fibulae which remind one of the so-called Gothic antiquities.

No one can say that Maria Tenisheva did not follow the right way.

Let us cite the names of those who at one time or other have collaborated with her and whom she held in high esteem. They were Vrubel, Nesterov, Repine, Serov, Levitan, Diaghileff, Alexander Benois, Bakst, Maliutin, Golovine, Somov, Bilibine, Naumov, Zioglinsky, Yakuntchikove, Polenova and also many others who had worked in Talashkino and in other studios and undertakings of Maria Tenisheva.

These names represent a brilliant epoch in Russian art; that epoch which brought Russia out of the narrow, national understanding and created her well-deserved reputation for her art, which it now holds. And Maria Tenisheva, by choosing precisely this group of artists pursuing daring and diverse ideals, showed thereby the correctness of judgment.

Maria Tenisheva loved the old Russian church painting and valued it very highly.

At the time when Russian church painting was still within the boundaries of the history of art and of iconographic investigations, Maria Tenisheva had already grasped the future artistic significance of this particular

---

[3] Martha Possadnitza stood at the head of the people of Novgorod when they were fighting Ivan III in the Fifteenth Century and urged them to unflinching resistance.

art. In her appreciation of the icons, as we now see, Maria Tenisheva had also followed the right road.

In promoting education and raising the level of the lower classes of Smolensk Maria Tenisheva accomplished a timely work, for the necessity of it was indeed evident. The correctness of her actions in this direction is incontestable.

Today a large street in the city of Smolensk bears the name of Tenishevskaya Street. Indeed, many were the people who had walked along Tenishevskaya Street to receive enlightenment and still more are bound to go seeking predestined cultural possibilities.

In enriching the museums by the best examples of creative ability, Maria Tenisheva wanted to point out the importance for future culture of furthering the understanding of art and the esteem for this type of creative work. One can always admire those who strive to lay the foundations of the future life.

About what has already been accomplished we speak briefly and lightly: *Let us remember all the schools, workshops, museums and the efforts to promote education.* It can be expressed in few words, yet think of all the labor, care and obstacles that each of these undertakings contain.

In turning to a broad understanding of religious principles it can be stated that here, too, Maria Tenisheva possessed opinions devoid of prejudices or superstitions, which were adequate to the demands of the near future.

Opinions, keen and to the point, can sometimes irritate small minds; but is not keenness of judgment an attribute of culture and civilization?

I look back on the work done by Maria Tenisheva with a feeling of joy. We must highly value people who are able to arouse in us such feeling of joy. May it follow her into the regions where she has departed, this feeling of joy, from the realization that she had yearned for a beautiful future and that her place is among those who are laying the steps of the coming culture.

Maria Tenisheva was a great woman—a true Martha Possadnitza.

Many years ago, when making excavations in the province of Tver, we visited the grave of Martha Possadnitza and heard the innumerable legends in which the people enshroud the name of this remarkable woman of Novgorod.

And I can now clearly visualize how gratefully the people of Russia will remember the name of Maria Tenisheva.

Many legends will be woven in Tenishevskaya Street and the name of Maria Tenisheva will be engraved among those of the true "constructors."

And once again we sit in the room of Princess Tenisheff. The same pictures are on the wall; the furniture is arranged as always. Here is the very writing desk with its same appointments. And here are the beloved memorable objects. The same dressing table. Everything has the air of the same care, as though its former occupant had just stepped out from her beloved study. As you sit at the working-desk of the Princess, it is difficult to imagine that she herself is no longer with us. But how solicitous must be that friend's hand which preserves so zealously the entire creative working atmosphere that surrounded the Princess.

Verily, such friends and fellow-warriors as Princess Ekaterina Constantinovna Swiatopolk-Chetvertinskaya are rare. She walked hand in hand with the late Princess upon all those upper paths of creative ascension. She knew the meaning of the life of the Princess; and she herself with untiring, vital creation, walked undeviatingly, and still walks towards the cultural, the spiritual, towards the Beautiful.

Only a high cultural spirit can impress and preserve the values of the near one. And Princess Ekaterina Constantinovna, not only preserves these, but herself unceasingly creates, spiritually enriching the whole atmosphere around her. It is a true joy to observe how she, with her worldly experience, encourages those who need encouragement and reproves those who fall in spirit, pronouncing a just word without releasing gossip and slander. She is always punctual. One can depend always upon her preciseness and exactness, because in these is the crest of nobility. To preserve the old, while creating new possibilities—what an unforgettable service to Culture has been the mission of the Princess Swiatopolk-Chetvertinskaya.

Himalayas, February, 1929.

A WREATH TO DIAGHILEFF

League of Composers' Magazine

DIAGHILEFF has gone. Something far greater than an individual force has passed with him. We may regard the entire achievement of Diaghileff as that of a great individual, but it would be still more exact to regard him as a true representative of an entire movement of synthesis, an eternally young representative of the great moment when modern art shattered so many conventionalities and superficialities.

The entire life of Diaghileff was a stormy one, as is the life of every true representative of vital art. More than once our personal relations were overshadowed and more than once renewed in the closest contact. Diaghileff was the first to express his faith in the artistic value of my painting "The Messenger." Then in 1900, at the time of the Paris Exhibition Universelle, he requested my painting, "The March," for his section, but this painting had been previously promised by me for the exhibition of the Imperial Academy of Fine Arts and in this way, because of my involuntary refusal, our relations became strained. Then I became Editor of the magazine *Art*, published by the Imperial Society for the Encouragement of Art, and Diaghileff was again taken aback, fearing that I would be combined with official circles. But again the waves of life brought us together and our great artist, Seroff, proved the splendid intermediary.

In 1906, Diaghileff again came to ask me for the designs for Polovetsky Camp for his ballet. It was a joyous period when the best French critics, such as Jacques Blanche, were heralding the Russian ballet and Russian art. I was no longer bound with the Academy of Fine Arts in its exhibitions, and thus without friction could partake in the exhibitions of Diaghileff and *Mir Iskustva*, of which I became President in 1910, closely participating in its movement. From this time, nothing clouded my relationship with Diaghileff.

Then came the productions of "Prince Igor," "Ivan the Terrible" and "Kitege" of Rimsky-Korsakoff, and our last work together was "Sacre du Printemps" and a revival of "Prince Igor" in 1920 in London when Diaghileff invited me there from Sweden. I met him for the last time in 1923, in Paris, and I recollect this meeting, so peaceful, so full of the memories of friendship.

One could have many disagreements with Diaghileff and yet not feel them as personal. Only the questions of art or of vital activity can permit such conflict and peace. And because of this quality, no one remembers his conflicts with Diaghileff, but recollects only the great constructive work accomplished in this stormy tide of art, in the hurricane of work for the benefit of humanity, introducing the best and most stirring.

Diaghileff was not one to advocate a drowsy life. From childhood, being himself a highly talented musician, he recognized the true future path of art. It was not superficial modernism. He was not a superficial "wearer of the green carnation," but a sincere knight of evolution in beauty.

I remember how, during the exhibition of *Mir Iskustva* in 1903, one evening I completely changed my painting "The Building of the City." During the process, late in the evening, came Diaghileff. When he saw the painting, he grasped my arm and said, "Not one stroke more! this is the real expression. Away with academic forms!"

This motto, "Away with academism," in the meaning of Diaghileff was not a destructive one. He understood and revealed with new splendor the beauty and genius of Moussorgsky. He valued the best moments of Rimsky-Korsakoff. Against contemporary pettiness, he evoked the power of Stravinsky, and it was he who so carefully caressed the art of Prokofieff and the most interesting French composers and artists.

Only one who knew him personally during the time of the most bitter fight for art, at the time of indescribable difficulties, could value his constructive genius and refined sensibilities. His co-workers may recollect how once in Paris, during the entire day he was as active as usual and no one sensed anything dangerous in the air. Only in the evening Diaghileff said to his gathered friends, "Now you deserve to have a calm supper, because today we were almost ruined, and only five minutes ago did I receive the news that all has been settled!"

And with this smile of a great consciousness, he encountered the beautiful new battles for art, assuming on his own shoulders all its responsibilities, and never did he spare his own name, because he knew that this sacred battle for the beatification of life was necessary.

Somebody has said that his enterprise was a personal one, and that he was an impresario working for himself. Only the most evil tongue and evil mind could have pronounced such a slander against this crusader in the service of beauty. Dispensing his own name liberally, he covered by his own responsibility many events and personalities. I remember when even in the time of difficulty, during the most critical moments he said: "Well, I alone shall sign. Please hold me alone liable for this." This was not the sign of egoism, but the sign of the great, lone fighter who knows why he holds his sword and shield.

Was he narrow in his opinions? Again, only a very ignorant person could say that he introduced only modernism. In his historical exhibitions of portraits, he showed the entire history of Russia from its very beginning, with equal reverence for the modern and for the old, even the icon-painters. In his magazine, *Mir Iskustva,* there were shown equally the most modern artists and the finest discoveries in old masters. Being most sensitive he felt the sources from which came the renaissance and the rejuvenation. And he showed the hidden treasures of ancient time and our hopes for tomorrow.

Could any one think him one-sided in music? Again, no! Equally did the Italian primitives and the most modern French composers attract his attention and aid. His productions were always real festivals of beauty. They were not extravagant fictions. No, they were feasts of enthusiasm, of faith in the enlightened future, where all the real values of the past were cherished as true milestones of human progress.

Without the slightest popularizing or vulgarizing of art, he revealed true art in all manifestations. To count all the productions, exhibitions and artistic enterprises of Diaghileff, is to write a history of Russian art from the nineties to 1928.

Recall the true sensation of the magazine *Mir Iskustva!* Remember his work with Princess Tenisheff! All the exhibitions—historical, foreign and modern Russian! And innumerable productions of ballets and operas through the world! Perhaps in time his name will be confounded with too many conceptions, of which he himself might not have agreed, but he was generous and he was never niggardly with his name. When he felt that it would be useful, he gave it freely—his one and only possession.

A refined, noble man, brought up under the finest conditions, he encountered war, revolution, all life's hurricanes, with the real smile of the Wise Man. This wisdom is, as always, the sign of synthesis. Not only did he expand his consciousness but he refined it and in this refined plane of mind, he could equally understand the past and the future.

When during the first productions of "Sacre du Printemps" we encountered the outburst of public opinion, he smiled and said, "This is victory! Let them hiss, let them cry! Because inwardly they already feel its value and only the conventional mask is hissing. You will witness the results." And in ten years came the real understanding and the result.

Recollecting the personality and work of Diaghileff, we recall one of the noblest and the most gigantic records of synthesis. His broad understanding, with unconquerable personal virility and faith in beauty provides a beautiful, unforgettable example for the young generation. Thus they learn how to guard the values of the past to serve the most constructive and beautiful victories of the future.

With unspeakable joy we recollect the glorious epopee of Diaghileff!

1930.

GRANDFATHER'S WORKING ROOM

"LET us go and visit Grandfather!"

Merrily we children run up the stairs. We pass the parlor and the alcove. We run through the library, over the gently creaking floor.

Old Feodor admits us through the high, dark door of grandfather's study. Everything belonging to Grandfather is unusual.

We like the chairs with dragons. If only we could have the same kind for our nursery! How fine is Grandfather's clock with its long-drawn-out music! Dark pictures hang on the walls. It seems to us that one of them has been hanging up-side-down for a long time. But Grandfather does not like any of his things to be touched.

Grandfather has many delightful things. The red table can be unfolded in ten different ways. One can touch the long, colored pipes on the high pipe-stand. One can feel the Masonic emblems (he does not permit us to put them on) and the screens with funny figures.

And when Grandfather is in good humor and his foot does not pain him, he opens the right drawer of the table!

There are interesting things, without end.

And Grandfather himself is such a dear! All white, all white! In a "Hussar's" dressing-gown.

We love to run to Grandfather after all sorts of pastimes. Grandfather gives us joy.

* * *

Something more.

"Grandfather orders you to come to him!"

Grandfather is so angry! So tall, so gray, so prickly! One does not know how to please him. He knows everything better than every one else! Everything that he has is better than any one's else. Everything must be just his way and no other! He scolds and always wants something or other...

"Ivan, tell Grandfather that we have gone for a walk!"

When we return it will be time for supper. And it will be just as good to go to him tomorrow. He will scold us

* * *

Everything is splendid while Grandfather's study is pleasant for us, while Grandfather is dear and white for us.

But when a gray, ireful Grandfather obscures our vital existence, which is strengthened only in the future, then it is bad. Then Grandfather's study is lost to us. Let us find a way gradually to leave it without disturbing anything.

In regard to the reverence for antiquity I have spoken even more than others. Nevertheless I fear it.

When antiquity is surrounded by general recognition, when antiquity is strengthened by all kinds of austere forbiddances, when the cherished and even persecuted antiquity rises up and forcefully demands submission, then the unceasing and tempestuous future should offer a very strong resistance. God forbid! after saving antiquity and cherishing it, one should not have to feel fatigue and, even more, doubt of the future of contemporary creation.

As long as Grandfather does not represent forbiddances or negation, but the sweet and precious moment of a wise antiquity, so long can we run to him. But just as soon as forbiddances, negations and threats resound near Grandfather's study, how is it possible that youth should not walk away? They will say, "The future is dearer to us!" Not so long ago we still were able to insist:

"It is a mortal sin to touch Grandfather's study; it is a sin to move anything around there in accordance with our own judgment. It is a sin not to run into the dear study of the wise, white Grandfather."

And it is true that at present, around antiquity, in the name of its glory, life is being filled with forbiddances and threats. Thus, in new laws regarding the observances of antiquity, are pre-supposed all sorts of chastisements for the disturbing of antiquity. But no similar reward is mentioned for its care. Of course, sometimes it is even necessary to threaten. But to build any kind of life upon forbiddances and storms is impossible.

And I feel that looking into the future, it is time to say:

"Let Grandfather's study remain the most dear, the most beloved place in the house. Let Grandfather not hinder the young life. Let us strive towards Grandfather in his best moments. Let Grandfather's laws be placed into the foundation. But *only* into the foundation of the structure of the future."

During the summer give extra thought to wise antiquity.

1912.

AN ANCIENT ADVICE

IN one of the old Italian manuscripts, possibly of the Fifteenth Century—the first pages and all the decorations of which have been torn out by the noble hand of some bibliophile—is related with simplicity the story of how a pupil came to the artist-teacher, Sano di Pietro, for advice regarding his painting.

The Teacher was working over a special order and could not answer the call of his pupil who had independently begun his picture, an "Adoration of the Magi," for a small village church in the Sienese district. The Teacher said:

"My dear boy, I have given my word to the Abbot of Montefalcone not to leave my house until I have completed the 'Coronation of the Holy Virgin,' commissioned by him. But, tell me, wherefore are your doubts? I am afraid that you have worked too much with me and are lost before your own work!"

"Revered Teacher," said the pupil, "my picture is complicated and it is difficult for me to coordinate its separate parts. Is it better to paint a dark olive grove against a red rock, at a distance? Are the tree-trunks visible and how distinct is the outline of the foliage?"

"My dear, paint as is necessary!"

"The mantle of the virgin is full of a golden design. Would it not be better to break it up into small folds and cover it with a pattern of large squares?"

"Do as is necessary!"

"Revered Teacher, thou art too busy with thine own resplendent works. I had better be silent until thy nearest moment of respite."

"My dear one, I do not expect any respite soon and you must not lose time if your picture has so much still unfinished. I am listening to everything and answer you, although with a certain surprise."

"The heads of the warriors which follow the kings are many. Is it necessary to find one line for them or to paint in each head and from these to have the outline of the crowd?"

"Do just as you need."

"I have made bushes on the distant fields and inter-crossed them with flowing rivers. But I wanted them quite clear cut, as is sometimes seen by the naked eye. I wanted to see the ripples in the water and a vessel on them and even an our in the hand of the oarsman. But it is all in the distance."

"Nothing is simpler. Do what is necessary."

"Master, I am frightened. Maybe you will in any case tell mo, should the crowns of the kings be made convex or only leave the applied gold for the crown?"

"Place the gold where it is necessary."

"I begin to think whether or not to make tufts of wool on the lambs, although they are hardly seen, but I remember what silky soft fleece the lambs have. I want to make them with a fine brush, but in the general picture they are almost unseen."

"Make them as is necessary."

"Master, I do not find any advice for my work in your answers. I know that all must be as is necessary. But what is 'Necessary'? It is obscure to me."

"Tell me, did Father Giovanni make any stipulation of work for you?"

"Outside of a date, no conditions. He said, 'Benvenuto, paint a good image of the Adoration of the three Magi before the Holy Child, and I will pay thee ten ducats out of the monastery funds.' Then he gave the date for the work and the measurements of the panel. But during the work I had various thoughts, in my desire to create a better image. And so, Master, I came to thee as before, for good advice. Tell me what is the meaning of 'as necessary'?"

" 'Necessary' means all must be as is well."

"But what means 'well'?"

"Poor, uncomprehending Benvenuto. What did I always speak about to you? What word did I often repeat to you? To make as well as possible, means only one thing: '*As beautiful.*' "

"And 'beautiful'?"

"Benvenuto, go out of this door and go to the shoemaker, Gabacuc. Tell him, 'Please hire me to soften leather, because I do not know the meaning of 'beautiful.' But do not come to me any more and, still better, do not touch your work."

After this story, the manuscript gives some recipes concerning the preparation of olive oil and about the use of olive pits. Then there is also a story about a citizen of Pisa, Chirilli Koda, who was buried alive.

But the last two stories do not concern us.

1906.

QUEEN OF HEAVEN

*Dedication to the Fresco, Church of Princess Tenisheff's
Estate*

FAR up lies the celestial path. The perilous river of life flows along. On its rocky banks perish inexperienced voyagers who are unable to discern the direction of good and of evil.

The All-merciful Queen of Heaven is solicitous about the inexperienced voyagers. The All-benevolent One speeds Her help to those on the hazardous paths. She wants to envelope the whole human sorrow of sin with a virgin veil.

Out of the resplendent city, from the wondrous abode of the angelic hosts rises the All-benevolent One. She gathers all her saintly helmsmen and lifts up Her prayers for humankind.

The angels marvel at the labors of the Queen. Out of the stronghold, legions arise in action. An effulgent, beatific host is pledged to the great achievement. They sound their trumpets in glory to the Queen.

From within the ramparts rise the Archangels. Cherubim and Seraphim gather about the Mother of the Lord. The Empowered, the Enthroned, the Ruling Ones aspire together. The Great Sources, which comprise the Mystery draw near. To the Holy Spirit, to the Great Lord, the Queen of Heaven transmits Her prayers; for the voyagers of limited understanding, for the visitations of God's paths, for salvation, protection, all-mercy. Thus the Great Spirit helps!

A great prayer rises unto Thee. The virgin prayer of the Mother of the Lord. Let us bring thanks to the Protectress! Let us proclaim the Mother of the Lord: Every living thing rejoices in Thee, Blessed One.

1910.